A

SKETCH OF THE DYNASTIES

OF

SOUTHERN INDIA

A

SKETCH OF THE DYNASTIES

OF

SOUTHERN INDIA

COMPILED UNDER THE ORDERS OF GOVERNMENT

ROBERT SEWELL

GYAN

Published by

Gyan Publishing House
5, Ansari Road
Daryaganj, New Delhi-110002
Phone: 011-47034999, 9811692060
E-mail: books@gyanbooks.com

Distribution Network
gyanbooks.com
India, USA, Canada, UK, Australia

ISBN: 978-93-6433-174-6 (PB)

First Published, 1883

2nd Impression 2024

Printed at: Gyan Press, Delhi.

A SKETCH OF THE DYNASTIES OF SOUTHERN INDIA
Author: ROBERT SEWELL

A

SKETCH OF THE DYNASTIES

OF

SOUTHERN INDIA.

Compiled under the Orders of Government

BY

ROBERT SEWELL,

H. M.'S MADRAS CIVIL SERVICE, MEMBER OF THE ROYAL ASIATIC SOCIETY
OF GREAT BRITAIN AND IRELAND, AND OF THE ASIATIC SOCIETY OF BENGAL.

MADRAS:
PRINTED BY E. KEYS, AT THE GOVERNMENT PRESS

1883.

PREFACE.

The contents of this volume are extracted from a larger work, Vol. II, of the Archæological Survey series of Southern India. It is thought that the separate publication of this slight historical sketch may be of use to many students of history who would not care to burden themselves with a larger work, much of which is taken up with lists of Inscriptions and Chronological Tables intended for the use of those practically engaged in making the bricks out of which the complete historical structure will hereafter be built.

This sketch of the Dynasties is, of course, not intended as a complete history. The subject of South Indian History is as yet in its infancy, and it is only because it is felt very strongly that a beginning must be made in some shape or another that this volume makes its appearance. Armed with this, readers will, it is hoped, feel themselves on fairly sure ground when they seek for information regarding some kingdom or sovereign of the peninsula, and little by little we shall advance in our knowledge.

Some of the principal families, not royal, who can boast of antiquity have been included in this list, since all information of that kind helps forward our knowledge of the march of events.

The arrangement is alphabetical, to assist reference.

R. SEWELL.

CONTENTS.

SKETCH OF THE DYNASTIES OF SOUTHERN INDIA.

SKETCH OF THE DYNASTIES OF SOUTHERN INDIA.

GENERAL HISTORICAL SKETCH.

In the earliest days of which we have any knowledge as to the sovereignties ruling the continent of India, it appears that the great Maurya dynasty held the north, while the south was divided amongst the Pāṇḍiyans of Madura, who governed the extreme south, the Choḷas, who held the country to their north and east, and the Cheras (Keraḷas), who ruled over the tracts to their north and west. This was in the fourth century B.C. I say "it appears" because, although we are certain of the Mauryas (probably B.C. 325–188) and the Pāṇḍiyans as existent in the time of Megasthenes (B.C. 302), we have only the fact of the Choḷas and Keraḷas (or Cheras) being mentioned in the inscriptions of Aśoka (B.C. 250) to verify their existence at that still earlier period. But tradition mentions no earlier kingdoms than those of Pāṇḍiya, Choḷa, and Chera in the south of India, and always speaks of them as contemporary. As we are certain of the Pāṇḍiyan, therefore, in B.C. 302, we may safely place the Choḷas and Cheras as far back as that date. The Keraḷas appear to have occupied the whole Western Coast under the ghāṭs, and it is probable that the Eastern Coast was also inhabited almost throughout its entire length; but there is no evidence of any kingdom having been in existence throughout the Dakhaṇ, and it is quite possible that almost the whole of its entire area was waste (the *Daṇḍakāraṇya* [1]) or inhabited only by a few half-wild tribes under their own chiefs, such as those so often mentioned in the *Purāṇas*. It is necessary for students of history to remember that very large areas now cultivated and populated were absolutely waste—mere barren tracts of rock, forest, and wild plains—till comparatively modern times, and this seems especially to have been the case with the Dakhaṇ country.[2] It must not be forgotten, however, that the earliest Buddhist legends speak of the kingdom of Kaliṅgā as then in existence.

At some period subsequent to that of Aśoka, the Pallavas[3] appear to have grown into importance on the Eastern Coast, and they gradually increased in power till they constituted themselves a great kingdom, with extensive foreign trade, and proved a source of danger to the Choḷas and their other neighbours. They appear to have held the entire Eastern Coast from Conjeeveram to the borders of Orissa. At present there is no evidence as to when they arose from obscurity into the dignity of a kingdom, but they seem to have been one of the principal southern powers when the first Chalukyas immigrated from Northern India about the fifth century A.D.

To the Mauryas in the north succeeded the Saṅga dynasty (B.C. 188–76) and this was followed by the short Kaṇva dynasty (B.C. 76–31). The last of these kings being murdered, the Andhra or Andhrabṛitya dynasty succeeded, and ruled from B.C. 31 to A.D. 436. (?) They were Buddhists, and it was by them that the magnificent marble *stupa* at Amarāvatī was erected. About this period, *i.e.*, the fifth century A.D., began to grow into importance the Chalukyan sovereignty of the Western Dakhaṇ, and it is in connection with the early Chalukyas that we hear of the Nalas (probably a Western Coast tribe), the Mauryas (possibly descendants of the earlier Mauryas) who inhabited part of the Koṅkaṇa, the Sendrakas, Mātaṅgas (apparently a barbarous tribe, perhaps aboriginal), the Kaṭachchuris,[4] the

---

[1] See Mr. Foulkes' article on the "Civilization of the Dakhaṇ down to the sixth century B.C." (*Ind. Ant.* VIII, 1—10.)

[2] According to the *Rāmāyana*, Bk. IV, Ch. 41, the races inhabiting the country south of the Tuṅgabhadrā where the Mekhalas, Utkalas, Daśarṇas, Vidarbhas, Ṛishikas, Mahiśakas, Matsyas, Kaliṅgas, Kaśikas, Andhras, Puṇḍras, Choḷas, Pāṇḍyas, and Keraḷas.

[3] Mr. Lewis Rice thinks that a dynasty of the *Mahāvali-kula* reigned over the eastern coast of the peninsula prior to the rise of the Pallavas, and that they gave their name to Mahāvalipuram, or the "Seven Pagodas." (*Ind. Ant.* X, 36.)

[4] Mr. Fleet's *Dynasties of the Kanarese Districts*, p. 10, and *note*. Their descendants (?) were called *Kāḷachuris*.

Gaṅgas of Maisūr, and the Ālupas or Āluvas, a tribe or dynasty apparently living to the south or south-west of the present Bombay Presidency. Early Chalukyan grants mention a number of other tribes, such as the Lāṭas (of *Lāṭadeśa,* in the north of Bombay), Mâlavas (Mâlwa), Gurjaras (of Gujarât), &c.

The Chalukyas divided into two branches in the beginning of the seventh century, an eastern branch conquering the Pallava kings of the Veṅgī country, or tract between the Krishṇā and Godāvarī rivers, and settling in that locality which they governed till A.D. 1023, the western remaining in their original home in the Western Dakhaṇ.

The Chinese pilgrim Hiwen-Thsang, who visited India A.D. 629 to 645, gives a graphic account of the state of the country in his time.

The Kadambas now began to grow into importance, and they fought with and defeated the Pallavas of Kañchī, and were perpetually at feud with the Chalukyas and their other neighbours. Their territory was in the South-west Dakhaṇ and North Maisūr. About the same period we find the Rāshṭrakūṭas giving great trouble to the Chalukyas. It is as yet uncertain whether these Rāshṭrakūṭas were "an Āryan Kshatriya, *i.e.*, Rājput, race which immigrated into the Dekkan from the north like the Chalukyas, or a Drāvidian family which was received into the Āryan community after the conquest of the Dekkan"—(*Dr. Bühler*). The wars with the Rāshṭrakūṭas seem to have resulted in the complete downfall for two centuries (A.D. 757-8 to 973-4) of the Western Chālukyas[1] and the consequent accretion of great power to the Rāshṭrakūṭas. The latter do not appear, however, to have attempted any conquests in the south. They were completely overthrown by the Western Chālukyas in A.D. 973-4, when the latter once more rose to great eminence. The overthrow of the Rāshṭrakūṭas, too, enabled the Raṭṭa *Mahāmaṇḍaleśvaras* to assert themselves, and their dynasty lasted till about A.D. 1253. About the same period we find the Śilāhāras and Sindas rising into importance, and, like the Raṭṭas, establishing independent dynasties which lasted for several centuries. The Śilāharas were overthrown by the Yādavas of Devagiri about A.D. 1220, and the Sindas cease to be heard of about A.D. 1182-3.

Little is known of the history of Southern India for two or three centuries immediately preceding the sudden rise of the Choḷas to great power,[2] which took place in the middle of the eleventh century. At the beginning of that century the Eastern Chālukyas held all the country along the Eastern Coast from the borders of Orissa as far south as the borders of the Pallava country. The Pallava kingdom was a powerful one, possessing the coast from its junction with the Chālukyas down to the northern border of the Choḷa territories, *i.e.*, just south of Kañchī. The Choḷas remained within their own borders and the Pāṇḍiyans in theirs, while the Koṅgu kings, who governed (apparently) the old Chera country east of the Malayāḷam tracts along the coast, although they were still independent and powerful, were beginning to feel the effect of the attacks of the little kingdom of the Hoyśala Ballāḷas, then rising into power and destined to subvert many of the surrounding monarchies.

In A.D. 1023, by an intermarriage between the two dynasties, the Choḷa sovereign acquired possession of the whole of the Eastern Chālukyan dominions. This was followed, apparently at the beginning of the reign of his successor, Rājendra Kulottuṅga Choḷa (1064–1113), by the complete subversion of the Pallavas by the Choḷas, and the annexation to the latter kingdom of their possessions. Rājendra also conquered the Pāṇḍiyans, and established a short dynasty of "Choḷa-Pāṇḍiyan" kings at Madura. A little later the Hoyśala Ballāḷas entirely overthrew the Koṅgu kings and seized their territories, so that the whole of the south of India passed at that time through a period of great political disturbance, which resulted in the Choḷas obtaining almost universal sovereignty for a short period, checked, however, by the power of the Hoyśala Ballāḷas above the ghāṭs in Maisūr.

This latter power was increased in importance by its conquest of the Kādambas[3] and Kālachuris to its immediate north about the beginning of the thirteenth century, and by the downfall of the great Western Chālukyan dynasty about A.D. 1184, which was caused partly by its wars with the Kādambas and partly by the rise of the Ballāḷas. A little later the Choḷas lost their northern possessions, which were seized by the Gaṇapatis of Oraṅgal.

We now find ourselves in the thirteenth century, the three great southern powers being the Choḷas and Pāṇḍiyans—both seemingly losing strength—and the Hoyśala Ballāḷas, rapidly growing in power.

---

[1] It seems to be now certain that the sovereigns of this dynasty were originally called *Chalukyas*, the adjectival form *Chālukya* being adopted by the later representatives of the family.

[2] We gather from the Singhalese chronicles that the Choḷas and Pāṇḍiyans were constantly at feud with Ceylon, and that the Tamils emigrated in large numbers into Ceylon.

[3] As with the *Chalukyas* and *Chālukyas*, the earlier and later dynasties of this kingdom seem to have been known respectively as *Kadambas* and *Kādambas*—(*Mr. Fleet*).

What might have occurred it is needless to enquire, though imagination readily depicts the impetuous Ballālas sweeping down from the ghāṭs and succeeding in subverting the ancient dynasties of the plains; but a new power now appears on the scene, which was destined to acquire universal dominion in course of time—the power of the Musalmāns.

Delhi had been captured by the Ghaznī Ghōrians in 1193, and a dynasty established there which lasted till A.D. 1288. The Khiljis succeeded (1288–1321), and 'Alāu-d-dīn Khilji despatched the first Muhammadan expedition into the Dakhaṇ in A.D. 1306. Four years later the Musalmān armies under Malik Kāfur swept like a torrent over the peninsula.

Devagiri and Orangal were both reduced to subjection, the capital of the Hoyśala Ballāḷas was taken and sacked, and the kingdoms both of the Choḷas and Pāṇḍiyans were overthrown. Anarchy followed over the whole south—Musalmān governors, representatives of the old royal families, and local chiefs being apparently engaged for years in violent internecine struggles for supremacy. The Ballāḷas disappeared from the scene, and the kingdoms of Devagiri and Orangal were subverted. A slight check was given to the spread of the Muḥammadan arms when a confederation of Hindu chiefs, led by the gallant young Gaṇapati Rāja, withstood and defeated a large Muḥammadan army; and the aspect of affairs was altered by the revolt of the Dakhāṇi Musalmāns against their sovereign in A.D. 1347, which resulted in the establishment of the Bāhmanī kingdom of the Dakhaṇ. But the whole of Southern India was convulsed by this sudden aggression of the Muḥammadans, and all the old kingdoms fell to pieces.

This period, then, about the year A.D. 1310, is to be noted as the second great landmark in South Indian history, the first being about the period 1023–1070, when the Choḷas became almost supreme over the south.

While the Bāhmanī rebels were consolidating their kingdom in the Dakhaṇ, another great power was being formed south of the Kṛishṇā. This was the kingdom of Vijayanagar. Established on the ruins of the Hoyśala Ballāḷas and the other Hindu sovereignties, it speedily rose to a height of power such as no southern kingdom had yet aspired to, and it held the Muḥammadans in check for two centuries. From 1336 till 1564 A.D. we have merely to consider, roughly speaking, two great powers—that of the Musalmāns north of the Kṛishṇā and that of Vijayanagar to the south.

The Bāhmanī kingdom fell to pieces at the close of the fifteenth century, being succeeded by five separate kingdoms founded by rival Musalmān leaders. Their jealousies aided the Vijayanagar sovereigns in their acquisition of power. In 1487 Narasiṁha of Vijayanagar completely subverted the Pāṇḍiyan country, Chola having fallen long before, and by the close of the fifteenth century the power of Vijayanagar was acknowledged as paramount through the entire peninsula. Small principalities existed, such as that of Maisūr, the Reḍḍi chieftainship of Koṇḍavīḍu south of the Kṛishṇā (which lasted from 1328 till 1427), and the always independent principality of Travancore, but Vijayanagar was supreme. At the beginning of the sixteenth century Kṛishṇadeva Rāya of Vijayanagar further extended the power of his house by the reduction of refractory chiefs far and wide, till his dynasty arose in his day to its greatest height of glory.

In 1564 (the third landmark) all this collapsed. The Muḥammadan sovereigns of the Dakhaṇ combined, and in one grand effort swept over Vijayanagar, sacked the capital, put to death the powerful chief who had ruled over the destinies of the empire, and for ever crushed out all semblance of independent Hindu power from the south of India. Even the very family that governed Vijayanagar divided, so that it becomes almost impossible to trace their history, and for a second time the whole of the peninsula was thrown into confusion.

Naturally the minor chiefs seized this opportunity for throwing off all fealty to their sovereign, and throughout the peninsula arose a large number of petty Poḷegars and small chieftains, whose quarrels and wars and struggles for supremacy kept the whole country in confusion for two-and-a-half centuries. The only chiefs that attained to real power were the Madura Nāyakkas, formerly viceroys of Vijayanagar, who speedily became independent and reduced to subjection almost the whole of the old Pāṇḍiyan kingdom, their compatriots, the Nāyakkas of Tanjore, holding sway over *Choḷadeśa*. The Rājas of Maisūr, too, became independent, and established a kingdom, though not a very powerful one.

Over all this distracted country the Muḥammadans gradually pressed downwards, securing the dominion of the countries south of the Tuṅgabhadrā, and eastwards to the sea, and encroaching southwards till they had reached the southern confines of the Telugu country by the middle of the seventeenth century, and by the beginning of the eighteenth were in power far south. The Mahrattas had established themselves in Tanjore in 1674 and remained there till the English supremacy. In 1736 the Musalmāns obtained possession of Madura.

The English, settled at Madras since 1639, now began to acquire more and more territory and power, and in the course of the century had conquered almost the whole of the south of India, the defeat of the Maisūr Musalmāns under Tīpū Ṣultān in 1799 finally laying the peninsula at their feet.

THE ĀLUPAS.

(Also called *Āluvas*. See Mr. Fleet's *Dynasties of the Kanarese Districts*, p. 14.)

They are mentioned in a Maisūr inscription on copper, known to many readers of scientific literature as "The Merkāra Plates." The age of this document is at present disputed. In a grant of A.D. 694 (Ś.S. 616)[1] the "Āluvas" are mentioned. The "Ālupas" are spoken of in a Kādamba inscription of A.D. 1169-70 (*Kaliyuga* 4270)[2] and in the *Vikramāṅkadevacharita* of Bilhaṇa.[3] Mr. Fleet locates them somewhere in the west or north-west of the Madras Presidency.

'ĀDIL SHĀHI DYNASTY OF VIJAYAPURA (BIJAPUR).

(*See* DAKHAṆ, Muḥammadan kings of the—.)

AHMADNAGAR, NIZĀM SHĀHI DYNASTY OF—

(*See* DAKHAṆ, Muḥammadan kings of the—.)

THE ANDHRA DYNASTY.

The earliest kings of whom we have any trace who ruled the north of this Presidency are the Andhras. The great Maurya dynasty of the north were, according to the *Purāṇas*, succeeded by kings of the Saṅga family, and these again by the Kaṇvas. The last Kaṇva, Suśarman or Siśuman, was murdered by his minister Śūdraka or Śipraka, who seized the throne and founded a dynasty which was called after the name of his tribe, the Andhras. These are the *Andaræ* of the Greek geographers.[4] Three dynasties successively ruled over their widely extended territories. These were the *Andhras* Proper, the *Āndhra-jātikas*, or "relatives of the Andhras," and the *Āndhra-bhṛityas*, or "servants of the Andhras."

The whole of the north of the Madras Presidency down, at least, to the Krishṇā river, and probably considerably to the south of it, belonged to them, and many of their leaden coins are found in the tracts near the great rivers. They were Buddhists in religion. About the beginning of the Christian era the Andhras were exceedingly powerful, possessing, according to Pliny, very large armies. They held the whole of Kaliṅgā.

In the IXth Volume of the *Asiatic Researches*, pp. 101–116, will be found an essay on the Andhras by Wilford, from which I extract the following comparative table of kings of the dynasty, taken from the several *Purāṇas*. I have corrected the spelling, and in the case of the list from the *Vishṇu Purāṇa* have added in italics notes by Mr. Edward Thomas. The list in the *Matsya Purāṇa* contains twenty-nine names.

---

1 *Ind. Ant.*, Vol. VII, p. 300.
2 J.B.B.R.A.S., Vol. IX, p. 278.
3 Bühler's Edition, V, 26. *Ind. Ant.* V, 320.
4 *Andræ Indi* in the Peutingerian Tables. Pliny calls them *Gens Andaræ*.

Bhāgavata-Purāṇa.	Vishṇu-Purāṇa.	Vāyu-Purāṇa.	Years.	Brahmāṇḍa-Purāṇa.	Years.
Balihita	Śipraka (or Śūdraka)	Sindhuka	23	Chhismaka	23
Kṛishṇa	Kṛishṇa	Kṛishṇa	18	Kṛishṇa	18
Śrī Śātakarṇī	Śrī Śātakarṇī	Śrī Śātakarṇī	...	Śrī Śātakarṇī	10
Paurṇamāsa	Pūrṇotsaṅga	Pūrṇotsaṅga	18	Pūrṇotsaṅga	18
......	Śātakarṇī	Śātakarṇī	56	Śātakarṇī	56
Lambodara	Lambodara	Lambodara	18	Lambodara	18
Ivīlaka	Ivīlaka (*Vikalā*?)	Āpīlaka	12	Āpīlaka	12
Meghasvāti	Meghasvāti	......		Saudāsa	18
Aṭamāna	Paṭumat (*Puḍumāyi*?)	Puṭumābi	24	Ābhi	12
......	Arishṭakarman	Nēmi Kṛishṇa	25	......	
Hāleya	Hala	Hala	1	Skandasvāti	28
Talaka	Pattalaka (*Maṇḍalaka*?)	Pulaka	5	Bhāvaka	5
Purīshbhoru	Pravillasena (*Purīkasena*?)	Purīkasena	21	Pravillasena	12
Sunandana	Sundara Śātakarṇin	Śātakarṇī	1	Sundara Śātakarṇī	1
Chakora	Chakora Śātakarṇin	Chakora Śātakarṇī	½	Chakora Śātakarṅī	6
......	......	......		Mahendra Śātakarṇī.	3
......	......	......		Kuntala Śātakarṇī	8
Vaṭaka	......	......		......	
Śivasvāti	Śivasvāti	Śivasvāmi	28	Svātisena	1
Gotamīputra	Gotamīputra	Gautamīputra	21	Yantramāti	34
Purīmān	Pulimān (or Pulomat)	......		......	
......	Śātakarṇin	......		Śātakarṇī	29
Madaśirā	Śivaśrī	......		Ābhi	4
Śivaskanda	Śivaskanda	......		Śivaskanda Śātakarṇī	2
Yajñaśrī	Yajñaśrī	Yajñaśrī	29	Yajñaśrī Śātakarṇī	19
		Śātakarṇī	60		
Vijaya	Vijaya	......		......	
Chandravijaya	Chandraśrī (*Daṇḍaśrī*?)	Daṇḍaśrī	3	Daṇḍaśrī Śātakarṇī	3
Lomadhi	Pulomārchis (*Pulomāvi*)	Puloma	7	Puloma	7

Of the above sovereigns, the descent of all is given as in the direct male line, with the exception of the second, Kṛishṇa, who was brother of the usurper, Śipraka. Śrī Śātakarṇī was son of Kṛishṇa, and thence the line proceeds direct.

Tables are also given in Prinsep's *Indian Antiquities, Useful Tables*, p. 241; and in the *Bṛihat Saṅhitā* (J.R.A.S., Vol. V, n.s., p. 82, etc.).

Mr. Fergusson, in his *History of Indian and Eastern Architecture* (p. 717), gives the following list[1] :—

Śipraka	B.C.	31	to	A.D.	8
Krishṇa	A.D.	8	to	"	10
Śātakarṇī I	"	10	to	"	28
Pūrṇotsaṅga	"	28	to	"	46
Śivasvāmi	"	46	to	"	64
Śātakarṇī II	"	64	to	"	120
Lambodara	"	120	to	"	138
Āpītaka	"	138	to	"	150
Saṅgha	"	150	to	"	168
Śātakarṇī III	"	168	to	"	186
Skandasvāti	"	186	to	"	193
Mṛigendra	"	193	to	"	196
Kuntalasvāti	"	196	to	"	204
Svātikarṇa	"	204	to	"	205
Pulomavit	"	205	to	"	241
Gorakshāśvaśrī	"	241	to	"	266
Hala	"	266	to	"	271
Maṇḍalaka	"	271	to	"	276
Purīndrasena	"	276	to	"	281
Sindara	"	281	to	"	284
Rājādhisvāti (6 *months*)	"	284			
Śivasvāti	"	284	to	"	312
Gautamīputra	"	312	to	"	333
Vāsiṭhīputra	"	333	to	"	335
Pulomat	"	335	to	"	363
Śivaśrī	"	363	to	"	370
Skandasvāti	"	370	to	"	377
Yajñaśrī	"	377	to	"	406
Vijaya	"	406	to	"	412
Chandraśrī	"	412	to	"	422
Pulomat	"	422	to	"	429 or 436

In J.B.B.R.A.S., XIII, 303, will be found a paper by Dr. Codrington and Bhagvānlāl Indrājī Paṇḍit on some Āndhrabhṛitya coins. They give the names of Vaḷivāya, son of Vasatī (*Vasiṭhī*),—Śivala, son of Madharī,—and Vidivāya, son of Gotamī.

In connection with this subject may be noted the succession of the predecessors of the Andhras mentioned above, as it seems certain that the sovereigns of those dynasties must have ruled over the northern portion of the Madras Presidency; though as yet, with the exception of the existence of the Edict of Aśoka at Jaugaḍa in Ganjam, I know of no remaining trace of their presence. These tables are taken from Mr. Fergusson's *Indian and Eastern Architecture*, p. 716.

Maurya Dynasty (137 Years).

Chandragupta	B.C.	325	to	B.C.	301
Bimbasāra	"	301	to	"	276
Aśoka[2]	"	276	to	"	240
Suyaśas	"	240	to	"	230 ?
Daśaratha	"	230 ?	to	"	220 ?
Saṅgata	"	220 ?	to	"	212 ?
Indrapālita	"	212 ?	to	"	210
Somaśarman	"	210	to	"	203
Śaśadharman	"	203	to	"	195
Vṛihadratha	"	195	to	"	188

[1] Dr. Oldenberg's paper on "*Ancient Indian Inscriptions and Coins*" in *Ind. Ant.* X, 213, may be consulted with reference specially to the older dynasties of the north-west.

[2] "Account of the great Hindu monarch, Aśoka," by Sir Erskine Perry, in J.B.B.R.A.S. for January 1851.

Saṅga Dynasty (112 Years).

Pushpamitra	B.C.	188 to	B.C.	152
Agnimitra	„	152 to	„	144
Sujyeshṭha	„	144 to	„	137
Vasumitra	„	137 to	„	129
Bhadraka, or Ārdraka	„	129 to	„	127
Pulindaka	„	127 to	„	124
Ghoshavasu	„	124 to	„	121
Vajramitra	„	121 to	„	112
Bhagavata	„	112 to	„	86
Devabhūti	„	86 to	„	76

Kaṇva Dynasty.

Vasudeva	B.C.	76 to	B.C.	67
Bhūmimitra	„	67 to	„	53
Nārāyaṇa	„	53 to	„	41
Suśarman (*murdered*)	„	41 to	„	31

ĀNDHRA-JĀTIKAS, ĀNDHRA-BHṚITYAS.

(*See* the Andhra Dynasty.)

AVUKU OR AUKU, ZEMINDARS OF—

(*See* Owk, Zemindars of—.)

BĀHMANĪ DYNASTY.

(*See* Dakhaṇ, Muḥammadan kings of the—.)

BALLĀḶAS, THE—

(*See* Hoysala Ballāḷas of Maisūr.)

BANAVĀSI, THE KĀDAMBAS OF—

(*See* Kādambas.)

BARĪD SHĀHI DYNASTY AT BĪDAR OR AHMADĀBĀD.

(*See* Dakhaṇ, Muḥammadan Kings of the—.)

BEDNŪR, RĀJAS OF—

(*See* Ikkeri).

BĪDAR OR AHMADĀBĀD, BARĪD SHĀHI DYNASTY OF—

(*See* Dakhaṇ, Muḥammadan kings of the—.)

BIJAPUR OR VIJAYAPURA, 'ĀDIL SHĀHI DYNASTY OF—

(*See* Dakhaṇ, Muḥammadan kings of the—.)

BĪRĀR, IMĀD SHĀHI DYNASTY OF—

(*See* Dakhaṇ, Muḥammadan kings of the—.)

THE CHALUKYAS.

The kingdom of the Chalukyas[1] was at one time widely extended, and for six centuries, from the sixth to the twelfth, they maintained a sovereignty, which, if sometimes merely nominal, was at others extremely powerful. We first hear of them in the Dakhaṇ in the sixth century, the third sovereign of the family ascending the throne in A.D. 566. Inscriptions of the dynasty are numerous, and those of the later sovereigns during the decay of the kingdom insert, in the genealogical portion of the document, a mythical series of kings, by which the descent of the family is traced, in the Lunar Race, through a succession of 59 sovereigns ruling in Ayodhyā, to one Vijayāditya, who is said to have journeyed southwards bent on conquest, but to have lost his life in battle. His widow fled, took refuge in the house of a Brahman, and there gave birth to a posthumous son—Vishṇuvardhana. Vishṇuvardhana is said to have acquired sovereignty and to have made extensive conquests, strengthening his authority by an alliance with the Pallava king of Kañchī, whose daughter he married. His son was Vijayāditya, and the latter's son was Pulikeśi Vallabha. The old inscription at Aihoḷe, published by Mr. Fleet in the *Indian Antiquary* (V, 67) names Pulikeśi's father Raṇarāga, and his grandfather, Jayasiṁha Vallabha. Mr. Fleet's estimate of this early history is that it is "a mere farrago of vague tradition and *Purānik* myths, of no authority, based on the undoubted facts that the Chalukyas did come originally from the north and did find the Pallavas in possession of some of the territories afterwards acquired by themselves, and on a tradition of the later Kādambas that the founder of their family was named Trilochana or Trinetra."

Pulikeśi's grandsons separated, and became the ancestors respectively of the Western and Eastern Chālukyas; the elder remaining in the Western Dakhaṇ, while the younger, Kubja Vishṇuvardhana, won for himself by the sword the sovereignty of the Eastern Coast by his conquest of the Śalaṅkāyana kings of Veṅgī (Pallavas). This conquest was very important, not only because of its political results, but because it was a triumph of the Brahmanical religion over Buddhism. The Veṅgī kings were Buddhists, and they seem to have succeeded the Buddhist Āndhra-bhṛityas on the Kṛishṇā river, while the Chalukyas were Vaishṇavas.

The following tables are taken mostly from Dr. Burnell's *South Indian Palæography*, page 18,[2] and Mr. Fleet's *Dynasties of the Kanarese Districts*, p. 18. The earliest sovereigns are called "Chalukyas." After the division between Satyāśraya I and Kubja Vishṇuvardhana the dynasties are respectively known as those of the "Western Chalukyas" and "Eastern Chalukyas,"—and the dynasty which commenced with Taila, or Tailapa, I called themselves "Chālukyas." Mr. Fleet has largely added to our knowledge since Dr. Burnell wrote, but I have retained some of that author's remarks.

Jayasiṁha I.

- Buddhavarmā.
  - Vijayarāja *or* Vijayavarmā,[3] (*Ś.Ś.* 394, *A.D.* 472).
- Raṇarāga.
  - Pulikeśi-Vallabha.
    - Kīrttivarmā Prithivī Vallabha I. (*Ś.Ś.* 489, *A.D.* 567.)
      - Satyāśraya I, Śrī Prithivī Vallabha, or S. Vallabhendra, or Pulikeśi II. *Began to reign separately in* 610 *A.D. Grant in Ś.Ś.* 556, *A.D.* 634.
      - Kubja Vishṇuvardhana, (*Eastern Chālukyas*). *Was probably reigning in* 607 *A.D.*
      - Jayasiṁha II,
        - Nāgavardhana.
    - Maṅgaliśa, Maṅgaliśvara *or* Maṅgalarāja. *Ascended the throne in* 567 *A.D. Reigned till Ś.Ś.* 532, *A.D.* 610.
      - ? Satyāśraya Indravarmā. (*Ś.Ś.* 532, *A.D.* 610).

[1] Mr. Fleet writes (*Ind. Ant.*, VIII. 105) regarding the habit of styling the early Chalukyas "Chalukyas of Kalyāṇapura,"—"This is nothing but a mistake. Kalyāṇa is nowhere mentioned in the earlier Chalukyan inscriptions; and, even if it existed as a city at that time, it was certainly not a Chalukya capital. The earliest mention of it that I have obtained is in a stone-tablet inscription of the Western Chalukya king Trailokyamalla or Someśvara I. It is dated *Śaka* 975 (A.D. 1053-4). . . . ."

[2] See Professor Dowson's Paper in J.R.A.S., New Series, I, 247 (1865).

[3] The Kaira grant (*Ind. Ant.* VII. 251).

Ādityavarmā.

Vijayabhaṭṭāraka (Chandrāditya).

Vikramāditya I, *about Ś.Ś.* 592 (*A.D.* 670) *to* *Ś.Ś.* 602 *or* 603 (*A.D.* 680 *or* 681). *According to the Koṅgudesa-Rājākkal, Śaṅkarāchārya lived during this reign—a statement nearly correct.—(Burnell.)*

Amberā (*daughter*).

Vinayāditya-Yuddhamalla I, (V. Satyāśraya), *Ś.Ś.* 602 *or* 603 (680 *or* 681 *A.D.*) *to Ś.Ś.* 618 (*A.D.* 696).

Vijayāditya, *Ś.Ś.* 618 (696 *A.D.*) *to Ś.Ś.* 655 (*A.D.* 733).

Vikramāditya II, *married* Lokamahādevī, *Ś.Ś.* 655 *to* 669 (*A.D.* 733 *to* 747).[1]

Kīrttivarmā II.[2] *Ś.Ś.* 669 *and* 679 (*A.D.* 747 *and* 757).

Bhīma I.

Kīrttivarmā III.[2]

Taila I.

Vikramāditya III.

Bhīma II.

Ayyana I.

Vikramāditya IV, Vijitāditya, Satyāśraya, *married Bontādevī* (*Ś.Ś.* 895—919 = 973—997 *A.D.*) *Restorer of the dynasty.—(Burnell.)*

Taila II, Tailabhūpa-Vikramāditya, or Āhavamalla I.

Satyāśraya II, *married Ambikādevī*, *Ś.Ś.* 919 *and* 930=997 *and* 1008 *A.D.*

Dasavarmā, *married Bhāgyavatīdevī.*

Vibhuvikrama, Vikramāditya V, or Tribhuvanamalla I. *Ś.Ś.* 930 *to about* 940=1008 *to about* 1018 *A.D.*

Ayyana II.

Akkādevī. *Ś.Ś.* 944 *and* 969 (*A.D.* 1022 *and* 1047).

Jayasiṁha III, (Jagadekamalla I). *About Ś.Ś.* 940 *to about* 964 = *about* 1018 *to about* 1042 *A.D.* *Mentioned in the Tanjore inscription.*

Someśvara I, (Āhavamalla II, Trailokyamalla I). *About Ś.Ś.* 964 *to about* 990 = *about* 1042 *to about* 1068 *A.D.*

---

[1] Mr. Rice's inscription (*Ind. Ant.* VIII, 23).

[2] At this point Dr. Burnell interpolates the following note :—"So far the flourishing older dynasty of the Chalukyas, which, after Vikramāditya II, appears to have been for a time almost overthrown by feudatories such as the Rashṭrakūṭa, Kalabhurya, and Yadava chiefs, and the history of this kingdom is, thus, very obscure for the eighth and ninth centuries. With Tailapa, the restorer of the Chalukya power in the later dynasty, all once more becomes tolerably certain, especially as regards the dates of the reigns. A very poetical account of the first sovereigns of this line is given in Bilhaṇa's *Vikramāṅkadevacharitra*; it is often contradicted in details by the Choḷa inscriptions."

Someśvara II, (Soyi *or* Sovideva *or* Bhuvanaikamalla). *About Ś.Ś.* 990—997 = *about* 1068—1075 *A.D.*

Vikramāditya VI, (Kalivikrama, *or* Tribhuvanamalla II). *Ś.Ś.* 997—1048 = 1075—1126 *A.D.*

Jayasiṁha IV, or Trailokyamalla II. (*Viceroy in Banavāsi.*) *Ś.Ś.* 1001 *and* 1003 (*A.D.* 1079 *and* 1081).

Children of Vikramāditya VI:

Jayakarṇa.

Someśvara III, *or* Bhūlokamalla. *Ś.Ś.* 1048—1060 = 1126—1138 *A.D.*

Mailaladevī, *married to Jayakeśi II of the Kādambas of Goa.*

Children of Someśvara III:

Jagadekamalla II, *Ś.Ś.* 1060—1072 = 1138—1150 *A.D.*

Taila III, *or* Trailokyamalla III. *Ś.Ś.* 1702 *to about* 1084 = 1150 *to about* 1162 *A.D.*

Son of Taila III:

Someśvara IV, Vīra Someśvara, or Tribhuvanamalla III. *Ś.Ś.* 1104 *to about* 1111 = 1182 *to about* 1189 *A.D.*

Pulikeśi Vallabha is said in an inscription at Aihoḷe (*Ind. Ant.* IV, 205) to have reduced Banavāsi to subjection. Mr. Fleet thinks that up to that time Banavāsi was the capital of an early branch of the Kādambas. Pulikeśi also seems to have conquered Bādāmi ("Vātāpi," which Mr. Fleet has satisfactorily identified with Bādāmi.—*Ind. Ant.*, V, 68, etc.)

Kīrttivarmā I is, in the last inscription mentioned, called "night of death to the Nalas, the Mauryas, and Kadambas." He claims to have entirely subverted the Kadambas.

His younger brother, Maṅgalīśa, is stated, in the same inscription, to have conquered the "Kaṭachchuris," whom Mr. Fleet identifies with the Kalachuris. He lost his life in an attempt to secure the kingdom for his own son. He conquered Revatidvīpa, the Mātaṅgas, and Kaḷachuris, part of the Koṅkaṇas, and a prince named Buddha, son of Śaṁkaragaṇa.

Satyāśraya was one of the most powerful princes of the dynasty. In later years poets were fond of styling the kings of this race and their descendants, "Princes of the House of Satyāśraya." His greatest achievement was his victory over Harshavardhana, king of Kanoj. He conquered a sovereign from the north named Govinda, whom Mr. Fleet takes to be one of the Rāshṭrakūṭas. He claims, in various inscriptions, to have subdued the Mauryas of the Koṅkaṇa, the "Lāṭas, Mālavas, and Gūrjaras." He reduced the fortress of "Pishṭāpura," acquired the sovereignty of *Mahārāshṭrakā*, terrified the "Kāliṅgas and Kosalas," drove the Pallavas behind the walls of Kāñchīpura, and prepared to conquer the Cholas with a large army. Too much trust must not be placed in the poetry of the inscriptions, but it is abundantly clear from other sources that Satyāśraya was a great conqueror. Hiwen-Thsang gives an interesting account of his kingdom, the manners and customs of the time, and the grandeur of the sovereign. Mr. Fergusson (*J.R.A.S.* XI, 155) points out that presents and letters were interchanged between him and Khosru II, contemporary king of Persia.

Mr. Rice has an inscription (*Mysore Inscriptions*, p. 298) mentioning Amberā, daughter of Satyāśraya.[1]

The Chalukyan supremacy, after the death of Satyāśraya, was interrupted, either by a confederacy of three kings over whom the Pallava lord of Kañchī claimed supremacy, or by three Pallava kings or viceroys in alliance (it is not yet certain which[2]), but Vikramāditya I defeated them and ascended the throne of his fathers. He suffered a reverse at the hands of the Pallavas, but afterwards crushed them and seized Kañchī, their capital. One of the inscriptions mentions that Devaśakti, king of the Sendrakas, was his vassal.

Vinayāditya claims to have conquered the "Pallavas, whose kingdom consisted of three dominions" at "the command of his father," (*Indian Antiquary*, VI, 85, *Mr. Fleet*). It seems not improbable that the Pallava confederacy which had checked the power of the Chalukyas was overthrown by Vinayāditya at the head of his father's armies, and that after Vinayāditya had acquired the throne of his father, he

[1] As corrected by Mr. Fleet (*Ind. Ant.* X, 133).

[2] The evidence as to this is summarised by Mr. Fleet in *Ind. Ant.* X, 133—135, in reply to an assertion by Mr. Rice that the evidence as to any such confederation is insufficient.

made war on and crushed the Pallavas, seizing their capital city. Vinayāditya seems to have possessed almost the whole of the Dakhaṇ country, and to have extended his conquests southwards. He claims to have conquered the Kaḷambhras (?), the Keraḷas, Haihayas, Viḷas, Mālavas, Choḷas, Pāṇḍiyans and others; and though a great deal of this may be vain boasting, he seems to have been a very powerful sovereign.

His son Vijayāditya boasts of conquests, but we do not hear much of him. His reign appears to have been peaceful.

Vikramāditya II claims to have conquered and slain the king of the Pallavas, and again to have victoriously entered Kañchī.[1] In other inscriptions he boasts of having conquered Kañchī, or the king of Kañchī, three times.

Kirttivarmā II claims another victory over the Pallavas.

But the power collapsed shortly afterwards, the feudatories revolting and the short-lived kingdom being overwhelmed by successful revolts and conquests by neighbouring powers.

With Taila II, who "acquired the earth, which had fallen into the hands of the Raṭṭas,"[2] the Western Chālukya kingdom again revived after a blank of two centuries. The territories governed by the new dynasty were greatly reduced in size, and appear to have extended no further than the limits of the Dakhaṇ Proper.

Jayasiṁha III claims to have overthrown a confederacy of Mālavas, and to have warred against the Cheras and Choḷas.

Someśvaradeva I, or Āhava Malla II, appears to have driven back the Choḷas, and to have been again defeated by the great Choḷa king, Kulottuṅga I.[3] In his reign the Kādambas and other neighbouring families began to assume independence. He married three wives, Bachalādevī, Chandalakabbe or Chandrikādevī, and Mailalādevī.

Someśvara II would appear to have checked the Kādambas, part of whose territories was acquired and held by his brother Vikramāditya VI.

Vikramāditya VI re-established the *Śaka* Era (Mr. Fleet in *Ind. Ant.* IV, 208, V, 175). He gave his daughter in marriage to a Kādamba prince, and married a Choḷa princess. He fought many battles, and seems to have been engaged in perpetual struggles to secure his sovereignty against members of his own family no less than against the armies of hostile sovereigns.[4] He was, however, very powerful, and a large number of inscriptions testify to the extent of his territories.

From this period the kingdom began to fall to pieces and nothing remarkable seems to have been achieved by the later sovereigns, though Someśvara IV re-established for a few years the power which had been rudely shaken by Bijjala the Kaḷachuri. The power of the Kaḷachuri and Gaṇapati kings and the rise of the Hoyśaḷa Ballāḷa dynasty of Maisūr sealed the fate of the Western Chālukyas, and nothing is heard of them after 1189 A.D.[5]

Eastern Chālukyas.

It has been already stated (p. 148) that the two great Chalukyan brothers, Satyāśraya and Kubja Vishṇuvardhana, separated and established two separate dynasties. The family of the former are called the Western Chālukyas. Kubja Vishṇuvardhana, marching to the Eastern Coast, conquered and dethroned the Śālaṅkāyaṇa sovereign of Veṅgī and established a dynasty which, gradually extending its conquests to the borders of Orissa and fixing its capital at Rajahmundry, ruled Kaliṅgā for four centuries.

The genealogy is as follows. The table is mainly taken from Dr. Burnell's *South-Indian Palæography*, (pp. 21, 22).

---

[1] An inscription published by Mr. Rice (*Ind. Ant.* VIII, 25) gives particulars of this event. It appears that after his coronation the king made war on the Pallavas, killed in battle Nandi Pōtavarma, their king, and victoriously entered Kañchī. He found that city richly decorated with sculptures which had been executed under the orders of a former king, Narasiṁha Pōtavarma, amongst them being images of *Rājasiṁha* (?) Vikramāditya II, when he left Kañchī, travelled on to the coast, and took up his residence there, for a time, in a town on the sea.

[2] *Ind. Ant.* V, 17.

[3] In Bilhaṇa's *Vikramāṅkakāvya*, it is claimed for Someśvara I that he conquered the Choḷas, apparently twice; and it expressly states that the Choḷa monarch had attacked him. But several inscriptions mention Kulottuṅga's defeat of the Chālukyan sovereign. (*Ind. Ant.* V, 318).

[4] (*Ind. Ant.* V, 319—623). While in camp on the Tuṅgabhadrā, Vikrama heard of the death of his father-in-law. He marched on Kañchī, crushed a rebellion there, put the rightful heir on the throne, and then seized Gaṅgaikoṇḍaśōrapuram. Shortly after he had retired he heard of the death of the newly enthroned monarch, and of the seizure of the Choḷa throne by "Rajiga, lord of Veṅgī," a member of the family. Vikrama offered battle, but was attacked in rear by his brother Someśvara, whom he defeated, while Rājiga fled. Vikrama then ascended the throne of the Chalukyas, A.D. 1076. He is said to have conquered the Choḷas on two subsequent occasions.

[5] J.R.A.S. IV, 17; M.J.L.S. VII, 209; Mr. Fleet's "*Dynasties of the Kanarese Districts*," 55, 59—63.

- Kubja Vishṇuvardhana I. 18 *years.* (?)
  - Jayasiṁhavallabha I. 30 *years.* (?)
  - Indra Bhaṭṭāraka or Indra Rāja.
    - Rājanandana Vishṇuvardhana II. 9 *years.* (?)
      - Maṅgi (Yuvarāja) 25 *years.* (?)
        - Jayasiṁhavallabha II. 13 *years.* (?)
        - Kokkili (Kokili or Kaikkili) 6 *months.* (?)
        - Vishṇuvardhana III. 37 *years.* (?)
          - (Śaktivarmā) Vijayāditya Bhaṭṭāraka I. 16 *or* 18 *years.* (?)
            - Vishṇuvardhana IV. 30 *years.* (?)
              - Vijayāditya-Narendra-Mṛigarāja II. 40 *or* 48 *years.* (?)
                - Kali Vishṇuvardhana V. 1½ *years.* (?)
                  - Guṇāṅka Vijayāditya III. 40 *or* 44 *years.* (?)
                  - Vikramāditya Yuvarāja.
                    - Chālukya Bhīma 30 *years.* (?)
                      - Kollabhiganda-Vijayāditya 6 *months.* (?)
                        - Amma Rāja I. (*surnamed* Vishṇuvardhana) 7 *years.* (?)
                          - Vijayāditya.
                          - Rāja Bhima 12 *years.* (?)
                            - Amma Rāja II. (*surnamed* Vijayāditya) 25 *years.* (?)
                            - Dānanṛipa 3 *years.* (?) — * * * — 25 *years.* (?) } Time of anarchy.
                              - Śaktivarmā, 12 *years.* (?)
                              - Vimalāditya, 7 *years.* (?)
                      - Vikramāditya 11 *months.* (?)
                  - Yuddhamalla.
                    - Tāṛapa 1 *month.* (?)
                      - Yuddhamalla 7 *years.* (?)

Vimalāditya married Kūndavā, daughter of Rājarāja of the Sūryavaṁśa, and younger sister of Rājendra Choḷa. His successor Rājarāja of the Chandravaṁśa married (A.D. 1022) Iramonaṅgā, (?)

daughter of Rājendra Chola, and their son Rājendra Chola was the first Chola ruler of Veṅgī, and succeeded in A.D. 1064.[1] The Veṅgī kingdom thenceforward became a mere northern province of *Choladeśa*. The succession of Cholas will be given below. Rājendra Kulottuṅga I made his son Rājarāja regent of the Chālukya country; but after ruling for a year the latter retired to the south, and the sovereign created his uncle Vijayāditya viceroy. Vijayāditya governed Kaliṅgā for 15 years. On his death Kulottuṅga gave the viceroyalty to his second son, Vīranātha, who ruled there till at least as late as A.D. 1102.

According to Dr. Burnell, the Cholas lost this country in 1228 A.D.

The number of years given to each sovereign's reign varies slightly in different inscriptions, and it is impossible yet to be quite certain of dates, as very few of the Eastern Chālukya inscriptions are dated.

Kubja Vishṇuvardhana's conquest is generally believed to have taken place about the year 605 A.D., and this may be taken as the approximate date. He seems to have finally separated from his brother in A.D. 610. The inscriptions of this dynasty unfortunately contain little more than mere lists of names with no details, and therefore it is impossible as yet to frame any connected narrative. The main landmarks are the conquest of Kubja Vishṇuvardhana;—the struggle for the throne between the two sons of Maṅgi the "Yuvarāja" and their half-brother Kokkili, resulting in the expulsion of the latter after he had ruled for six months;—the usurpation of Tārapa who drove out Amma Rāja I's son Vijayāditya and seized the throne;—his own ejection at the hands of Chālukya Bhīma's son Vikramāditya, a month later;—the struggles which ensued between rival claimants ending with the triumph of Rāja Bhīma, who reigned for 12 years;—the accession of Amma Rāja II in 945 A.D., a date which is fixed by an inscription;—the anarchy of 27 or 30 years (duration not certain) which ensued;—and the extinction of the dynasty when the Cholas succeeded to the sovereignty. For the subsequent history of the Eastern Chalukyas, see under "THE CHOLAS" (p. 154).

In the reign of one of the sovereigns bearing the name of Vishṇuvardhana at Rajahmundry, lived Nannayya Bhaṭṭa, who, at the command of the king, composed the Telugu version of the *Mahābhārata*, (see Campbell's *Telugu Grammar*, *Introd.*, IX—X, where the original passage relating to the authorship of the poem is quoted).

The Eastern Chālukyas may be considered as having ruled during these four centuries more or less peaceably over the whole of the Veṅgī and part at least of the Kaliṅgā countries; being disturbed probably more by the Gajapatis of Orissa on the north than by any power on their south and west.

At the end of the twelfth and beginning of the thirteenth centuries, the Gaṇapati sovereigns of Oraṅgal were acquiring power in the Eastern Chālukyan territories, and they finally ejected the Chola-Chālukyas about the year 1228 A.D. (*Dr. Burnell*).

THE CHERAS.

There has been much difference of opinion in scientific quarters as to the Chera and Koṅgu Dynasties, some writers asserting that they were identical, some that they were totally different. The territories ruled by them have been variously assigned. The opinion seems to be gaining ground that the Cheras were the dynasty that preceded the Koṅgus in the same kingdom, in other words that the first seven sovereigns of the Koṅgu Dynasty, as given below (p. 189), ought properly to be styled Cheras. Others believe that the Cheras ruled almost the whole of the Western Coast and the country far inland, north of the Pāṇḍiyans, west of the Pallavas and Cholas, and south of the Koṅkaṇa, from the earliest known historical times, their territories, of course, varying perpetually as their arms were victorious or the reverse in their wars with their neighbours, until the Koṅgus, who occupied the eastern and northern portion of their dominions, including Maisūr, overwhelmed the old sovereignty and succeeded to the most part of their dominions, the Western Coast being excluded.

The Cheras were mentioned by the oldest known European geographers as well as by the most ancient writers yet known in India. They are spoken of as contemporary with the Cholas and Pāṇḍiyans, and are so mentioned in the edicts of Aśoka, where their sovereign is called Keralaputra. According to Ptolemy (VII, I, 86), Karūr was their capital then. Hiwen-Thsang does not mention the kingdom, but refers to part of it under the name of *Koṅkaṇapura* (Koṅkaṇahaḷḷi). (Dr. Burnell's *South-Indian Palæography, p.* 33, *notes* 1 *and* 2 ; *Ind. Ant.* VIII, 145, 146.)

---

[1] This is Sir Walter Elliot's account. I confess it puzzles and perplexes me at present, because it does not seem to tally with other contemporary statements, but all will soon become clear, it is to be hoped, and meanwhile it is fitting that I should quote the opinions of the best authorities.

Those who desire to study the subject should read Mr. Foulkes's historical sketch of the country in question in the *Salem District Manual*, and Professor Dowson's Paper in Vol. VIII of the *Royal Asiatic Society's Journal*. See also Dr. Burnell's *South-Indian Palæography*, p. 33, &c.; the Markāra Plates (*Ind. Ant.* I, 361—366; II, 271, *note*, and V, 133); the Nāgamangalam Plates (*Ind. Ant.* II, 155; III, 152 *and* 262); Mr. Rice's note on the Ganga Kings (*Ind. Ant.* VII, 168).

THE CHOḶA KINGS.

The Choḷa [1] Kingdom forms one of the three great divisions of Southern India, which existed from the earliest known historical times. The Choḷas held the east, the Pāṇḍiyans the south, and the Cheras the west. This distinction existed as far back as the days of Aśoka, and is confirmed by Greek writers. Unfortunately Choḷa history is almost a blank till the days of Rājarāja (1023 A.D.). We have not even a legendary list of names to guide (or mislead) us as with the Pāṇḍiyans.

The Choḷa capital seems to have been at Uṛaiyūr (Warriore) close to Trichinopoly in the second century A.D., at Malaikūṟṟam (Kumbakōnam?)[2] in the seventh, and at Tanjore (?) in the tenth—(*Dr. Burnell*). It was at Gangaikoṇḍaśōṛapuram at one time, probably in the tenth century, being fixed finally at Tanjore early in the eleventh. The ancient name for the Choḷa country, according to Dr. Burnell (*South Indian Palæography*, 47, note 4,) was *Malakūṭa*. "The Choḷa banner had a tiger on it, which the kings of this dynasty must have taken from the Pallavas." (*ib.* 107.)

I have met with only two lists, which can be at all depended upon, of Choḷa sovereigns reigning prior to Rājarāja. The first is given by Mr. Lewis Rice (*Mysore and Coorg*, I, 212) as that of Choḷas reigning in the east of Maisūr.

	A.D.
Ādityavarmā, Rājendra Choḷa	867 to 927
Vīra Choḷa, Nārāyaṇarāja	927 to 977
Dasoditya Rāya	?
Parandaka Rāya, Hari Māli	?
Divya Rāya, or Deva Rāja Choḷa	?
Harivari Deva, or Tribhuvana Vīra Deva Choḷa	986 to 1023

But Mr. Rice adds, "There is no certainty regarding either the names or the dates," and he does not give his authority for the list. The second is by Mr. Foulkes (*Salem District Manual*, Vol. I, p. 39).

Vijayādi Rāya.
|
Ādityavarma Rāya
or Vijaya Rāya Āditya Varmā.
? *about A.D.* 878.
|
Vīra Choḷa Rāya
alias Vīra Choḷa Nārāyaṇa Rāya.
Builder of the Kanaka-sabhā at Chidambaram.
|

Hariñjaya Rāya *or* Aruñjeya Rāya.	Desotya Rāya *or* Dāsoditya Rāya, *died sonless.*	"*Many sons,*" "*a great many other children.*"
|		

[1] Lists of the Choḷas will be found in the following works:—
Buchanan's *Mysore, Canara and Malabar*, iii, 472, (Higginbotham's 8vo Edition of 1870, Vol. ii, p. 532,) taken from a native Manuscript.
J.A.S.B., vii, 371, 389, 507, 512. Taylor's Oriental Manuscripts.
Wilson's *Catalogue of the Mackenzie MSS.*, I, pp. xc and 181.
Taylor's *Catalogue Raisonnée of Oriental MSS.*, III, 391, 440, 518, 522.
Prinsep's "Useful Tables" in Thomas's Edition, II, 275, 279. The lists are taken from Buchanan and Wilson.
Taylor's notices of the Manuscripts in the several volumes of the M.J.L.S.
None of them, however, must be depended upon for a moment as they come from most untrustworthy sources.

[2] *Malai* = "hill," *kuṟṟam* = "subdivision." The place seems also to have been called "Malakūṭa." (*Ind. Ant.* VII, 39). Apparently it gave its name to a tract of country, for mention is made of a Brahman village, "the ornament of Malakūṭa." Dr. Burnell thinks that "Malakūṭa" was "the kingdom comprised, roughly speaking, in the delta of the Kaveri."

Parāntaka Rāya
alias Hari Māli, *or* Ari Malli,
married Chittiri, daughter of Setu Rāya, or Chati Rāya.

Divi Rāya *or* Divya Rāya, *alias* Hari-Tittu Rāya *or* Arititu Rāya, *died sonless.*

Rājarāja Narendra, *also called* Harivarideva, *married an Eastern Chalukyan princess.*

Many other children, "sons."

"Elder sons."

Rājendra Choḷa.

I have cut the genealogy short as it is unnecessary here to give the whole.

Dr. Burnell thinks that the Choḷas were extending their power to the northwards about the period from 850 to 1023 A.D. by warfare and inroads, and he attributes the thirty (or twenty-seven) years' anarchy in the Eastern Chālukyan dominions to Choḷa invasions. With Rājarāja (1023 A.D.) the history becomes all more clear, but previons to that reign we are as yet very much in the dark. Dr. Burnell tentatively fixes Karikāla Choḷa about the year 950 A.D., but this is not as yet conclusive.

The Choḷa kingdom was in existence as early as 250 B.C., being mentioned in the inscriptions of Aśoka where it is called "Choḍa." It was also known to the Greek Geographers and is noticed in the *Periplūs Maris Erythrœi,*[1] and in Ptolemy (130 A.D.), the capital being then at Uṛaiyūr. It is clear from the legends in the Madura *Sthala Purāṇa* and the *Śrītāla* Book that, according to Pāṇḍiyan tradition, the kingdom of Choḷa was as old as that of the Pāṇḍiyans, or even older, since the son of the founder of Madura is stated to have married the daughter of the Choḷa king. These legends allude perpetually to wars between the Choḷas and Pāṇḍiyans, but there is no need to discuss the question as to their authenticity. If the two nations were contemporary, it is almost certain that they must have been constantly at feud, but the particular battles mentioned in the legends are probably purely mythical.

At the beginning of the seventh century we read in an inscription[2] of the celebrated Satyāśraya or Pulikeśi II of the Chalukyan dynasty, that that sovereign ruined the Pallavas of Kañchī, and had proposed to himself to annihilate the Choḷas; but the expedition seems to have been abandoned. A few years later, viz., about the year 640 A.D., Hiwen-Thsang heard of the kingdom though he did not visit it. Vikramāditya I of the Western Chalukyas (670—680 ?) claims[3] to have conquered Choḷa, though the statement is not necessarily to be credited. He, however, seems certainly to have defeated the Pallavas, and to have seized Kāñchīpura. (The "Seven Pagodas" probably date from this reign.) Vinayāditya[4] (A.D. 680 ?--696), his successor, also claims, and probably with equal want of truthfulness, to have conquered the Choḷas. About 60 years later the Western Chalukyan Kingdom seems to have collapsed, and to have only risen again to power after a lapse of two centuries. In Wilson's Mackenzie Manuscripts (I, pp. 198-9) mention is made of an inscription which shows that in 894 A.D. the Choḷas, under their king Ādityavarmā, conquered the Chera or Koṅgu country. The date seems to be somewhat uncertain but there can be little doubt that this conquest really did take place, and that the Choḷas held the Koṅgu country (Maisūr mainly) till the tenth century, when the Hoyśala Ballāḷas arose on the ruins of the Koṅgu kings. Tailabhūpa Vikramāditya of the Western Chālukyas states that he was victorious over the Choḷas; and Jayasiṁha III (1018--1042) makes a similar boast. This brings us down to the reign of the Choḷa sovereign Rājarāja, who was a contemporary of Jayasiṁha's, and was one of the most powerful chiefs of his time. He raised the Choḷa kingdom to great eminence. Dr. Burnell thinks that it is certain that the Choḷas were conquered by the Chālukyas shortly before the beginning of the eleventh century, *i.e.*, shortly before the reign of Rāja Rāja (1023—1064 A.D.) He writes of Rāja Rāja;—"This king must have restored Tanjore, which, according to Al-Bīrūnī, was in ruins at the beginning of the eleventh century.[5] This fact confirms the earlier Chālukya boasts of conquest, and was certainly owing to them."

---

1 The date of the *Periplūs* is fixed by Reinaud as A.D. 246 or 247 (*Ind. Ant.* VIII, 331, 334, 337). For translation, with notes and commentary, see *Ind. Ant.* VIII, 107.

2 *Ind. Ant.*, VIII, 237.

3 *Ind. Ant.*, VI, 75.

4 *Ind. Ant.*, VI, 35, 83, 91.

5 Al-Bīrūnī wrote at the beginning of the eleventh century. He died A.D. 1039. He is quoted by Rashīd-ud-dīn (1310 A.D.). (Sir Henry Elliot's *History of India*, I, 66; Reinaud *Fragments*, pp. 92, 121; *Mémoire*, p. 284). The king had built "another city on the shore called Padmar."

During the early period, before the eleventh century, the Choḷas were repeatedly attacked by powers other than those above mentioned, and we hear of them in succession as being conquered by or conquering the Kāḍambas, the Pāṇḍiyans, and others.

Singhalese annals give us an invasion of Ceylon by Choḷas about the year 247 B.C. (the date is quite unauthenticated), in consequence of which the Choḷas ruled the island for 44 years; also a second invasion a hundred years later, and a third in the year 110. A.D. A counter invasion of Choḷa territories by Singhalese took place in 113 A.D., and subsequent to this, warfare between the two races was of constant occurrence. In the middle of the tenth century it is said that the king of Ceylon sent an army to the assistance of a Pāṇḍiyan king who was then at war with the Choḷas, but that the Pāṇḍiyans were defeated, and the Choḷas, in revenge, invaded Ceylon but were repulsed. The next thing we hear of relates to the reign of Rājarāja, a period when, as before stated, the chronicles appear more trustworthy.

Dr. Burnell has given the succession thus (*South-Indian Palæography*, p. 40, *note* 1).

Karikāla Choḷa,
? about 950 *A.D.*

Rājarāja Choḷa
alias Narendra,
40 *or* 41 *years—A.D.* 1023 *to* 1064.

|

Vīra Choḷa
alias Kulottuṅga Choḷa I,
alias Rājarājendra (Rājarāja) Koppākeśarivarmā.
49 *years—A.D.* 1064 *to* 1113.
His Abhisheka took place in 1079.

|

Vikrama Choḷa,
15 *years—A.D.* 1113 *to* 1128.

|

Kulottuṅga Choḷa II,
A.D. 1128 *to* ? *Ruled over the whole Tamiḻ Country for at least* 30 *years.*

|

* * *

|

Vikramadeva,
reigning in A.D. 1235.

Rājarāja, owing to an intermarriage between the Choḷas and Eastern Chālukyas, united the whole of Veṅgī and Kaliṅgā to the Choḷa territories. (M.J.L.S. XIII, Pt. 2, p. 40). He came to the throne in the same year as King Mihindu IV. of Ceylon, *i.e.*, in 1023 A.D. Ten years later—years during which constant emigration was taking place from the mainland to Ceylon—King Mihindu, overwhelmed with the perpetual influx of foreigners, lost his authority both over his own people and the strangers, and fled to Ambagalla. Rājarāja invaded the island twenty-six years after this event, *i.e.*, in 1059 A.D., and was completely successful. He seized the government, took Mihindu prisoner, and sent him with his queen and the crown jewels to the mainland, appointing a Choḷa Viceroy to govern the conquered territory. Mihindu died in 1071 A.D., still in captivity.

Previously to this, however, viz., in 1064, the throne of the Choḷas passed to Kulottuṅga I or Rājendra Choḷa, one of the greatest princes of his day.[1] Besides assuming the sovereignty over his own territories, which, by the union of the Choḷa and Eastern Chālukya countries, extended up to the borders of Orissa, he conquered in A.D. 1064 and annexed for a time the whole of the Pāṇḍiyan kingdom, and by the prowess of his illegitimate son Āḍoṇḍai (according to native tradition) completely and for ever crushed the power of the Pallavas of Kañchī. Although it must be admitted that proof is as yet wanting, I incline to the belief that there is at least a basis of historical truth underlying this

---

[1] He was crowned in 1071 A.D. The name of his principal queen seems to have been "Ulaha Muṟuduḍaiyaḷ," a Tamiḻ translation of "*Loka Mahādevī.*" It is also given in inscriptions as "*Bhuvana-*, or *Avani-Muṟuduḍaiyāḷ*, all meaning the same thing. It has become a question, however, whether this is not a mere title assumed by many South Indian Queens. It has been found in connection with more than one Pāṇḍiyan sovereign, and the wife of Vikramāditya II of the Western Chalukyas bore the same name.

native tradition. At any rate it seems certain that the annexation of the kingdom of the Pallavas to that of the Choḷas took place at this period. It is further stated in the great inscription round the temple at Tanjore that the Choḷas, towards the beginning of the eleventh century, conquered Bengal (Burnell's *South Indian Palæography, p.* 22, note 6). Either in the reign of Rājarāja or in that of Kulottuṅga I—probably the former—the Choḷas swept over the Western Chālukya country. It was during the reign of Someśvara I of the latter dynasty. (Mr. Fleet's *Kanarese Dynasties*, p. 46 *and note* 2). They destroyed a number of Jain temples at Puligere or Lakshmeśvara, but their success was only temporary. They were driven over the Tuṅgabhadrā and their leader killed. The date of this event is possibly 1059-60 A.D. In the *Vikramāṅkadevacharita* of Bilhaṇa, Someśvara I is said to have "penetrated as far as Kañchī itself, stormed it, and driven its ruler into the jungles," but this is probably a mere poetical exaggeration and really alludes to the victory above mentioned. A little later the Choḷas are again found fighting with the Western Chālukyas, this time with a Pallava (?) of Veṅgī.

Vikramāditya VI, of the Western Chālukyas, who reigned from 1075 to 1126 A.D., was, previous to his accession, always at feud with his elder brother Someśvara II, and during his reign occupied himself in warfare on his own account against the enemies of his country. At this period he is said to have repeatedly defeated the Choḷas and plundered Kañchī (it is almost impossible to believe this, and the authority seems to be only the *Vikramāṅkadevacharita*), to have destroyed the sandalwood forests of the Malaya hills, to have slain the king of Keraḷa, and conquered the cities of Gaṅgaikoṇḍapuram (*Gāṅgakuṇḍa*—Mr. Fleet), Veṅgī and Chakrakōṭa or Chakragotta (?) He had married a daughter of the Choḷa king, and on the occurrence of a rebellion in the Choḷa country, in which his brother-in-law was killed (this, if true, *must* have been Rājarāja and the date A.D. 1064), he heard that Rājigā, king (?) of Veṅgī, had marched down and seized Kañchī. Vikramāditya marched to the south to meet Rājigā, and his brother Someśvara followed with another army "promising outwardly to assist his brother, but intending to play the traitor." A battle ensued in which Rājigā was defeated and fled, and Someśvara was taken prisoner (*i.e.*, the Choḷas were victorious at all points). Vikramāditya then proclaimed himself king.

The above account is all taken from Mr. Fleet's new publication, and he draws his information from Bilhaṇa, who, being a Hindu poet, is almost certain to be absolutely wrong in details, though his story may be based on the truth. I do not therefore discard the tale on account of the discrepancy in dates, for it is quite possible that the latter part of the story may refer to a date eleven years later than the rebellion which caused the Choḷa king's death—the date, that is, of Vikramāditya's accession to the throne.

Kulottuṅga I was a man of many names. Thus he is called "Vīra," "Rājendra," "Koppākēsarivarmā," or "Kopparakēsarivarmā," "Kōvirāja Kēsari," and others. He conquered Āhavamalla, or Someśvaradeva I of the Western Chālukyas in a battle near the Tuṅgabhadrā, a fact which is recorded in several inscriptions. The Pāṇḍiyan king whom he conquered was Vīra Pāṇḍiyan, son of Vikrama Pāṇḍiyan. (*Inscriptions at Chidambaram.* Dr. Burnell's *South-Indian Palæography, p.* 45, *note* 1.) Kulottuṅga placed his younger brother Gaṅgaikoṇḍān Choḷa on the throne of Madura.[1]

Reverting to Ceylon we find that Kulottuṅga held firmly to his father's conquest for the first few years of his reign. Young prince Kāśyapa, however, son of Mihindu, who was at the most 26 years' old at the capture of his father, had been gradually consolidating his power while in exile amongst the hills, and he succeeded in beating back the Choḷa Viceroy's army when it marched against him, even though the latter was aided by a force of 10,000 men sent over from the mainland to its assistance. Mihindu died in 1071, and Kāśyapa, proclaiming himself King of Ceylon, was making great preparations for driving the usurpers out of the island, when his career was cut short by his early death. He could not have been more than 38 years old. The throne of Ceylon was seized by the son of the minister Lokeśvara on the demise of Kāśyapa, there being no other claimants for the purple. He called himself Vijaya Bāhu I, and proclaimed war against the Choḷas. The natives flocked to his standard, and fighting soon afterwards commenced. A general action was, after a protracted and desultory warfare, fought under the walls of Pollonnaruwa, and the Choḷas were defeated and driven into the town. After a siege of six weeks the town was carried by storm, and the defenders put to the sword. The king's authority was soon recognized all over the island. Shortly after this, Vijaya Bāhu insulted the Choḷa king by giving the first place in precedence at an audience to the envoy from Siam in preference to the Choḷa ambassador, and this so enraged Kulottuṅga that he seized the Singhalese envoy at his court and cut off his nose and ears. War ensued. The Choḷas landed at Mantotte, defeated the Singhalese army, and marched on the capital. The king fled, and the Choḷas demolished the city. Recovering himself

[1] Dr. Burnell states, on the authority of an inscription at Karuvūr, that this prince assumed the title of "Sundara Pāṇḍiyan."

soon, however, Vijaya Bāhu returned to the attack, defeated the invaders, and drove them from the island.

Kulottuṅga died in 1113, and three years later, during the reign of his son and successor, Vikrama Choḷa, the Singhalese invaded the Choḷa country but were driven back without difficulty.

All the old native chronicles unite in narrating the glories of Kulottuṅga's illegitimate son Ādoṇḍai, the conqueror of the Pallavas. An inscription at Tiruttaṇi (*Vol. I, p.* 158) in the Pallava country gives a genealogy of five generations, and the local chronicle of Nārāyaṇavanam (*ib., pp.* 157, 158) mentions four, of which the names correspond, thus :—

Tiruttaṇi Inscription.	Nārāyaṇavanam Chronicle.
Karikāla Choḷa.	
Chakravarti.	Ādoṇḍai.
Sudhāmā.	Sundama Rāja.
Ruchira.	Surasira Rāja.
Nārāyaṇa Rāja.	Nārāyaṇa Rāja.

These evidently refer to the same persons, and "Chakravarti" is a common title of Ādoṇḍai. Ādoṇḍai is always declared to be the son of Kulottuṅga I. Was, then, "Karikāla Choḷa" another of the latter's numerous names? This point is interesting and important.

If native chronicles are to be believed in this respect, Kulottuṅga I had a brother Śāraṅgadhara, another son of Rājarāja Choḷa. In the *Appakāviyamu* or Appa Kavi's Commentary on the Grammar of Nannayya Bhaṭṭa, Śāraṅgadhara is stated to have been the son of Rājarāja, and this is repeated in the *Śāraṅgadharacharita*.[1] A question arises whether this prince could possibly be identical with Śāraṅga, also called "Rudradeva" *alias* "Churaṅga" "*alias* Chōṟ Gaṅga" (*Choḷa* or *Sōṟa Gaṅga*), who, summoned from Karṇāṭaka by the chiefs of Orissa after the collapse of the Kesari Dynasty of that kingdom, founded the Gāṅgavaṁśa family of Orissa about the year A.D. 1132. The dates seem at first sight fatal to the theory, but our Orissan chronology is as yet very imperfect. It is to be observed that Kulottuṅga claims to have reduced Bengal.

The facts noted above enable some slight additions to be provisionally made to the genealogy of the eleventh century Choḷas. All will doubtless become clear when the many extant inscriptions are carefully studied, but at present the following is put forward tentatively. The main points are taken from Dr. Burnell's *Palæography*, which, in some respects, follows Dr. Caldwell.

?

A sister, married Vallavarai Yāvadyadeva. (*Inscriptions at Tanjore.*)	Rājarāja Choḷa, *alias* Rājarāja Narendra, *or simply* Narendra, (1023--1064). *Killed during a rebellion* (?)	? Vijayāditya, *Governor of Vengī or Kaliṅgā for* 15 *years under his nephew; died A.D.* 1079.	(*A sister* ?) *married Vikramāditya VI of the Western Chālukyas* (?)

Children of Rājarāja Choḷa:

Vīra, *alias* Rājendra Choḷa, *alias* Kulottuṅga I, *alias* Rājarājendra, *alias* Koppā (*or* Koppara) Kēsarivarmā, *alias* Kōnēri Nanmai Koṇḍān, *alias* Kōvirāja Kesarivarmā. *A.D.* 1064–1113. *Crowned* 1079. *Married* Loka Mahādevī, *alias* Ulaha-Bhuvana– *or* Avani– Muṟuduḍaiyāḷ.	Gaṅgaikoṇḍān, *ascended the throne of Madura after his father's conquest of the Pāṇḍiyan country, and was called "Sundara Pāṇḍiyan."*	Kūndavā, *married* Vimalāditya *of the Eastern Chālukyas.*	Śāraṅgadhara ?

[1] Appa Kavi declares that Śāraṅgadhara studied Telugu Grammar directly under Nannayya Bhaṭṭa, but if the prince was son of Rājarāja Choḷa, this is impossible. For he would not have been born much before A.D. 1023, while Nannayya Bhaṭṭa's date must have been earlier by a century. The latter was contemporary with an Eastern Chālukyan sovereign named Vishṇuvardhana, residing at Rajahmundry (*Introd. to Nannayya Bhaṭṭa's Telugu Translation of the Mahābhārata. Campbell's Telugu Grammar, Introd., pp.* ix, x) and the last sovereign of that name that we as yet know of was Amma Raja I, who bore that title (*Ind. Ant.*, VIII, 76). His date is A.D. 918–925, or thereabouts. On the other hand it is noticeable that "Vishṇuvardhana" was a title of the Eastern Chālukyan Dynasty borne by many sovereigns, and especially the later ones (*Vol. I, p.* 105, *note*).

Vikrama Choḷa, A.D. 1113 to 1128.	*(By a dancing girl)* Ādoṇḍai, *also called* Toṇḍamān Chakravarti. *Conquered and ruled over the Pallava country.*	Rājarāja, *ruled Veṅgī or Kaliṅgā for one year under his father.*	Vīradeva, *alias* Vīranātha, *alias* Saptama Vishṇuvardhana.[1] *Governor of Kaliṅgā from A.D.* 1079 *till at least A.D.* 1102.	*(A daughter). The mother of Chōḍagaṅga, alias Anantavarmā of Kaliṅgā.*
Kulottuṅga Choḷa II, *A.D.* 1128 *to ? Ruled over the whole Tamil country for at least* 30 *years.*				
Rājendra, *mentioned in inscriptions about the Godāvarī and Kṛishṇā Rivers.*				

Little seems to be known of the sovereign Vikrama. Kulottuṅga Choḷa II[2] succeeded. His reign came to an end at some time subsequent to the year 1158 A.D. Dr. Burnell then gives us Vikramadeva Choḷa reigning in A.D. 1235. If the copies sent to me of inscriptions about the Godāvarī and Kṛishṇā Rivers are accurate, Kulottuṅga II had a son Rājendra, whose inscriptions are found in that tract between A.D. 1165 and 1194. He was succeeded there by, apparently, an anarchy, when petty rulers held sway, preparing the way for their complete overthrow by the Gaṇapatis of Orangal, who seized and held the country firmly till the fourteenth century. So fell the Choḷa sovereignty north of the Pennār.[3]

According to Singhalese annals Parākrama Bāhu I (1153–1186) attacked Kulaśekhara, the Pāṇḍiyan king, at one period of his reign (the date is not given), subdued Rāmeśvaram and the six neighbouring provinces, and drove the king from the throne of Madura. Vīra Pāṇḍiyan, son of Kulaśekhara, was installed as king of Madura. The ousted monarch sought aid from the Cholas and attacked the Singhalese. The allies were defeated, and a considerable portion of the Choḷa country was captured by the invaders, on which Kulaśekhara submitted. He was then restored to his throne, Vīra Pāṇḍiyan being comforted by the gift of the conquered Choḷa country as a principality. After this, the Singhalese retired.

If the copies of two of the Conjeeveram inscriptions which, by the kindness of Mr. Foulkes, I had access to are correct (*Nos.* 178 *and* 204 *of my List, Vol. I, pp.* 184-85), there was a second Rājarāja Choḷa, of whom we now hear for the first time, who came to the throne in A.D. 1216, and ruled till at least A.D. 1232. Vikrama (ruling in A.D. 1235) probably succeeded him. It was in the reign of this Rājarāja II that Kaliṅgā was lost to the Cholas, if the date of this event, as given by Dr. Burnell (A.D. 1228), is accurate.[4] (*South Indian Palæography*, p. 40, note 4.)

---

[1] Amma Rāja I being Vishṇuvardhana the sixth.

[2] Dr. Burnell writes of him (*South Indian Palæography*, p. 40, note 37): "He was reigning in 1134 A.D. . . . . . . In his time there must have been a great many Buddhists in Tanjore, as Parākrama Bāhu (King of Ceylon, 1155 to 1186) fetched his priest from there according to the Mahāwaṅso."

[3] The deductions of Sir Walter Elliot from inscriptions vary from those of Dr. Burnell regarding the relatives of Rājendra Kulottuṅga I. I therefore append extracts from the former's writings on the subject (*Numismatic Gleanings*, No. 2, in M.J.L.S., Vol. IV, N.S., 1858, p. 94, *etc.*; O.S., Vol. XX:—"Rājendra Choḷa was succeeded by his son Vikrama Dēva surnamed Kulōttuṅga Choḷa. On the death of his uncle, Vijayāditya, who had been viceroy of Vengidēsam, the king deputed his son Rājarāja to assume the office, but after holding it for one year, A.D. 1078, he resigned it in favor of his younger brother Vira Dēva Choḷa, who assumed the title of Kulōttuṅga Choḷa. His grants are found in great numbers from A.D. 1079 up to the year 1135, when a partial restoration of the Chalukya line appears to have taken place, and they maintained a divided and feeble influence till the latter part of the twelfth century, when the country fell under the sway of the Kakatiya dynasty of Warangal." On page 40 he gives the succession thus:—

26. Rājarāja Narēndra.
27. Rājēndra Choḷa.
28. Vikrama Dēva Kulōttuṅga Choḷa.
29. Rājarāja Choḷa, viceroy for one year.
30. Vīra Dēva Kulōttuṅga or Saptama Vishṇuvardhana, viceroy from A.D. 1079 to 1135.

[4] Inscriptions in the Veṅgi country will doubtless throw light on this important point. At Kuṅkulaguṇṭa, in the Narasarāvupēta Taluk of the Kistna District, is an inscription which would point to the Gaṇapatis of Orissa having acquired power in that country as early as A.D. 1197; while there is a Gaṇapati inscription at Drakshārāma in the Godāvarī District, dated in 1175 A.D. The latest Gaṇapati inscription in that tract is dated A.D. 1336.

Another of the Conjeeveram inscriptions gives, according to the copy, Peruñjiṅga or Kopperuñjiṅga Choḷa as commencing to reign in A.D. 1242 (*Inscription No.* 265), his grant being in A.D. 1260. He reigned at least twenty years (*No.* 191).

Again, another (*No.* 101) gives a sovereign as commencing to reign in A.D. 1250, his grant being in 1266. Inscription No. 194 determines his name to have been "Vijayakaṇḍa Gopāladeva," and the coincidence seems to show that this is probably correct. The dates, however, conflict, and until the originals are examined nothing can be definitely stated.

The next date that I find is that of Mathurāntaka[1] Poṛṛapi Choḷa, who began to reign A.D. 1286, and held the sovereignty till the Musalmān invasion of A.D. 1310. (*No.* 74 *of the Conjeeveram Inscriptions.*)

These names and dates, though at present put forward doubtfully, seem to afford reasonable hope of our being soon able, after careful examination of the original inscriptions, to carry on a connected narrative of the history of the Choḷas down to the Musalmān conquest of A.D. 1310; and if so, a considerable step forward will have been made.

The Musalmān conquest seems to have finally crushed the power of the Choḷas. I am only acquainted with two allusions to Choḷas after that event. One is to be found in one of the inscriptions at Conjeeveram (*No.* 98), which consists of a command issued by Sadāśiva of Vijayanagar to "Rājakumāra Bhaṅgappadeva Choḷa" to conduct certain festivals at the temple at Conjeeveram. The other will be noticed below.

The Musalmāns seem to have held the country till A.D. 1347, when they were driven across the Krishṇā by a powerful Hindu confederation. According to one of the Conjeeveram inscriptions (*No.* 60), just at that period a chief by name Nārāyaṇa Śambuva Rāyar claims sovereignty at Kañchī and dates his grant in his ninth year, placing his accession in A.D. 1337. He seems to have ruled for at least eighteen years (*Inscription* 58), which brings us down to A.D. 1355.

It now becomes a question whether the almost extinct power of the Cholas once more and for the last time asserted itself in the person of a second Vijayakanda Gopāladeva. The usurpation of a family of Uḍaiyārs, probably from the Kanarese country, whose earliest recorded date at Kañchī is that of Kampaṇa, son of Bukkaṇa Uḍaiyār, in A.D. 1365, is well established by inscriptions at various localities. And amongst the Conjeeveram inscriptions are two, by the same local chieftain, one of which is dated in the twentieth year of Vijayakaṇḍa Gopāladeva, and the other in the reign of Kampaṇa Uḍaiyār. This, if authentic, would help us to bridge the interval of nine years between A.D. 1356 and 1365. Kampana was succeeded by Arayaṇṇa or Āryēna Uḍaiyār in or before the year 1377, for we have an inscription of the latter's reign dated in that year. Āryēna was succeeded by his son Vīruppaṇṇa.[2] The latter seems to have been conquered or superseded by King Harihara of Vijayanagar, and it is, indeed, not improbable that these Uḍaiyārs were either generals or chiefs of the early Vijayanagar sovereigns. There seems reason, however, to believe that for a century and a half the Vijayanagar sovereignty was not very firmly established till, in the reigns of the kings of the Narasiṁha dynasty, the whole was finally reduced to subjection.

Then followed the supremacy of the Nāyakkas of Madura during the decline of the great sovereignty, and these were followed by the Mahratta dynasty, who ruled the country precariously till it passed into the hands of the English.

---

[1] *Mathura-antaka,* "the cause of the end of Madura," or the "*Yama* (god of death) of Madura." It cannot yet be decidedly stated whether this was a mere title significative of the inveterate hatred existing between the Choḷa and Paṇḍiyan kingdoms, or whether it perpetuates an event in history. The title still exists in the Choḷa-Pallava country in the name of the town of "Mathurāntakam" in the Chingleput District, a flourishing place which gives its name to a taluk, and which probably was called after the sovereign.

[2] I think the succession is as follows:—

Bukkaṇṇa,
married Janemādevī, and gave her the town of Pennakoṇḍa.

Vīrupaṇṇa.
Inscriptions A.D. 1344, 1354, 1364 (*Pennakoṇḍa*),
His minister constructed the fort at Pennakoṇḍa.

Kampaṇa.
Inscriptions A.D. 1365, 1368 (*Kañchī*),
1371, 1374 (*Rāmnād*).

Arayaṇṇa *or* Āryēna.
Inscriptions A.D. 1377 (*South Arcot*), 1378 (*Kañchī*).

Vīrupaṇṇa.
Inscriptions A.D. 1385, 1396 (*South Arcot*).

It must be considered as not quite conclusively proved that the Bukkaṇṇa who is mentioned as father of Vīrupaṇṇa, and the Bukkaṇṇa who is mentioned as father of Kampaṇa, were one and the same person, but there is little reason to doubt it.

DAKHAṆ, MUHAMMADAN KINGS OF THE—.

By way of preface to a sketch of these Musalmān sovereignties of the Dakhaṇ, it will be well to insert a few notes on the previous transactions of the Delhi kings in Southern India.

The first expedition of the Muḥammadans into the Dakhaṇ took place in A.D. 1306, when the Emperor 'Alāu'd-dīn sent an ennobled slave, by name Malik Kāfur, to bring to his senses the Rāja Rāmadeva of Devagiri (*see the* YĀDAVAS OF DEVAGIRI), who had withheld tribute for three years. The Rāja made no defence, but, being defeated in March 1307, accompanied his opponent to Delhi, where he received honourable treatment.

In 1309 Malik Kāfur was again sent to the Dakhaṇ to reduce the Gaṇapati king of Orangal, Rudradeva, better known as Pratāpa Rudra II. The expedition was successful. The city was captured and the Rāja made terms.[1] Next year he was again despatched on a similar errand against the Hoyśala Ballāḷas of Dvārasamudra. The general pushed forward with great energy and speed, passed Devagiri, and reached the Malabar Coast, where he built a mosque to commemorate the event. He attacked and stormed the city of Dvārasamudra, sacked the celebrated Hallabīḍu temple, and returned to Delhi.[2]

In 1312 the Devagiri Yādavas again became troublesome, in the person of Śaṅkaradeva, son of Rāma, and Malik Kāfur was once more sent to reduce the Rāja to a proper sense of his inferiority. In the campaign which ensued the Musalmāns were completely successful and the Rāja lost his life. Four years later 'Alāu'd-dīn died and Malik Kāfur was at once murdered.

Mubārak Khilji became Emperor of Delhi in 1317, and one of his first acts was to make war for the third time on Devagiri. He captured the person of the Rāja, Haripāladeva, son-in-law of Rāma, and flayed him alive. The *Nuh Sipihr* of Amīr Khusrū gives a circumstantial account of a defeat of the Rāja of Orangal by "Khusrū Khān," generally known as Malik Khusrū, in the reign of this sovereign, but no such event is recorded by Ferishta. The chief is said to have been commanded to go to "Arangal in Tillang," and to have obeyed. In the end, it is said, the Muḥammadans were victorious, and retired after taking from the Rāja all his moveable property.

Mubārak was murdered in A.D. 1321 by Malik Khusrū, and the latter was killed by Ghāzi Beg Toghlak, Viceroy of Lahore, who,—all the royal family having been barbarously murdered by Malik Khusrū,—was chosen sovereign of the empire under the title of Ghiyāṣu'd-dīn.

In 1321 he sent his eldest son, Ulugh Khān, against Orangal. The capital was invested and a close siege took place. The garrison was on the point of capitulating when a panic seized on the Muḥammadans owing to mischievous rumours spread about the camp that the Sultān was dead. Several of the generals fled, and the army became disorganized; so that, on a desperate sally being made by the garrison, the besiegers were beaten at all points and hastily retreated.

In 1323, however, the Sultān again made war on Pratāpa Rudra with complete success. Orangal was captured and the Rāja carried captive to Delhi. Ghiyāṣu'd-dīn was succeeded in 1325 by Muḥammad.

In 1327 the Musalmān Viceroy of the Dakhaṇ rebelled, and the Emperor sent an expedition against him. He fled to Kampḷi close to Vijayanagar, whence the king's troops were compelled to retreat, the Vijayanagar king being too strong for them. The rebel fled to the Hoyśala Ballāḷa king at Tānūr in Maisūr, but the latter was too much in fear for his own safety to show any hospitality to the fugitive. He accordingly delivered him up to his master, who flayed him alive for his rebellious conduct.

Either in 1338 or 1339 the capital of the Muḥammadan empire was arbitrarily removed to Devagiri, which was rechristened Daulatābād by the sovereign Muḥammad.

In 1341 ensued a revolt in Malabar, and Muḥammad started to quell it, but fell sick on the way and returned to his capital. Shortly after this Orangal revolted, and the Sultān was powerless to effect its reduction.

Three years later, in 1344, a Hindu confederation, consisting of the son (?) of Rudradeva of Orangal, Krishṇa "Nāyakka," the Rāya of Vijayanagar, and Ballāḷadeva of Dvārasamudra, with an immense force drove the Muḥammadans out of Orangal and rolled back the tide of their advance.

This reverse was followed, three years later, by a revolt in the Muḥammadan dependencies in the Dakhaṇ. The Viceroy of Daulatābād proclaimed his independence, the royal troops were defeated, and the Viceroy became the first Bāhmanī king of the Dakhaṇ.

Hasan, the Viceroy, now monarch, was originally a poor man who rose to eminence at court mainly by the help of a Brahman, one Gangu, whose name he, in gratitude, assumed when he established the new kingdom.

---

[1] The campaign is graphically described by Amīr Khusrū in his *Tārīkh-i 'Alāī* (Sir Henry Elliot's *History of India*, III, 80), and in the *Tārīkh-i Fīrōz Shāhī* of Ziāu'd-dīn Barnī (*Id.* 189).

[2] Ferishta states that Malik Kāfur marched as far as Rāmeśvaram and built a mosque there, but this statement is beginning to be discredited, as it is not shown to be supported by other testimony.

He fixed his capital at Kulbarga or Aḥsanābād. The kingdom lasted about two and a half centuries, being succeeded by five separate kingdoms with capitals at Bīdar, Bijapur (or Vijayapura), Golkoṇḍa, Birār, and Aḥmadnagar.

I append a list of Bāhmanī kings as given by Prinsep. Mr. Eastwick's List, published in his *Handbook for Madras* (p. 41), and founded on information supplied to him at Kulbarga, does not appear to me to be so accurate.

BĀHMANĪ KINGS OF THE DAKHAN.

(*Prinsep's List.*)

		A.D.
1.	'Alāu'd-dīn Hasan Shāh Gango Bāhmanī	1347—1358
2.	Muḥammad Shāh I	1358—1375
3.	Mujāhid Shāh	1375—1378
4.	Dā'ūd Shāh	1378
5.	Maḥmūd Shāh I	1378—1397
6.	Ghiyāṣu'dīn	1397
7.	Shamsu'dīn Shāh	1397
8.	Fīrōz Shāh	1397—1422
9.	Aḥmad Shāh Wali (Khān Khānān)	1422—1435
10.	'Alāu'd-dīn Shāh II	1435—1457
11.	Humāyūn the Cruel	1457—1461
12.	Niẓām Shāh	1461—1463
13.	Muḥammad Shāh II	1463—1482
14.	Maḥmūd II	1482—1518
15.	Aḥmad Shāh II	1518—1520
16.	'Alāu'dīn Shāh III	1520—1522
17.	Waliu'llāh	1522—1525
18.	Kalām Ullāh	1525—1527

The following table gives the genealogy of the family :—

- 1. 'Alāu'd-dīn Hasan Gango Bāhmanī, (1347 *to* 1358).
  - 2. Muḥammad I, (1358 *to* 1375).
    - 3. Mujāhid, (1375 *to* 1378).
    - Ruhparva Āgha.
  - 4. Dā'ūd, (1378).
    - Muḥammad Sanjar.
    - 8. Fīrōz, (1397 *to* 1422).
      - Hasan.
    - 9. Aḥmad Shāh Wali (Khān Khānān), (1422 *to* 1435).
      - 10. 'Alāu'd-dīn II, (1435—1457)
        - 11. Humāyūn, (1457 *to* 1461).
          - 12. Niẓām, (1461 *to* 1463).
          - 13. Muḥammad II, (1463 *to* 1482).
            - 14. Maḥmūd II, (1482—1518).
          - Aḥmad.
        - Yehāya or Yahyā.
        - Hasan.
      - Muḥammad.
  - 5. Maḥmūd I, (1378 to 1397).
    - 6. Ghiyāsu'dīn, (7 *weeks in* 1397).
    - 7. Shamsu'd-dīn, (1397, *deposed*).

15. Aḥmad II, (1518 *to* 1620).	16. 'Alāu'd-dīn III, (1520 *to* 1522).	17. Waliu'llāh, (1522 *to* 1325).
	18. Kalām Ullāh, (1525 *to about* 1527).	

1. 'Alāu'd-dīn's reign was uneventful. He died on February 10th, 1358.

2. Muḥammad plundered the country of the Gaṇapatis up to Orangal, and then made peace. He again invaded Orangal territories, and captured and put to death the Rāja's son, Vināyaka or Nāgadeva, obtaining Golkoṇḍa and its dependencies. Next he wantonly made war on Vijayanagar, and was guilty of terrible cruelties. This was in 1365-66. He was successful, and dictated terms of peace. He died March 21st, 1375.

3. Mujāhid again wantonly attacked Vijayanagar and more than once invested the city, on one occasion penetrating into the second line of works; but he was compelled to retire. In the retreat he was murdered by his uncle Dā'ūd on April 14th, 1378.

4. Mujāhid's sister conspired against Dā'ūd in revenge, and on May 19th, 1378, Dā'ūd was assassinated. Maḥmūd, the youngest son of 'Alāu'd-dīn, was raised to the throne.

5. Maḥmūd reigned peaceably and well for 19 years. He died April 20th, 1397.

6. His son, Ghiyāsu'd-dīn, was blinded and imprisoned by a slave on June 9th of the same year, and (7) Shamsū'd-dīn was raised to the throne; but the sons of Dā'ūd attacked him and deposed him on November 15th, 1397.

8. Fīrōz, Dā'ūd's second son, succeeded and ruled for 25 years. In 1398 Deva Rāja of Vijayanagar invaded the Bāhmanī territories, and war ensued which was abruptly ended by the treacherous murder of Deva Rāja's son, when the Rāja fled and Fīrōz was victorious at all points. Another war broke out in 1401 owing to the Rāja of Vijayanagar's attempt to carry off a girl from Muḍgal. Fīrōz invested Vijayanagar successfully, dictated terms, and married the Rāja's daughter. In 1417 the king again attacked Vijayanagar, but was defeated. He died September 15th, 1422, leaving a son Hasan, who, however, was quietly set aside, and acquiesced in the arrangement.

9. Aḥmad (otherwise called Khān Khānān) made war on Vijayanagar soon after his accession, and was guilty of much unnecessary cruelty. He defeated the Rāja and obtained payment of tribute. A war with Orangal followed, which resulted in the death of its Rāja and the permanent destruction of the kingdom. He founded the city of Bīdar and died there February 19th, 1435.

10. His son 'Alāu'd-dīn II succeeded. His brother Muḥammad revolted, but was defeated and kindly treated. Muḥammad, on this occasion, received aid from Vijayanagar. The capital of the Bāhmanī kingdom was definitely removed to Bīdar. In 1437 Deva Rāja of Vijayanagar again provoked a war, and some very severe battles were fought, after which a peace was arranged which lasted for some years. The king died in 1457.

11. He was succeeded by his son Humāyūn, a cruel and unscrupulous prince, who was murdered four years later, viz., on September 3rd, 1461.

12. His son Niẓām Shāh was a boy of eight when he came to the throne, but his mother, who was a very remarkable woman, conducted the government for him with great success, assisted by the celebrated minister, Maḥmūd Gawān. Their territories were invaded in 1461 by a large army from Orissa and Telingāna, which was driven back. The Muḥammadan King of Mālwa attacked Bīdar, and invested it while the queen and the young king fled. But a Gujarāti army in jealousy attacked Mālwa and the invaders retreated with great loss. In 1462 the king returned to Bīdar. He died suddenly on July 29th, 1463.

13. His brother Muḥammad was placed on the throne. In 1468 the young king, then fourteen years' old, took Maḥmūd Gawān as his chief minister. In 1469 he reduced the Konkaṇa, wresting it from the power of Vijayanagar. In 1471 a relative of the King of Orissa, who had been ousted from the throne, begged aid from Muḥammad Shāh for the recovery of his rights. This was given, and Muḥammad invaded Telingāna. He captured Koṇḍapalle and Rajahmundry and stayed for some time in that country, residing for three years at Rajahmundry. In 1477 occurred another expedition into Orissa, and the king marched to the sea-coast at Masulipatam. He took the opportunity to make a dash southwards along the coast as far as Conjeeveram, which he sacked, returning with an immense booty. In 1481 the king by a great misfortune lost the services of Maḥmūd Gawān. A plot was raised against the latter by the chief of a rival faction, Niẓāmu'l-mulk Bhairi, and the King, believing Maḥmūd to be false to him, put him to death. This act resulted in the downfall of the kingdom. The principal

chiefs absented themselves from court and remained on their estates with all their forces. Yūsuf 'Ādil Khān, adopted son of Maḥmūd Gawān, was shortly afterwards sent to defend Goa against the Rāja of Vijayanagar. Soon after this the king died, viz., on March 24th, 1482.

14. His son Maḥmūd II succeeded, Niẕāmu'l-mulk Bhairi being his minister. Yūsuf 'Ādil returned to court, but, on an attempt against his life being made, he retired to his estate at Bijapur. Maḥmūd went on an expedition to Teliṅgāna, and while there Niẕāmu'l-mulk was murdered. His son Malik Aḥmad promptly proclaimed his independence at Jūnĕr. 'Imādu'l-mulk, Governor of Bīrār, also revolted. At Bīdar, Kāsim Barīd, a Turki or Georgian slave, was minister. The King betrothed his daughter to Yūsuf 'Ādil in 1497. Kāsim Barīd died in 1504, and his son Amīr Barīd held the king in absolute subjection. In 1512 Quṭbu'l-mulk, Governor of Teliṅgāna, declared his independence at Golkoṇḍa. Some fighting between the royal troops and those of Bijapur and Bīrār followed. Maḥmūd died on October 8th, 1518.

15. Aḥmad, son of the late king, was nominally placed on the throne by Amīr Barīd, but had no power, and died in 1520.

16. His brother 'Alāu'd-dīn was next placed on the throne, but, on his attempting to rid himself of his minister, he was deposed in 1522 and shortly afterwards murdered.

17. His younger brother Wali was then installed but after two years was poisoned, and Amīr Barīd married his widow. This was in 1524.

18. Kalām Ullāh, son of Aḥmad, was then enthroned, but he escaped in 1527 and fled to Aḥmadnagar, where he remained till his death.

Amīr Barīd at once threw off all pretence at subjection, and established a new dynasty at Bīdar, or Aḥmadābād. And thus ended the Bāhmanī dynasty. The five kingdoms which sprung from it were as follows :—

1. The Barīd Shāhi Dynasty at Bīdar, or Aḥmadābād.				
2. ,,	'Ādil	do.	do.	Bijapur.
3. ,,	'Imād	do.	do.	Bīrār.
4. ,,	Niẕām	do.	do.	Aḥmadnagar.
5. ,,	Quṭb	do.	do.	Golkoṇḍa.

These will be considered in order.

The Barīd Shāhi Dynasty at Bīdar, or Ahmadābād.

	A.D.
1. Kāsim Barīd I, a Turki or Georgian slave	1492—1504
2. Amīr Barīd I (son)	1504—1549
3. 'Alī Barīd Shāh (son), the first who assumed royalty ...	1549—1562
4. Ibrahīm Barīd Shāh (son)	1562—1569
5. Kāsim Barīd Shāh II (brother)	1569—1572
6. Mīrzā 'Alī Barīd Shāh (*deposed*) (son)	1572—1609
7. Amīr Barid Shāh II	1609

Kāsim Barīd was minister to Maḥmūd Bāhmanī. Dying in 1504, his son Amīr became minister. He held the young Bāhmanī king in complete subjection, raised in succession four puppet sovereigns of that dynasty to the throne of Bīdar, and, on the flight of the last to Aḥmadnagar about 1527, became independent at the ancient Bāhmanī capital. Not long after this Ismā'īl 'Ādil Shāh took Bīdar, but made it over again to Amīr Barīd, who then became almost a dependent of the Bijapur kings. His successor 'Alī Barīd first assumed the title of "Shāh." He lost almost all his possessions in a war with Burhān Shāh of Aḥmadnagar.

The dates of this dynasty are greatly confused as, according to Ferishta, 'Alī Barīd reigned 45 years.

For an account of Bīdar, I beg to refer readers to Dr. Burgess's Third Archæological Report, Bombay, published in 1878 (*pp.* 42—46).

The 'Ādil Shāhi Dynasty at Bijapur (Vijayapura).

	A.D.
1. Abū'l Muẕaffar Yūsuf 'Ādil Shāh, son of Āghā Murād, or Amurath II, of Anatolia	1489—1511
2. Ismā'īl 'Ādil Shāh	1511—1534
3. Malū 'Ādil Shāh	1534—1535
4 Ibrahīm 'Ādil Shāh I	1535—1557

	A.D.
5. 'Alī 'Ādil Shāh	1557—1579
6. Ibrahīm 'Ādil Shāh II	1579—1626
7. Muḥammad 'Ādil Shāh	1626—1656
8. 'Alī 'Ādil Shāh II	1656—1659
9. Sultān Sikandar (an infant at his accession)	1659—1686

(1.) Yūsuf 'Ādil, in 1493, defeated the Vijayanagar King and took immense treasure and 200 elephants. He surrounded Bijapur with a stone rampart. In 1510, the Portuguese captured Goa, and Yūsuf 'Ādil recaptured it the same year. Albuquerque, however, made another successful attack, and Goa was finally ceded to the Portuguese (1510) by (2.) Ismā'īl 'Ādil. In 1519 there was another war with Vijayanagar, in which the Raya Krishṇadeva was victorious. (5.) 'Alī 'Ādil made a league with the Vijayanagar Rāya Rāma, and defeated the Musalmān King of Aḥmadnagar; but in 1565 the Muḥammadan sovereignties united and completely crushed the power of Rāma Rāya in the great battle of Talikōṭa. Vijayanagar was sacked and the temples and palaces ruined. In 1555, or ten years previous, Ibrahīm had unsuccessfully attacked Goa. In 1568 or 1570, 'Alī 'Ādil attacked Goa, but was repulsed. He took the fortress of Ādōni (*Ādhvani*), and in 1577 compelled Rāma Rāya's brother, Tirumala, to retire to Chandragiri. During the reign of (7.) Muḥammad 'Ādil Shāh, the Mahrattas began to rise to power. Śivājī revolted in 1648, and by 1662 had wrested from Muḥammad the whole of the Koṅkaṇa from Kalyāṇa to Goa. From then till 1680 he constantly defeated the King of Bijapur In 1686 the kingdom was seized and annexed by the Emperor Aurangzīb, being finally brought under the government of Delhi in 1688.

The following is the genealogy of the family :—

- 1. Abū'l Muzaffar Yūsuf 'Ādil. 1489—1511.
  - 2. Ismā'īl 'Ādil Shāh. 1511—1534.
    - 3. Malū 'Ādil Shāh. 1534—1535.
    - 4. Ibrahīm 'Ādil. 1535—1557.
      - 5. 'Alī 'Ādil. 1557—1579.
      - Tahmāsp.
        - 6. Ibrahīm 'Ādil. 1579—1626.
          - 7. Muḥammad 'Ādil. 1626—1656.
            - 8. 'Alī 'Ādil, 1656—1659.
              - 9. Sikandar. 1659—1686.
        - Ismā'īl.
    - (*A daughter*) *married 'Alāu'd-dīn 'Imād Shāh of Birār*).
  - A daughter, (*married Ahmad Shāh Bāhmanī*).
  - Maryam (*married Burhān Shāh of Ahmadnagar*).

The 'Imād Shāhi Dynasty of Bīrār (Capital Ellichpur).

	A.D.
1. Fathu'llāh 'Imād Shāh Bāhmanī	1484—1504
2. 'Alāu'd-dīn 'Imād Shāh	1504—1528
3. Daryā 'Imād Shāh	1528—1560
4. Burhān 'Imād Shāh	1560—1568
5. Tufail Khān	1568—1572

The following is the genealogy of the family. They come little in contact with the countries now forming the Madras Presidency.

1. Fathu'llāh 'Imād Shāh Bāhmanī,
(1483—1504. *A Hindu boy of Vijayanagar. Turned Musalmān and rose to distinction under the Bāhmanīs. Declared himself independent.*

|

2. 'Alāu'd-dīn 'Imād Shāh,
(1504 *to* 1528. *Constantly at war. Married daughter of Ismā'il 'Adil Shāh of Bījapur*).

|

3. Daryā 'Imād Shāh,,
(*Peaceful reign.* 1528–1560.)

|

4. Burhān 'Imād Shāh,
(1560–1568. *He was captured and imprisoned by* (5) *Tufāil Khān, who seized the throne, but was murdered by the Ahmadnagar King. The kingdom then fell under Ahmadnagar.*)

Bībī Daulat,
(*a daughter; married Husain, king of Ahmadnagar.*)

The Nizām Shāhi Dynasty of Ahmadnagar.

		A.D.
1.	Aḥmad Nizām Shāh	1490—1508
2.	Burhān Nizām Shāh I	1508—1553
3.	Ḥusain Nizām Shāh	1553—1565
4.	Mūrtazā Nizām Shāh I	1565—1587
5.	Mīrān Ḥusain Nizām Shāh	1587—1589
6.	Ismā'il Nizām Shāh	1589—1590
7.	Burhān Nizām Shāh II	1590—1594
8.	Ibrahīm Nizām Shāh	1594
9.	Aḥmad Ibn Shāh Tāhir	1594—1595
10.	Bahādur Nizām Shāh	1595—1598
11.	Mūrtazā Nizām Shāh II	1598—1607
12.	Malik Ambar	1607—1626

1. Aḥmad was son of Nizāmu'l-mulk Bhairi, minister of the Bāhmanī State. He declared his independence in 1490 A.D., and founded the city of Aḥmadnagar. He took Daulatābād (Devagiri) in 1499. Dying in 1508, he was succeeded by his son Burhān, then a boy seven years' old.

2. Burhān in 1523 married Maryam, the daughter of Yūsuf 'Ādil Shāh of Bijapur. In 1531 he suffered a serious defeat at the hands of his brother-in-law Ismā'il 'Ādil Shāh. He was after this constantly at war with the Bijapur State. In 1545 he made an alliance against Bijapur with the young king of Vijayanagar through his minister, and in 1549 another arrangement was come to with Vijayanagar for the partition of the Bijapur State. Burhān died in A.D. 1553.

3. Ḥusain was only thirteen years' old when he succeeded. He at once suppressed a rebellion raised by his brother Abdu'llāh. Shortly afterwards Aḥmadnagar was besieged by an immense army sent by a confederation of the Bijapur and Vijayanagar States, Rāma Rāja being at the actual head of the latter. Hard terms were accepted and the siege was raised. In 1562 the same confederacy again attacked Aḥmadnagar in consequence of Husain's attempt to recover Kalyāna, the ancient seat of the Chālukyas, which had been ceded to Bijapur. The capital was invested, but the siege was raised after a disastrous flood which swept away many thousands of the besieging army. In 1565 Ḥusain joined the other Muḥammadan princes in their grand attack on Vijayanagar, which resulted in the downfall of that kingdom, but he died the same year, June 7th.

4. His son Mūrtazā succeeded. The war with Bījapur broke out afresh, but a peace was arranged on the understanding that Aḥmadnagar should attack Birār, and Bijapur should seize the territories of Vijayanagar, each unopposed by the other. The Emperor Akbar sent an order to Mūrtazā directing him not to interfere with Birār, but Mūrtazā, disregarding the order, annexed that State to his own dominions in 1572. He was murdered by his son in 1587,

5. Mīrān gave way to excesses of all kinds, and murdered all the royal family. The minister, becoming terrified for his safety, sent for the king's cousin, Ismā'īl, then twelve years' old, intending to depose Mīrān. A revolt of troops followed. The minister had the king beheaded, but was himself murdered.

6. Ismā'īl succeeded and nominally ruled for two years, but his father Burhān deposed him.

7. Burhān in 1592 despatched against the Portuguese an army which suffered a very severe reverse, the Muḥammadan general being captured and sent to Portugal, where he became a Christian. The king died in 1594.

8. At his death, Burhān passed over his eldest son Ismā'īl and declared Ibrahīm to be his successor. Ibrahīm at once made war on Bijapur, but was killed in the first battle, four months after his accession to the throne.

9. Then ensued great confusion. Ibrahīm's son was an infant, and the army proclaimed for a boy named Aḥmad, erroneously supposed to be of royal descent. The minister sent to the Moghuls for aid and defeated the leader of the military faction. He discovered too late his error in addressing the Moghuls, for Akbar's son Murād advanced with a large army to Aḥmadnagar. The city was invested, and a desperate defence was made by the heroic Queen, Chānd Bībī, Prince Murād only withdrawing on receiving the cession of Birār. The infant king was then crowned, and a new minister selected; but the latter treacherously plotted with the Emperor Akbar, who invaded the territory of Aḥmadnagar. After a brave defence the city was captured, and Chānd Bībī was foully murdered. The infant king was sent to Gwalior, and Mūrtaẓā, grandson of Burhān I, proclaimed himself king. He ruled well, but was deposed by his minister, the Abyssinian soldier Malik Ambar, in 1607.

The kingdom then virtually passed under the Moghul empire, but Malik Ambar held nominal rule at Aḥmadnagar till his death in 1626, when the kingdom was finally annexed to Delhi.

The following table shows the genealogy of the family:—

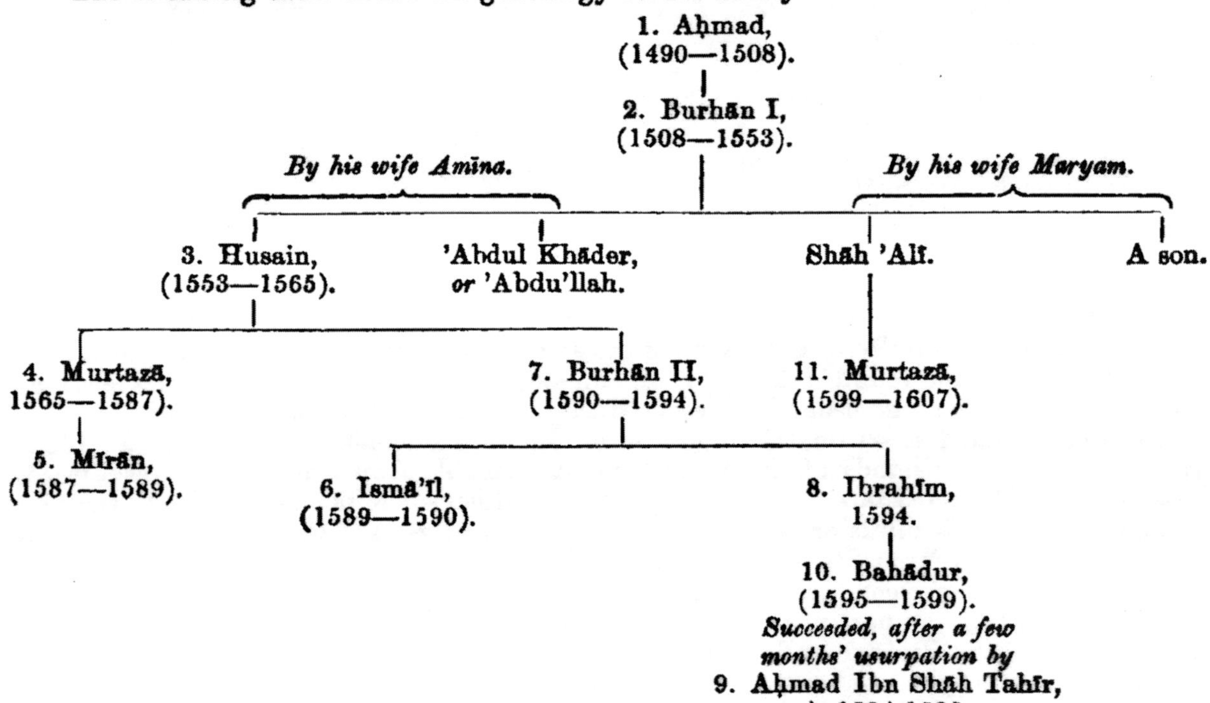

The Quṭb Shāhi Dynasty at Golkoṇḍa.

	A.D.
1. Ṣultān Qulī Quṭb Shāh	1512—1543
2. Jamshīd Qulī Quṭb Shāh	1543—1550
3. Ibrahīm Quṭb Shāh	1550—1581
4. Muḥammad Qulī Quṭb Shāh	1581—1611
5. 'Abdu'llāh Quṭb Shāh	1611—1672
6. Abū Hasan	1672—1688

1. Quṭbu'l-Mulk was Governor of Teliṅgāna under Muḥammad Bāhmanī, and withdrew from court after the death of Maḥmūd Gawān, the minister, residing at Golkoṇḍa. He remained loyal to his sovereign till the minister Kāsim Barīd's tenure of office, when he proclaimed his independence, A.D 1512. The new king gradually extended his conquests. Krishṇadeva Rāya of Vijayanagar conquered all the country east of the ghāṭs about the year 1516, but Ṣultān Qulī defeated the Hindus at Koṇḍapalle, and seized all the country between the Kṛishṇā and Godāvarī. Rajahmundry was then under the Gajapatis, who had received that province from Kṛishṇadeva Rāya. He also captured the fort of Orangal. There is an inscription at Koṇḍapalle recording this sovereign's capture of the fort. The king was murdered at the instigation of his second son, Jamshīd.

2. Jamshīd blinded his elder brother and seized the throne. His reign is not remarkable. He died in 1550.

3. He was succeeded by his son Subhān, a boy of seven, but the latter was set aside by the nobles, and the late king's brother, Ibrahīm, appointed. Ibrahīm had, up to the time of his accession, lived at Vijayanagar under the care of Rāma Rāya. But he joined in the attack on Vijayanagar in 1565 A.D. Immediately after his return from this great victory, Ibrahīm planned the capture of Rajahmundry from the Gajapatis of Orissa. This had been attempted in 1564, but the Hindu army collected in such force that the Musalmāns were powerless. In 1567, however, the attack on Rajahmundry was perfectly successful, and the whole territory was annexed to Golkoṇḍa as far north as Chicacole. Many Hindu Rājas, south of the Kṛishṇā, were also overcome. He died suddenly in 1581. The king having poisoned his eldest son 'Abdu'l Qādir, and another having died, his third son, Muḥammad, succeeded him.

4. Muḥammad kept up constant warfare with the princes of Vijayanagar, then residing at Pennakoṇḍa, and held with great difficulty the province of Koṇḍavīḍu, now known as Guṇṭūr. In 1589 he founded the present city of Ḥaidarābād, then called Bhāghnagar. It is believed that Muḥammad conquered Gandikōṭa, Cuddapah, and all the country south of the Pennār, but this seems rather doubtful.

5. "Muḥammad Koolli leaving no son, was succeeded by his brother Mahummud, who was succeeded by Abdoolla Koottub Shaw." (Scott's *Ferishta*, I, 410.) I have not been able to ascertain the exact relationship of 'Abdu'llāh to Muḥammad.

During the reign of Shāh Jahān, Aurangzīb attacked and defeated 'Abdu'llāh and compelled him to submit to very hard terms. In 1667 the Mahratta Śivājī attacked the capital and exacted a large payment as tribute. 'Abdu'llāh died in 1672, and was succeeded by his son-in-law Abū Hasan.

6. This king made an alliance with the Mahrattas in 1676, but was attacked by the Moghul troops in 1678. In 1685 he was attacked and completely defeated by Aurangzīb in person, and was confined for life as a prisoner at Daulatābād.

In 1688 Golkoṇḍa was finally annexed.

The genealogy is as follows :—

- 1. Ṣultān Qulī Qutb Shāh, (1512—1543).
  - Qutbu'd-dīn, (*blinded by Jamshīd*).
  - 2, Jamshīd, (1543—1550).
    - Subhān.
  - Haidar, (*died without issue*).
  - 3. Ibrahīm, (1550—1581).
    - 'Abdu'l Qādir, (*poisoned by his father*).
    - *A son*, (*died before his father*).
    - 4. Muḥammad, (1581—1611).

DELHI, MUHAMMADAN KINGS AND EMPERORS OF—.

Delhi was captured from its Hindu Rāja and converted into a seat of Muḥammadan Government by Muḥammad, brother of Ṣultān Ghiyāṣu'd-dīn Ghōri of Ghaznī in A.D. 1193. Muḥammad, otherwise known as Shahābu'd-dīn, succeeded his brother and was murdered in 1205 A.D. Ghiyāṣu'd-dīn's son Maḥmūd succeeded, and one of his first actions was, in A.D. 1206 to create the Viceroy of his Northern Indian possessions King of Hindustān. The new monarch was Quṭbu'd-din, an ennobled slave. He established the dynasty generally called the "Slave Kings."

"Slave Kings of Delhi."

Qutbu'd-dīn Aibak, (A.D. 1206—1210).

- **Arām,** (*deposed*).
- **A sister,** *married* **Shamsu'd-dīn Altmish,** (1210—1236).
  - **Nāṣiru'd-dīn Maḥmūd,** (*died early*).
  - **Ruknu'd-dīn Fīrōz,** (1236), (*dethroned*).
    - **'Alāu'd-dīn Mas'ud,** (1242—1246), (*assassinated*).
  - **Sultān Razīya,**[1] (1236—1239), (*assassinated* 1239).
  - **Mu'izzu'd-dīn Bahrām,** (1239—1242), (*assassinated*).
    - **Nāṣiru'd-dīn Maḥmūd,** (1246—1266), *On his death the throne was seized by* **Ghiyāsu'd-dīn Balban,** *his minister*.

Ghiyāsu'd-dīn Balban, (1266—1286).

- **Muḥammad,** *killed in battle in his father's lifetime.*
  - **Kai-Khusrū,** *murdered by Kai-Kubād.*
- **Bughrā Khān,** *acquiesced in his son's accession.*
  - **Kai-Kubād,** (1286—1288), *dethroned by the family of the Khiljis, who seized the throne.*

The Khilji Dynasty.

- **Jalālu'd-dīn Fīrōz Khilji,** (1288-1295), (*murdered by 'Alāu'd-dīn*).
  - **Khān-i Khānān,** (*murdered*).
  - **Arkali Khān,** (*murdered*).
  - **Qādir Khān,** (1295-1296). *Crowned by his mother after the murder of his father, his brothers being absent. Fled.*
- **'Alāu'd-dīn,** (1296-1316).
  - **Khizr Khān,** (*blinded*).
  - **Shādī Khān,** (*blinded*).
  - **Mubārak Qutbu'd-dīn,** (1316-1321), (*murdered by Malik Khusrū*).
  - **Shahābu'd-dīn,** (*blinded*).

Ghiyāṣu'd-dīn Tughlik, an ennobled slave, seized the throne and established the dynasty of Tughlik.

---

[1] Her name would properly be *Raẓiya Begam Ṣultānā*, but she was always known as *Ṣultān*.

The Tughlik Dynasty.

Ghiyāsu'd-dīn Tughlik,
(1321–1325).

- Muḥammad Khān, Ulugh Khān, (1325–1353).
- Sipah-sālār Rajab.
  - Fīrōz Tughlik, (1351–1388).
    - Muḥammad Tughlik Nāṣiru'd-dīn, (1390–1394).
      - Humāyūn, (1394), *(died without issue).*
      - Maḥmūd, (1394–1414). *The sack of Delhi by Taimūr the Moghul took place in this reign. Mahmūd fled and his successor was appointed by Taimūr.*
    - Zafar Khān.
      - Abū Bakr, (1389–1390). *Deposed and imprisoned by Nāṣiru'd-dīn.*
    - Fath Khān.
      - Tughlik Shāh Ghiyāsu'd-dīn, (1388–1389). *Seized the throne, but was deposed.*

Saiyid Rulers of Delhi.

Saiyid Khizr Khān,
(1414–1421).
Placed on throne by Taimūr. He had been Viceroy of Lahore.

Saiyid Mubārak,
(1421–1435).
Murdered.

Saiyid Muḥammad,
(1435–1445).

Saiyid 'Alāu'd-dīn,
(1445–1450).
Removed his capital from Delhi, which was immediately seized by Bahlol Lodī, Governor of the Panjāb.

The Dynasty of Lōdī.

Bahlōl Lōdī,
(1450–1488).

Sikandar Lōdī
Nizām Khān,
(1488–1506).

Ibrahīm Lōdī,
(1506–1526).
Conquest of Delhi by the Moghuls under Bābar. The Sultān was killed.

Mogul Emperors of Delhi.

- **1. Bābar,** Zahīru'd-dīn Muḥammad, *King of Ferghāna,* 1494. *Seized Delhi* 1526. *Died* 1530.
  - **2. Humāyūn** Nāṣiru'd-dīn, (1530–1543 *and* 1555–56). *Between* 1543 *and* 1555 *the rule of Shēr Khān intervened.*
    - **3. Akbar,** Abū'l Fatḥ, Jalālu'd-dīn, (1556–1605).
      - **4. Jahāngīr,** Abū'l Muzaffar Nūru'd-dīn, (1605–1627).
        - **Khusrū,** (*imprisoned. Died before his father*).
        - **Parvīz,** (*incompetent*).
        - **5. Shāh Jahān,** Shahābu'd-dīn Ghāzi, (1627–1658).
          - **Dārā Sheko.**
            - **Solimān,** (*murdered*).
          - **Shujā,** (*fled*).
          - **6. Aurangzīb,** 'Ālamgīr, Abū'l Muzaffar, Muḥāiyiu'd-dīn, (1658–1707).
            - **Muḥammad Ṣultān.** (*Died in prison. No issue.*)
            - **7. Bahādur Shāh,** Shāh 'Ālam, Muḥammad Qutbu'd-dīn, (1707–1711).[1]
              - **8. Jahāndar Shāh,** Mu'izzu'd-dīn, (1711–1712). *Murdered by Farrukhsiyar. No issue.*
                - **14. 'Ālamgīr II,** Abū-l'Ādil'Āzīzu'd-dīn Muḥammad, (1754–1759). *Murdered.*
              - **Jahān Shāh.**
                - **12. Muḥammad Shāh,** Roshan Akhtar, Abū'l fatḥ, Nāṣiru'd-dīn, (1719–1748).
                  - **13. Aḥmad Shāh,** 'Abū'l Nāṣir, (1748–1754). *Deposed and blinded.*
              - **Rafī'u-sh Shāh.**
                - **11. Rafī'u'd Daulah,** (1719). *Died after 3 months' reign.*
                - **10. Rafī'u'd Darajāt,** (1719). *Died after 6 months' reign.*
                - **Muḥammad Ibrahīm.**
              - **'Azīmu-sh Shāh.**
                - **9. Farrukhsiyar,** (1712–1719). *Murdered. No issue.*
            - **'Azīm,** (*killed* 1707).
            - **Kambaksh,** (*killed* 1708).
            - **Akbar,** (*fled*).
          - **Murād,** (*murdered*).
      - **Murād,** (*died before his father*).
      - **Danial,** (*died before his father*).
    - **Hakīm,** *Governor of Kābul.*
  - **Kamrān,** *Governor of Kābul.*
  - **Hindal,** *Governor of Sambal.*
  - **Mirzā Askeri,** *Governor of Mewat.*

[1] Authorities differ as to the exact date. See Sir Henry Elliot's *History of India* (VII, p. 428, note).

15. Shāh 'Ālam,
Jalālu'd-dīn, Mirzā 'Abdu'llāh Wālā Gauhar,
(1756–1806).
Empire overthrown by the Mahrattas, 1761. *Lived under British protection.*

16. Akbar II,
'Abū'l Nāṣir, Mun'aim'd-dīn Muḥammad,
(1806–1837).

17. Muḥammad Bahādur,
(1837–1857).
Transported to Rangoon after the Mutiny of 1857.

DEVAGIRI YĀDAVAS, THE—.

(*See* YĀDAVAS.)

DVĀRASAMUDRAM YĀDAVAS, THE—.

(*See* HOYŚALA BALLĀḶAS.)

EASTERN CHĀLUKYAS.

(*See* CHALUKYAS.)

GAṆAPATIS OF ORAṄGAL,[1] THE.—

Very little is as yet known about the kings of this dynasty, and it is to be hoped that inscriptions exist which will throw light on the subject.

Prinsep's List, and that given in the *Madras Journal* XV, 219, in a paper called "A Statistical Report on the Circar of Warungul," by Dr. Walker (1849), are practically useless. So also is the manuscript analyzed by the Rev. W. Taylor and published in his Report on the Mackenzie MSS. (No. 32, countermark 722, republished in the *Madras Journal* X, 18–22). No inscriptions that I have yet met with (except one which will be mentioned below) carry the genealogy of the family further back than Prōlē or Prōla Rāja, who seems to have flourished about the early part of the twelfth century. From the spelling of the names in his list, it is clear that Dr. Walker received his information orally, and not from any written chronicle or inscription. According to him the first king conquered the Choḷa country and married the daughter of the king of Ceylon. His son became insane, and his two grandsons succeeded and ruled jointly, having their capital at Nandēr on the Godāvarī. After these comes a break in the history, which commences again with a king living at Khandhar, from whom the crown descended directly in the male line to Prōla Rāja. Including the first king of this new dynasty ten sovereigns are named before Prōla Rāja. The names are hopelessly badly spelt and no good can be derived from reproducing them.

The succession appears to be as follows :—

1. Tribhuvana Malla.

2. Prōla Rāja,
or Prōlē, *married* Muppammadevī.

---

[1] This name is variously spelt *Voraṅgallu, Voraṅgōlu, Oraṅgallu, Oraṅgōlu, Vōruvakallu, Voruvakallu,* now generally *Vōrukallu*. I think that *Oraṅgal* is perhaps the best mode of transliteration, and have adopted it in this volume, considering *Oraṅgallu* a trifle too pedantic, while all such renderings as *Warangal, Warangul, Warungul* are positively wrong.

|

3. Pratāpa Rudra I.

|

4. Gaṇapatideva,
after whose death his widow
5. Rudramma
ruled for 38 *years,* 1257 *to* 1295 *A.D.*

|

A daughter.

|

6. Pratāpa Rudra II,
(1295 to 1323 A.D.)

|

Krishṇa.

|

Vināyaka
alias Nāgadeva.

1. We know nothing as yet of Tribhuvana Malla except that his name appears as father of Prōla in an inscription at Anumakoṇḍa, which was published in J.A.S.B. VII, 901, in J.B.B.R.A.S. X, 46 by Dr. Bhāu Dājī, and quite recently by Mr. Fleet in the *Indian Antiquary* for January 1882 (XI, 9).[1]

2. According to tradition on the spot, Prōla built the city of Oraṅgal, eight of his predecessors having ruled at Anumakoṇḍa. He is said to have been a minor at his accession, to have defeated the Gajapati of Orissa, and to have been killed accidentally by his son, thus fulfilling a prophecy which foretold his fate exactly as it occurred. The Anumakoṇḍa inscription above-mentioned states that Prōla captured and afterwards released "Tailappadeva," whom Mr. Fleet identifies with Taila III of the Western Chālukyas (A.D. 1150—1162). In Prōla's time, too, occurred a siege of Anumakoṇḍa by Jagaddeva, one of the Sāntara kings of Maisūr, the besiegers being successfully repulsed by the garrison (*Ind. Ant.* XI, 10).

3. Rudra, or Pratāpa Rudra I, seems to have been a powerful prince. The inscription above-mentioned is dated in his reign (A.D. 1162). It mentions the death of Tailapa III, and narrates some conquests made by the Gaṇapatis, especially over one Bhīma, and the capture of the city of Chōḍōdaya.[2]

4. If Dr. Burnell (*South-Indian Palæography, p.* 40, *note* 4) is right in his assignment of the date A.D. 1228 for the loss of the Kaliṅgā country to the Choḷas, it was probably in the reign of (4) Gaṇapatideva that that king conquered Kaliṅgā, but there are, I think, reasons for not being too certain at present. The inscriptions in *Kaliṅgadeśa* are numerous, and await careful examination. It will very possibly be found that the Gaṇapatis had acquired power in those territories previous to that date.

5. Queen Rudramma was in many respects a very remarkable character. On her husband's death there was no heir to the throne, and she at once assumed the reins of government. Her long reign of thirty-eight years was marked by a most able system of administration, as is testified to by Marco Polo, who visited the coast south of the Krishṇā River at Mōtupalle just at the close of the reign. He writes, —"This was formerly under the rule of a king, and since his death some forty years past it has been under his queen, a lady of much discretion, who, for the great love she bore him, never would marry another husband. And I can assure you that during all that space of forty years she had administered her realm as well as ever her husband did, or better, and as she was a lover of justice, of equity, and of peace, she was more beloved by those of her kingdom than ever was lady or lord of theirs before." (Colonel Yule's *Marco Polo*, II, 295.) In A.D. 1295 Rudramma's daughter's son having attained his majority, the queen abdicated in his favour.[3]

6. This was the celebrated Pratāpa Rudra II (A.D. 1295—1323), one of the most powerful princes of his time, but destined to be virtually the last of his line. In A.D. 1295 the Muhammadans under 'Alāu'd-dīn, Governor of Oudh and nephew of Jalālu'd-dīn Khilji of Delhi, marched into the Dakhaṇ and wantonly plundered the city of Devagiri, the capital of the kingdom bordering on Oraṅgal. They exacted large tribute and retired. In 1306 'Alāu'd-dīn, who by the murder of his uncle had raised himself to the throne, again sent an army into the Dakhaṇ under the command of Malik Kāfur to

---

[1] Mr. Fleet published a short note on this inscription in *Ind. Ant.* X, 211, for the purpose of fixing the date, viz., A.D. 1162.

[2] Possibly a Choḷa king or viceroy (*Choḷa-udaiyar*).

[3] Dr. Gustav Oppert publishes (*Madras Journal* for 1881) some inscriptions and extracts from local records which seem to show that during the reign of Queen Rudramma one Gōre (*or* Gorre) Gaṅgayya Reḍḍi was a general of considerable power and influence.

reduce Devagiri in consequence of the Rāja having refused to pay tribute. The Rāja was captured and taken to Delhi. In 1309 the arms of the Musalmāns were directed against Orangal. The first campaign was unsuccessful, but in the second Rudradeva was completely defeated and compelled to become tributary to Delhi, his capital being captured.[1] In 1310 Malik Kāfur was again sent southwards to reduce the Hoysala Ballālas of Dvārasamudra. In this he was completely successful and reached the Malabar Coast, where he built a mosque to commemorate the event. He captured the capital, sacked the celebrated temple of Hallebīḍu, and returned in triumph to Delhi. In 1312 Devagiri was again reduced by Malik Kāfur, and the crown prince put to death. Six years later Mubārak Khilji of Delhi marched against, seized, and flayed alive Haripāladeva, son-in-law of Rāja Rāmadeva of Devagiri. Amīr Khusrū, in his *Nuh Sipihr*, gives an account of an expedition sent by the sovereign of Delhi under the leadership of Malik Khusrū against Orangal, which resulted in the entire defeat of the Rāja; but the circumstance is not recorded by Ferishta.[2] Whether it occurred or not, the open hostility of the Muḥammadans seems to have roused to the highest pitch the terror and anxiety of the Dakhaṇi princes, and about the year 1326 Pratāpa Rudra made an alliance with the Rāja of Devagiri and threw off all semblance of fealty to the king of Delhi. He was probably incited to this important step by the disturbances at Delhi, which resulted, in 1321, in the subversion of the house of Khilji and the establishment of the dynasty of Tughlik. If so, he was very ill-advised, for one of the first actions of the new sovereign was to despatch an army (1321) to Orangal under his eldest son Ulugh Khān to reduce the refractory Rāja.[3] The expedition was, however, unsuccessful. The Muhammadan troops invested both the mud fort and the stone fort of Orangal, but were attacked during the siege by a terrible epidemic disease, became dispirited and panic-stricken, and, on being beaten at all points and driven from their camp by a courageous sally of the garrison, retired hastily and raised the siege. In 1323, however, a second large Musalmān force marched southwards and captured Orangal. Pratāpa Rudra was made prisoner and sent to Delhi. His son Krishṇa succeeded him, but with a much reduced kingdom. He revolted and turned the tables in 1344 by making a grand combination of Hindu States, and driving the Muḥammadans out of the country. No attempt seems to have been made by the sovereigns of Delhi again to subvert the Orangal monarchy, but in 1358 Muḥammad Shāh Bāhmanī plundered the country up to the capital, and only retired on being paid the expenses of the war. The Muhammadan writers speak of Vināyakadeva ("Vinaik Deo"), *alias* Nāgadeva, as the son of the Rāja, and it may be presumed that the Rāja was then Krishṇa "Nāik." In 1371 war again broke out between Orangal and the Bāhmanī sovereign, which resulted in the disastrous defeat of the former, the fortress of "Vellumputtan" being captured and Prince Nāgadeva being cruelly put to death (*Scott's Ferishta, I*, 18—20). The Hindus, however, so harassed the retreat of the victorious enemy that only a third of their number reached Kulbarga in safety. The Rāja vainly attempted to induce the sovereign of Delhi to aid him, and on being again attacked, submitted and made over an immense treasure to the Dakhaṇi Muḥammadans. A treaty was drawn up and boundaries fixed to the two kingdoms.

In 1424 Aḥmad Shāh Bāhmanī made war on Orangal, and the then Rāja was killed. (I have been unable to ascertain his name, or relationship to Pratāpa Rudra's family.) This is the last we hear of the Orangal Kingdom.

GANGAS OF KALINGĀ.

(*See* KALINGĀ.)

GANGAS OF MAISŪR.

(*See* KONGUS.)

[1] See the *Tārīkh-i 'Alāī* of Amīr Khusrū, who gives full particulars (Sir Henry Elliot's *History of India*, III, 80), and the *Tārīkh-i Fīrōz Shāhi* of Ziāu'd-dīn Barnī (*Id.* 189). The outer walls of the city were then made of mud, and its circumference was 12,546 yards. The ramparts were stormed, after an unsuccessful night attack by the garrison.

[2] Several points of interest may be observed in the narrative of Amīr Khusrū (Sir Henry Elliot's *History of India*, III, 558—561). Orangal's two lines of defences, one of mud and one of stone, are mentioned. Before the engagement, "Hindus made an attack upon Hindus to try their respective strength." "Fire-worshippers of Buddha" are alluded to as residing in the city. The latter were very possibly Jains, though why styled "Fire-worshippers" is not clear.

[3] The *Tārīkh-i Fīrōz Shāhi* of Ziāu'd-dīn Barnī (Sir H. Elliot's *History of India*, III, 231).

GOLKONḌA, QUTB SHĀHI DYNASTY OF—

(*See* DAKHAṆ, Muḥammadan Kings of the—.)

GUTTAS.

(See Mr. Fleet's *Dynasties of the Kanarese Districts*, pages 6, 7.)

In the sixth century a dynasty of "Mauryas" was reigning in the Koṅkaṇa, who claimed to be descendants, and possibly were so, of the Maurya dynasty of Pāṭaliputra (*see under* ANDHRAS, p. 144). The ancient dynasty was founded by Chandragupta, and Mr. Fleet thinks that the Gutta family, who called themselves *Mahāmandaleśvaras* in the twelfth and thirteenth centuries, were later offshoots of the same family. They were feudatories of the Western Chalukyas, and seem to have lived in Dhārwāḍ and Maisūr. Mr. Fleet notes inscriptions (1) of the reign of Vikramāditya VI of the Western Chalukyas (A.D. 1075-1126), (2) of A.D. 1179-80, (3) of A.D. 1181-82, (4) of A.D. 1187-88, (5) of A.D. 1191-92, (6) of A.D. 1213-14, (7) of A.D. 1237-38, and (8) of A.D. 1262-63, all of which mention chiefs of this Gutta family.

HAIDARĀBĀD, NIZĀMS OF—.

1. Nizāmu'l-mulk,
(1713–1748).
His real name was Mīr Kamrū'd-dīn Khān. *His other titles were* Nizāmu'l-mulk Āsaf Jāh, *and* Fath Jang Nizāmu'd-daulah. *He is also known by one of his earlier titles,* Chin Kalich Khān. *He rose to distinction under Aurangzīb, and was Wazīr to Muhammad Shāh. He was recognized as Subahdār of the Dakhaṇ in* 1713, *and became independent on the downfall of the Moghul dynasty. Died* 1748.

His sons:

- **Ghāzi-ud-dīn Khān.** *Remained absent from the Dakhaṇ till* 1752, *when, attempting to wrest the Subahdāri from Salābat Jang, he was poisoned.*
- **2. Nāṣir Jang,** (1748–1750). *Killed in* 1750 *by the Navāb of Cuddapah.*
- **4. Salābat Jang,** (1750–1761). *Deposed in* 1761 *by Nizām 'Alī and murdered January 26th,* 1763.
- **5. Nizām 'Alī Khān, Āsaf Jāh i Sānī,** (1761–1803).
- **Basālat Jang.**

3. Muzaffar Jang, Hidāyat Muhī-ud-dīn. (*Dec. 5th,* 1750 *to Jan. 30th,* 1751). *Grandson of Nizāmu'l-mulk by a daughter. Allied himself with Chandā Ṣāhib and fought against Nāṣir Jang. He was killed* 1750 *in a moment of triumph, leaving an infant son, who never came to power.*

Descendants of Nizām 'Alī Khān:

6. Sikandar Shāh, (1803–1829).

7. Farkhundah 'Alī Khān, Nāṣiru'd-daulah, (1829–1857). *Sir Sālar Jang was made his Dewān in* 1853.

8. Afzūl-ud-daulah, (1857–1869). *Sir Sālar Jang was his Dewān.*

9. Mīr Mahbūb 'Alī Khān Bahādur Fath Jang, Nizāmu'd-daulah, Nizāmu'l-mulk (1869), *the present Nizām. Sir Sālar Jang died* 1882.

THE HOYŚALA BALLĀLAS.[1]

This was a dynasty that ruled over most part of the present Maisūr territories from about the beginning of the eleventh till the beginning of the fourteenth century. They were probably feudatories of the Kaḷachuris, whom they succeeded on the downfall of that kingdom. The Musalmān raids of 1310 A.D. caused the subversion of the family. The Ballāḷas were Yādavas by origin, and resided, during the time of their greatest power, at the old Yādava capital, Dvārasamudra (modern Halebīḍu). The founder of the family is by tradition called Śala or Hoyśala, and in the *Chenna Basavanna Kālajñāna* he is given a long reign, from A.D. 984 to 1043; but it is possible that the name is mythical. Mr. Rice states that two inscriptions insert a son Kari between Śala and Vinayāditya, making Vinayāditya grandson of the former. Vinayāditya is the earliest authentic sovereign. The genealogy of the family is as follows:—

Vinayāditya.
Also called Tribhuvana Malla I. Married Keleyabbe, or Keleyaladevī. Inscriptions A.D. 1047, 1076.[2] *He was a feudatory of the Western Chālukya Vikramāditya VI.*

|

Ereyaṅga or Eregaṅga,
married Echaladevī.

|

Sons of Ereyaṅga:

- Ballāḷa I.
  Married Padmaladevī, Chāvalidevī, and Boppadevī. Inscription in A.D. 1103. *Overcame the Śāntara king Jagaddeva.*
- Vishṇuvardhana.
  Also called Bittideva, Bittiga, Tribhuvanamalla II, Bhujabalagaṅga, Vīragaṅga, *and* Vikramagaṅga. *Inscriptions A.D.* 1117, 1137. *Married Śāntaladevī. Took Talakāḍ, the capital of the Gaṅgas. He is said to have made many conquests. This is believed to be the sovereign who was converted to the worship of Vishṇu by Rāmānujāchārya.*
- Udayāditya.

|

Narasiṁha I. (son of Vishṇuvardhana)
Also called Vīra Narasiṁha *or* Vijaya Narasiṁha. *Married Echaladevī. A.D.* 1142—1191.

|

Ballāḷa II.
or Vīra Ballāḷa. *Married Padmalādevī. Mr. Fleet limits the Inscriptions to A.D.* 1192—1211. *Defeated the Kāḷachuris and assumed royal titles. Fought against Pāṇḍiya, Choḷa, &c.*

|

Narasiṁha II.
or Vīra Narasiṁha. *Was defeated by the Devagiri Yādavas, and lost much territory. Inscription, A.D.* 1223.

|

Someśvara.
Married Bijjaladevī and Somaladevī. Inscription of A.D. 1252. *Resided at "Vikramapura," a place he had established "in the Choḷa country."*

|

---

[1] Fleet's *Dynasties of the Kanarese Districts*, p. 64; Rice's "*Mysore and Coorg,*" I, 213; "*Mysore Inscriptions,*" by the same author, lxxv.

[2] Mr. Rice adds an inscription in A.D. 1039.

Narasiṁha III.
Inscriptions range from A.D. 1254 *to* 1286. *Reigned at Dvārasamudra.*

Ballāḷa III.
or Vīra Ballāḷadeva. *Reigned till the Musalmān conquest of A.D.* 1310.

In A.D. 1310 'Alāu'd-dīn, Emperor of Delhi, sent Malik Kāfur to reduce the Yādava kings of Dvārasamudra.[1] The invaders were completely successful. They destroyed the capital, sacked the temples, and subverted the dynasty. Ballāḷa seems to have been captured, but afterwards to have been released and allowed nominally to rule. This continued till A.D. 1326–1327, when a second Musalmān invasion completed the destruction of the kingdom. It appears, however, that princes of the dynasty continued, as might be expected, to claim a nominal dignity as heads of the family, for we read of the rebel Muḥammadan Viceroy fleeing in A.D. 1337 to the Hoyśala king at Tānūr for safety (he was delivered up and flayed alive by his sovereign), and in 1347 it seems that the Hoyśala prince Ballāḷadeva of Dvārasamudra sent a contingent to help the great Hindu confederation that stemmed the torrent of Musalmān successes, and checked for two centuries their advance southwards.

IKKĒRI, KELAḌI, OR BEDNŪR, RĀJAS OF.—

This was a principality in Maisūr which lasted from A.D. 1560 to 1763, the capital being at Ikkēri. The chiefs do not appear to have been very powerful at any time.

In 1560 Sadāśiva Rāya of Vijayanagar is said to have conferred on a man of the Śūdra caste a small government, which the family held, increased, and finally usurped as their own. To the first chief the Vijayanagar sovereign gave his own name. This was Sadāśiva Nāyakka, eldest son of Basavappa-gauḍa.

Basavappa-gauḍa.

1. Sadāśiva Nāyakka, *A.D.* 1560–1576.

2. Bhadrappa Nāyakka, *A.D.* 1576–1585.

Sons of No. 1:

(By first wife).
3. Doḍḍa Suṅkana Nāyakka, *A.D.* 1585–1596. *Lived in retirement, leaving government to his brother.*

6. Veṅkaṭappa Nāyakka, *A.D.* 1604–1626. *A weak prince, who left all government to Śivappa Nāyakka.*

7. Bhadrappa Nāyakka, (*A.D.* 1626– ?). *It was either this chief or his son who declared himself independent in A.D.* 1637. *He and his son both left all the affairs of State to the management of Śivappa.*

8. Bhadrappa Nāyakka, *A.D.* ? –1649. *See note to No.* 7. *Died without issue.*

(By second wife).
4. Chikka Suṅkana Nāyakka, *A.D.* 1596–1603. *Retired from government.*

5. Siddhappa Nāyakka, *A.D.* 1603–1604.

9. Śivappa Nāyakka, *A.D.* 1649–1671. *Daḷavai and real ruler in reigns of Nos.* 6, 7, 8. *On death of No.* 8 *he became chief, and was the greatest prince of the house. Defeated the Jain Rājas of Tuḷuva and acquired Kanara.*

10. Bhadrappa Nāyakka, *A.D.* 1671–1681.

11. Somaśekhara Nāyakka, *A.D.* 1681–1686. *He was succeeded by his widow,* Doḍḍa Chinnamājī, *A.D.* 1686–1698,

[1] The expedition is described by Amīr Khusrū in his *Tārīkh-i 'Alāī* (Sir H. Elliot's *History of India*, III, 80, &c.), and by Ziāu-d-dīn Barnī in the *Tārīkh-i Fīrōz Shāhī* (*Id.* 203).

(*adopted*)
12. Basavappa Nāyakka, *A.D.* 1698–1714. *The ruling house was extinct. This prince was son of a Bednūr (Biderūru) merchant of the Śeṭṭi caste.*

13. Somaśekhara Nāyakka, *A.D.* 1714–1740.

Vīrabhadra.

14. Buddhi Basavappa Nāyakka, *A.D.* 1740–1753. *Married Vīrammāji, who adopted a son, and, after the latter's death, another.*

(*adopted*)

15. Chinna Basavanna Nāyakka, *A.D.* 1753–1755. *He is supposed to have been murdered by his adoptive mother.*

16. Somaśekhara Nāyakka, *A.D.* 1755–1763. *He and his adoptive mother were confined by Haidar 'Alī, and deposed.*

In 1763 Haidar 'Alī seized the territories of this house, which thenceforth ceased to exist. No. 16 died without issue.

(*See* Buchanan's *Mysore*, etc., II, 289; Wilks' *History of Mysore*, I, 36, 37; Rice's *Mysore and Coorg*, II, 355.)

IMĀD SHĀHI DYNASTY OF BĪRĀR.

(*See* DAKHAṆ, Muḥammadan Kings of the—.)

JEYPORE RĀJAS.

The Rājas of Jeypore belong to an ancient family, but unfortunately dates and genealogical descent cannot be traced. The family chronicler[1] names a line of eighty-seven sovereigns, after whom came a prince named Vināyakadeva, who is said to have founded a new dynasty at Nandāpuram, the ancient capital of Jeypore. Others believe this chief to have been a dignitary at the court of the Gajapatis of Orissa. The family are Rājputs of the lunar line. The following is the list of Rājas, kindly given me by Mr. P. W. Moore, C.S :–

Vināyakadeva.
Vijayachandrakshayadeva.
Bhairavadeva.
Viśvanāthadeva.
Balarāmadeva.
Dasalnantadeva.
B. Vikramadeva.
B. Kṛishṇadeva.
Viśvambaradeva.
Malki Mardana Kṛishṇadeva.
Harideva.
Balarāmadeva.
Raghunātha Kṛishṇadeva.
Rāmachandradeva.
Balarāmadeva.
Viśvambaradeva.

[1] *Vizagapatam District Manual*, page 284 *et seq.*

Lālā Krishṇadeva.
Ejected by force of arms by Sītārāma Rāja of Vizianagrum in A.D. 1760 *in favour of his brother.*

Vikramadeva.
Installed by Sītārāma Rāja of Vizianagrum in A.D. 1760. *Ceded much territory to the latter. Jeypore became tributary to Vizianagrum.*

Rāmachandradeva.
Vikramadeva.
Rāmachandradeva,
(*the present Mahārāja*).

Vikramadeva.

KADAMBAS AND KĀDAMBAS, THE—.

In Mr. Fleet's recent publication "*The Dynasties of the Kanarese Districts*" he points out (*pages* 7—10, 84, *&c.*) that there were three families having similar names. The kings of the ancient dynasty called themselves *Kadambas*, while those of the two latter dynasties were styled *Kādambas*. These will be considered in order.

The ancient dynasty was that of the KADAMBAS of PALĀŚIKĀ, or Halsi in Belgaum, and Vaijayanti or Banavāsi in North Kanara. The various grants of this dynasty supply the following genealogy:—

Kākusthavarmā.

Śāntivarmā. — (*A son.*)

Mrigeśavarmā. *Conquered the Gaṅgas and Pallavas* (*Ind. Ant. VI*, 25). — (*A son.*)

Ravivarmā. *Re-established the family at Palāśikā by overthrowing Chaṇḍadaṇḍa, Lord of Kañchī, a Pallava* (*Ind. Ant. VI*, 30; VII, 33). — Bhānuvarmā. — Śivaratha.

Harivarmā. *An inscription of his reign mentions the Sendraka King, Bhānuśakti.*

In an inscription of Mrigeśavarmā's reign, his third year is called *Pausha* and his eighth *Vaiśākha*, while the years are divided, in the primitive method, into three seasons instead of four. Mr. Rice assigns the dates A.D. 538 to Kākustha, A.D. 570 to Mrigeśa, and A.D. 600 to Bhānu. Mr. Fleet doubts the authenticity of the grant on which the first date is founded, and places these sovereigns at about the close of the fifth century A.D., anterior to the subjugation of the Kadambas by Kīrttivarmā I of the Chalukyas, whose date is A.D. 567.

The Devagiri grants mention a Krishṇavarmā and his son Devavarmā, who may have been anterior or posterior to the above kings. Krishṇa's sister married the Gaṅga king Mādhava II.

These Kadambas were, like the Chalukyas, of the *Mānavya gotra*, "Sons of Hāriti." [1] They were Jains.

Next come the KĀDAMBAS OF BANAVĀSI AND HĀṄGAL.

Mr. Fleet thinks that the difference in the name implies that the later chiefs cannot claim direct lineal descent from the Kadambas. Three lists of sovereigns are given. The first, by Wilson (*Mackenzie*

---

[1] Mr. Fleet gives an interesting note on the title *Hāritiputra*, on page 5, n.

Collection I, ciii, enlarged by Mr. Lewis Rice in his *Mysore and Coorg* I, 193, &c.), relates to the founders of the dynasty and is probably purely mythical. The genealogy given stands as follows:—

Jayanta.
"Trilochana or Trinetra Kadamba."
Founder of the dynasty. Capital at Banavāsi.
Madhukeśvara.
Mallinātha.
Chandravarmā.

- Chandravarmā.
  - Mayūravarmā. *Married Śaśāṅkamudrā, daughter of Rāja Vallabha of Kalyānapura.*[1] *Introduced Brāhmans into his kingdom from the north.*
    - Kshetravarmā. "Chandragada" *or* "Trinetra Kadamba."
    - (*Daughter.*) Kanakāvatī. *Married a kinsman, Lokāditya, son of Chandrasena, governor of Southern Tuḷuva. He murdered a chief in the Maisūr country and seized his territory.*
- Purandara.

The second list is given in a number of inscriptions, but there is nothing extant to prove its authenticity; and Mr. Fleet points out that a number of Rāshṭrakūṭa inscriptions show that at any rate up to A.D. 947 a family of *Mahāmaṇḍaleśvaras* of a different name preceded the Kādambas in the government of Banavāsi.

Mayūravarmā I.
|
Kṛishṇavarmā.
|
Nāgavarmā I.
|
Vishṇuvarmā.
|
Mṛigavarmā.
|
Satyavarmā.
|
Vijayavarmā.
|
Jayavarmā I.
|
Nāgavarmā II.
|
Śāntivarmā I.
|
Kīrttivarmā I.
|
Ādityavarmā.
|
Chaṭṭaya, Chaṭṭa or Chaṭṭuga.
|
Jayavarmā II *or* Jayasiṁha.

[1] One of the Chalukya kings.

From this point commences the third list, which is probably accurate. Mr. Fleet, however, states that the first historical name is that of Kīrttivarmā II.

Jayavarmā II
or Jayasiṁha.

- **Māvulideva.**
- **Taila I** *or* Tailapa I. *Married Chavundalādevī.*
  - **Kīrttivarmā II** *or* Kīrttideva I, *alias* Tailana-Siṅga. *A.D.* 1068, 1076, 1077. *He was feudatory of the Western Chālukya Vikramāditya VI.*
- **Śāntivarmā II,** Śānta, *or* Śāntaya. *A.D.* 1088. *Married Siriyādevī of the Pāṇḍiyan family.*
  - **Taila II** *or* Tailapa II. *A.D.* 1099, 1108, 1122, 1124. *Feudatory of the Western Chālukya Vikramāditya VI. Died in A.D.* 1135-6 *probably.*
    - (*By first wife Bāchalādevī of the Pāṇḍiyan family.*)
      - **Mayūravarmā III.** *Governing in conjunction with his father, probably in A.D.* 1131.
      - **Mallikārjuna I.** *Governing, in conjunction with his father, in A.D.* 1132 *and* 1135-6, *as feudatory of Someśvara III, and in A.D.* 1144 *as feudatory of Jagadekamalla II. He was also called* Tribhuvanamallarasa.
    - (*By second wife Chāmalādevī.*) **Tailama.**
      - **Kīrttideva II.**
      - **Kāmadeva.** *Married Ketalādevī. Governing in A.D.* 1189 *as feudatory of Someśvara IV. Conquered "Male," Tuḷu, the Koṅkaṇa, and the Western Ghāṭs. He commenced to reign A.D.* 1181. *Is last heard of in A.D.* 1203-4.
- **Chokideva** *or* Jokideva.
- **Vikrama** *or* Vikramāṅka.

We hear in these inscriptions of a siege of Hāṅgal by the Hoyśala Ballāḷas in A.D. 1135, when King Vishṇuvardhana wrested from the Kādambas for a time the provinces of Banavāsi and Hāṅgal. In A.D. 1196 the Hoyśala king Ballāḷa II besieged Hāṅgal, but was repulsed by Kāmadeva. Soon afterwards, Mr. Fleet thinks, Ballāḷa II completely subjugated the Kādambas and annexed their territory, all that is known being that in A.D. 1203-4 Kāmadeva was still struggling.

THE KĀDAMBAS OF GOA.—These belonged to a distinct family connected with the Banavāsi Kādambas, but in a manner not yet known. They ruled at Goa and Halsi (*Palāśikā*). The genealogy is as follows:—

Guhalla.
|
Shasṭhadeva,
Chaṭṭa, Chaṭṭala, or Chaṭṭaya,
A.D. 1007.
|
Jayakeśi I,
A.D. 1052.
|
Vijayāditya I.
|
Jayakeśi II,
A.D. 1125.
|

Permādi *or* Śivachitta. *A.D.* 1147—1175. *Married Kamalādevī.*

Vijayāditya II *or* Vishṇuchitta. *A.D.* 1147 *and* 1171. *Married Lakshmīdevī.*

Jayakeśi III, A.D. 1175 and 1188.

Tribhuvanamalla, *Married Māṇikyādevī.*

Shasṭhadeva II. *Began to reign A.D.* 1246. *Reigning in* 1250.

A daughter. Married to Kāmadeva or Kāvana.

Shasṭhadeva I and Jayakeśi I were feudatories of the Western Chālukyas. Vijayāditya I married Chaṭṭalādevī, sister of Bijjalādevī, the mother of Jagaddeva of the Śāntara family. Jayakeśi II was also a feudatory of the Chālukyas, though at first he seems to have attempted to rid himself of their supremacy. He fought with the Sindas, and was for a time defeated. He was also defeated by the Hoyśalas. Permādi and Vijayāditya II seem to have reigned conjointly. Mr. Fleet thinks that, at the death of Jayakeśi III, the kingdom of the Kādambas of Goa was practically at an end, and that Shasṭhadeva II had very little real power.

KAḶACHURIS OR KAḶACHURYAS, THE—.

A dynasty of KAṬACHCHURIS is mentioned in an inscription of Maṅgalīśa of the early Chalukyas (A.D. 567—610), and Mr. Fleet (*Dynasties of the Kanarese Districts*, pp. 10, 11) considers them to be the predecessors of the KAḶACHURIS. Their king Buddha, son of Śaṁkaragaṇa, seems to have been conquered by Maṅgalīśa.

With the more northern branch of the family, as described by Mr. Fleet, we have nothing to do in the Madras Presidency, but the existence of the southern branch was felt in its day. Mr. Fleet gives the following genealogy :—

Jogama.

Permādi. *A.D.* 1128. *Feudatory of the Western Chālukya Someśvara III.*

Bijjala.[1] *Feudatory of the Western Chālukyan Jagadekamalla II. Commander-in-Chief of Taila III.* (*A.D.* 1156—1167.) *Assumed royal titles about A.D.* 1161-2. *Established his power in the south of the Chālukyan dominions, including part of Maisūr, and eventually established himself at Kalyāṇa. Was murdered by the celebrated Basava, the Liṅgāyat, whose sister Padmāvatī he had married.*

Siriyādevī. *Married Chāvuṇḍa II of the Sindas of Erambarage.*

Someśvara. *A.D.* 1067—1175. *Also called* Sovideva *and* Rāyamurāri.

Saṅkama, A.D. 1175—1180.

Āhavamalla, A.D. 1176 to 1188.

Siṅghana, A.D. 1183.

The three brothers were united in the government, but their power in the Chālukyan dominions had waned. An inscription of Āhavamalla's speaks of wars with the Choḷas, the Hoyśalas, and a Vijayāditya, possibly a Kādamba of Goa.

The Kaḷachuris were overthrown by Ballāḷa II of the Hoyśalas in, or soon after, A.D. 1183-4.

---

[1] "Also called Bijja, Bijjana, Vijjala, Vijjana, Tribhuvanamalla, and Nissaṅkamalla I."—(*Mr. Fleet.*)

KĀḶAHASTI, THE ZEMINDARI OF—.

This is an ancient Zemindari in the North Arcot District, but very little is known regarding the family to whom it belonged. They claim to have received their territory by grant from one of the two Pratāpa Rudras of Orangal in the thirteenth century, who created Dāmarla Javi Rāya (or *Rāyuḍu, Tel.*), first chief of Kāḷahasti.

In 1639, Dāmarla Veṅkaṭādri Nāyuḍu, the then Poḷegar, gave the village of Chennakuppum to the English, who obtained a *sanad* for it from the Rāja of Chandragiri, the expatriated prince of Vijayanagar. The Poḷegar stipulated that the new settlement was to be called "Chenna-paṭṭaṇam" after his father Chennappa or Chennayya Nāyuḍu. On the site so obtained, Mr. Day, the Superintendent of the Company's factory, built Fort St. George, and founded the city now called "Madras" by the English, but "Chennapaṭṇam" by the natives of the country. (See Mr. Cox's *Manual of North Arcot*, p. 216.)

KALIṄGĀ, GAṄGAS OF—.

We have still a great deal to learn about the sovereigns and princes of Kaliṅgā, for though it is certain that they were powerful and independent sovereigns at a very early stage of the history of Southern India, as yet we know nothing of their names. They governed the country south of Orissa and north of the Godāvarī. (See Mr. Foulkes's "*Civilization of the Dakhaṇ down to the Sixth Century B.C.*" in *Ind. Ant. VIII*, 1.)

The people and the reigning house of Kaliṅgā are alluded to in the oldest extant chronicles of India and Ceylon, and were known equally to the classical writers of Greece and Rome and to the inhabitants of the far East. They appear to have been hardy and adventurous traders by sea to distant countries. The oldest Buddhist legends speak of the Kaliṅgā monarchs as then rulers of a civilized country.

An ancient inscription [1] found at Chicacole in Ganjam gives the name of Nandaprabhañjanavarmā, King of Kaliṅgā, at a period probably previous to the Chālukyan conquest of Veṅgī at the beginning of the seventh century A.D. Like the Veṅgī kings, the sovereign was probably a Pallava by origin. His grant is dated from the city of Sārapalle.

Two other inscriptions of later date give the name of King Indravarmā. His grants are dated from the city of Kaliṅgānagara, in the years 128 and 146 of the "Victorious reign" (of the dynasty ?).

Later on we come to the descendants of this Indravarmā in the tenth century. After the Chālukyan conquest in the seventh century, we hear little or nothing of the Kaliṅgā Gaṅgas till about the year 977 A.D.[2] At that period there ensued a period of anarchy in the Eastern Chālukyan territories which lasted for twenty-seven years at least, and the Kaliṅgā princes again rose to power for a time at Kaliṅgānagara. The following short genealogy is gathered from inscriptions of this period :—

Jayavarmadeva.
- Anantavarmadeva (*reigning in* A.D. 985).
  - Rājendravarmadeva.
  - Devendravarmadeva.
    - Satyavarmadeva.

Two inscriptions found at Chicacole[3] record grants made by Devendra and his son Satya in the same year, namely, the "fifty-first year of the reign of the *Gāṅgēya-vaṁśa*," at Kaliṅgānagara, and it would seem natural to suppose that they date from the commencement of the reign of some king (Jayavarmā ?) who re-established for a time the fortunes of the family. Another grant of Devendravarmā[4] is dated in the "254th year," but without stating the era. Here also the order is issued from the city of Kaliṅgānagara. If pure conjecture may be allowed a place in a publication of this kind, I would note, as a possible explanation of these figures, that as the Kaliṅgā country lay between the territories of Orissa and those of the Eastern Chālukyas, it is possible that the ancient family may have

---

[1] Pages 21, 22 of this Volume. *Indian Antiquary*, X, p. 243.
[2] Dr. Burnell's *South Indian Palæography*, p. 53, note 4.
[3] Page 22 of this Volume. *Indian Antiquary*, X, 243.
[4] Pages 14, 15 of this Volume. *Indian Antiquary*, X, 243.

partially re-established themselves and founded a dynasty about the end of the seventh or beginning of the eighth century, when, seemingly, the Orissan kings lapsed into a condition of weak peacefulness for four and a half centuries (*Stirling*), but being afraid of their powerful neighbours on the south, they dared not assert any considerable independence till the period of anarchy in the Eastern Chālukyan dominions, which commenced about the year A.D. 977. The fifty-first year would then refer to the era of independence, the 254th to the original establishment of the dynasty.

On pp. 31—34 *ante*, I have noted a dynasty of kings professing to belong to the Gaṅga family, of whom a complete genealogy is given for three and a-half centuries, ending in A.D. 1119 with Chōḍagaṅga *alias* Anantavarmadeva, whose father married a daughter of Rājendra Choḷa (A.D. 1064—1113). They seem to be unconnected with the Gaṅgas mentioned above, and yet they claim to have ruled the Kaliṅgā country during the whole of that long period. I can at present offer no explanation of this apparent confusion.

KAṆVA OR KAṆWA DYNASTY, THE—.

(*See* the ANDHRA Dynasty.)

KĀRVĒṬINAGARA, ZEMINDARS OF—.

Sir Walter Elliot ("*Numismatic Gleanings*," in the *Madras Journal*, No. VII., N.S., p. 96, Vol. XX, O.S.) states that from a "local history of some merit" he finds that the ancient possessors of the "Kārvēṭinagaram" estate were a family of Sālva Reḍḍis, who migrated from the neighbourhood of Piṭṭāpuram in the delta of the Godāvarī, about the eighth or ninth century. One of them, Sālva Narasā Reḍḍi, obtained the favour of the last of the Eastern Chālukyas, Vimalāditya (A.D. 1016—1023),[1] and was appointed chief of the country about Tirupati, where he founded a town called Narasāpuram.

From the account that follows I obtain the following pedigree :—

Sālva Narasā Reḍḍi,
1st chief, about A.D. 1020.
|
* * *
|
Sālva Veṅkaṭapati Nāyuḍu
dispossessed by the Choḷas.
|
Sālva Bhīma Nāyuḍu
recovered his patrimony.[2]
|
Sālva Narasiṁha Nāyuḍu
assumed independence after an inroad by the Chera (?) king Kīrttivarmā whom he assisted. Ruled 35 years with much ability.
|
Sālva Bhujaṅga Nāyuḍu
was reduced to subjection by the Western Chālukya king, Somēsvaradeva (I or II) and taken prisoner to Kalyāṇa where he died.
|
* * *
|
* * *
Recovered the estate.

---

[1] Sir Walter Elliot's date, A.D. 930, is wrong.

[2] Another wrong date, Ś.Ś. 898 (A.D. 976), given.

In Ś.Ś. 1152 (A.D. 1230), it is said that the estates were curtailed to 24 villages by Rāja Rāja II of the Choḷa dynasty, but during the next four generations, as the power of the Choḷas decayed, the fortunes of the Kārvēṭinagara family rose, and in Ś.Ś. 1236 (A.D. 1314) the chief was able to obtain as his son-in-law Prōli, or Prōlaya, Reḍḍi, the first of the Koṇḍavīḍu Reḍḍi dynasty. Shortly after this the family became feudatories of Vijayanagar, and remained so for about two hundred years, when the family became extinct and the present Bomma Rāzu family succeeded. The last of the old family was Śeshāchala Reḍḍi, who stipulated that his family-name should be retained. This is still done, the name *Sālva* being one of the titles of the present Zemindar.

The founder of the family, Narasā Reḍḍi, was granted permission by his patron, the Chālukya, to use the royal seal and boar-signet of the Chālukyas, a proud distinction still kept up.

Mr. Cox (*Manual of North Arcot, p. 222, etc.*) gives an account of the origin and fortunes of the Bomma Rāzu family. Geddi Makha Rāzu and Boppa Rāzu, two scions of a family in the Northern Sarkārs, travelled southwards, and were successful in beating off a band of robbers. The chief of Kārvēṭinagara heard of this and sent for them. They took service under him, and Makha Rāzu eventually became his prime minister, and succeeded to the estate on the death of his patron without heirs (the widows becoming *satīs*). Boppa Rāzu became his prime minister. The present Zemindar is descended from them.

The family profess to be pure Kshatriyas.

KELAḌI, RĀJAS OF—.

(*See* Ikkēri Rājās.)

KERAḶA KINGS.

(*See* Rulers of the Malayāḷam country.)

KIMEDI, ZEMINDARS OF—.

There are at present three estates in the Ganjam District, Parla Kimedi, Pedda Kimedi, and Chinna Kimedi. The Zemindars of these estates belong to the same family, which is of considerable antiquity and claims to be descended from the Keśari sovereigns of Orissa. It is impossible, however, to ascertain anything reliable regarding their origin, or the ancestry of the present chiefs of Pedda Kimedi or Chinna Kimedi. I append a list of the Parla Kimedi family as given to me by Mr. C. F. Macartie, C.S., who compiled it from the Zemindari records and believes it to be authentic.

Kapiladeva.
(1227—1245).
|
Narasiṁhadeva,
(1245—1265).
|
Madanadeva,
(1265—1290).
|
Nārāyaṇadeva,
(1290—1309).
|
Ānandadeva,
(1309—1317).
|
Ananta Rudradeva,
(1317—1325).
|
Jaya Rudradeva,
(1325—1367).
|

|

Lakshmi Narasiṁha Bhānudeva,
(1367—1392).

|

Madhukarṇadeva,
(1392—1423).

|

Mṛityuñjaya Bhānudeva,
(1423—1457).

|

Mādhava Madana Sundara Bhānudeva,
(1457—1494).

|

Chandra Betāla Bhānudeva,
(1494—1527.)

|

Suvarṇa Liṅga Bhānudeva,
(1527—1566).

|

Śivaliṅga Nārāyaṇadeva,
(1566—1590).

|

Suvarṇa Keśari Nārāyaṇadeva,
(1590—1630).

|

Mukunda Rudra Nārāyaṇadeva,
(1630—1656).

|

Mukundadeva,
(1656—1674).

|

Ananta Padmanābha Nārāyaṇadeva,
(1674—1686).

|

Sarvajña Jagannātha Nārāyaṇadeva,
(1686—1702).

|

Narasiṁhadeva,
(1702—1729).

|

Vīra Padmanābha Nārāyaṇadeva,
(1729—1748).

|

Vīra Pratāpa Rudra Nārāyaṇadeva,
(1748—1766)
Having no son, adopted

|

Jagannātha Nārāyaṇadeva,
(1766—1806).

|

Gaura Chandra Gajapati Nārāyaṇadeva,
(1806—1839).

|

Purushottama Gajapati Nārāyaṇadeva,
(1839—1843).

|

Jagannātha Gajapati Nārāyaṇadeva,
(1843—1850).

|

Vīra Pratāpa Rudra Gajapati Nārāyaṇadeva,
(1850).
Present Zemindar.

KONḌAVĪḌU, REḌḌI CHIEFS OF—.

Konḍavīḍu is a strong hill-fortress in the Kistna District, south of the Krishṇā river and eight miles west of Guntūr. After the subversion of the Gaṇapati Rājas of Oraṅgal by the Muḥammadans in A.D. 1323, the Reḍḍi chiefs in different parts of the Eastern Coast rose to power. Amongst these the Konḍavīḍu chiefs were, for a century, so important that their government rises to the dignity of a kingdom, and their family to that of a dynasty.

The succession is as follows:—

	A.D.
Pōliya (Prōle, or Prōlaya) Vēma Reḍḍi, son of Donti Allā Reḍḍi (?)	1328—1339
Ana Vēma Reḍḍi	1339—1369
Aliya Vēma Reḍḍi	1369—1381
Komāragiri Vēma Reḍḍi	1381—1395
Komaṭi Veṅkā Reḍḍi	1395—1423
Rācha Veṅkā Reḍḍi	1423—1427

The dynasty was overthrown by the Muḥammadans in A.D. 1427.

Native tradition at Konḍavīḍu states that Prōlaya Vēma Reḍḍi was not connected with the family of Donti Allā Reḍḍi, but was "a guest in his house." Allā Reḍḍi is said to have lived at Dharaṇikōṭa near Amarāvatī, and his family are stated to have "entered" that place in A.D. 1225. Prōlaya Vēma Reḍḍi is said to have built (or rebuilt ?) the "Puttakōṭa" at Konḍaviḍu. His daughter married one of the Sālva Reḍḍis of Kārvēṭinagara.

Ana Vēma Reḍḍi rebuilt the *Amarēśvara* Temple at Amarāvatī, as is proved by an inscription there.

Komāragiri Vēma Reḍḍi has a bad character for unpopularity.

Native tradition makes Rācha Veṅkā Reḍḍi brother of Komaṭi Veṅkā Reḍḍi.

History of the Rulers of Konḍavīḍu from Native Sources.

Several Telugu chronicles are extant, which profess to give an account of the history of Konḍavīḍu, the ruins of the forts and temples of which are extensive.

The following is an abstract of one, by repute the most authentic of them, which is held in high estimation among the educated natives of that part of the country. It is so accurate in the main (though the dates are sometimes wrong) that I consider it very necessary that it should be examined in detail, as several assertions are made in it referring to events hitherto unknown or little known to English writers.

The history commences with a Gajapati Rāja from Orissa named Viśvambaradeva, who ruled twelve years and built the first fort or *Puttakōṭa*.[1] He had four sons, Gaṇapatideva, Bāla Bhāskaradeva, Hariharadeva, and Viśvambaradeva. Gaṇapatideva gave a village away in charity in Ś.Ś. 1067 (A.D. 1145). He "gave up his government" to Kākatīya Rudradeva.[2]

During the period of 100 years after the Gajapati sovereignty, the Reḍḍi chiefs began to grow into importance, and an inscription proves that in Ś.Ś. 1147 (A.D. 1225) one Donti Allā Reḍḍi was in possession of the fort of Dharaṇikōṭa, close to Amarāvatī on the river. Subsequently Prōlaya Vēma Reḍḍi, a member of Allā Reḍḍi's family, acquired power, defeated the officers of Kākatīya Pratāpa Rudra at Dharaṇikōṭa, proclaimed himself independent, came to Konḍavīḍu, and rebuilt the *Puttakōṭa*.[3] He ruled from Ś.Ś. 1242—1253 (A.D. 1320—1331).

Then follows an account of the Reḍḍi dynasty corresponding with that given above.

---

[1] Mr. Boswell in his report to Government printed with G.O. of 7th November 1870, reprinted in the *Indian Antiquary* (I, 182), says that the *Puttakōṭa* at Konḍaviḍu was built by "Odiya sovereigns when they held this part of the country."

[2] This would imply a conquest of this country from the Gajapatis by the Oraṅgal Gaṇapatis a few years (?) subsequent to A.D. 1145. This remains to be proved; also that the Gajapatis conquered the Choḷa sovereigns of Kaliṅga previous to that date. At present we know nothing of this. Dr. Burnell states that the Choḷas lost Kaliṅga in A.D. 1228 (*South Indian Palæography*, p. 40), and we know that they gained it in A.D. 1023. It has always been supposed that they held it undisturbed during those two centuries. I learn from a paper in the "*Asiatic Researches*" (XV, 269) that Ánaṅga Bhīmadeva, the Gajapati King of Orissa, visited Puri in the twelfth year of his reign, and after making a solemn declaration of conquests made by him, which extended the frontier of his kingdom from Chicacole to Rajahmundry, built the new temple of *Jagannātha* in honour thereof. According to Stirling the reign of this king commenced in 1174 A.D. Hunter makes the date 1175, and the writer of the above article places it in 1196. This would make the date of the conquest in question previous either to 1186, to 1187, or to 1208 A.D.

[3] See above, p. 174. It is very possible that this defeat occurred as stated. Pratāpa Rudra II was completely defeated by the Muḥammadans in A.D. 1323.

Ignoring the Muhammadan chiefs the Hindu historians pass on to Lāṅgūla Gajapati, who succeeded the Reḍḍi sovereign Rācha Veṅkā Reḍḍi. He is said to have ruled from S.Ś. 1342—1353 (A.D. 1420—1431).[1]

This Gajapati was followed by two sovereigns of the Ānegundi family, (*i.e.*, the Vijayanagar dynasty) whose names were Pratāpadeva and Hariharadeva. They reigned respectively seven and fifteen years, viz., from 1431 to 1454 A.D.[2]

This history then gives us another Gajapati named Kapileśvara as having conquered Harihara, and we have the following genealogy :—

Kapileśvara Gajapati,[3]
27 *years*, *A.D.* 1454—1461.
|
Śrī Vīra Pratāpa Purushottama Gajapati,
35 *years*, *A.D.* 1461—1496.
In 1479 (*Ś.Ś.* 1411, "*Kīlaka*"). *This king exempted the people of Konḍavīḍu from taxation, as is testified to by an inscription.*
|
Pratāpa Rudra Gajapati,
1 *year*, *A.D.* 1496-1497.
|
Vīrabhadra Gajapati,
18 *years*, *A.D.* 1497—1515.

Vīrabhadra was defeated by Krishṇadeva Rāya of Vijayanagar in A.D. 1515, who marched up from the south (Udayagiri, etc.), carrying all the fortresses that lay on his march.[4] After his conquest, Krishṇadeva Rāya went to Orissa and married the Orissa Gajapati's daughter.

He left as Governor of Konḍavīḍu a nephew of Sālva Timmarasu, by name Nādenḍla Gōpamantrī. Krishṇadeva Rāya built a temple at Konḍavīḍu and had an inscription engraved on a slab in Ś.Ś. 1443 (A.D. 1521).

Achyuta's reign is mentioned. He is said to have been succeeded by his minister Rāmayya Bhāskaruḍu. He it was who murdered the 72 chiefs of the Reḍḍis at Konḍavīḍu. (See Boswell's Report, *Indian Antiquary* I, 183.) During the reign of Sadāśiva Rāya at Vijayanagar, the Governor at Konḍavīḍu was Viṭhaladeva, son of Mūrti Rāja, who was son of Kanḍanavōli Rāma Rāja.

Sadāśiva's reign was followed by a Muhammadan conquest.[5]

Tirumaladeva of the Vijayanagar family collected a large army and drove the Musalmāns across the Krishṇā, fairly reconquering all the country south of that river. He left as Governor of Konḍavīḍu one Raṅga Rājayyadeva, his son.[6] This Governor in Ś.Ś. 1494 (A.D. 1572) granted a village to a temple. Tirumaladeva ruled till Ś.Ś. 1496 (A.D. 1574) and was succeeded by Śrī Raṅgadeva, who in Ś.Ś. 1499 (A.D. 1577) granted another village to a temple. In his reign Ibrahīm Pādshāh (Ibrahīm Quṭb Shāh of Golkonḍa) sent a force under a Brahman, Rāya Rāu (a Mahratta ?) who seized the Palnāḍ country and the country about Kurnool and Nellore, and finally attacked Konḍavīḍu, the Governor of which place, being bribed, treacherously surrendered it in Ś.Ś. 1502 (A.D. 1580).

Here the history closes, but it ends with a mysterious statement that "afterwards Pratāpa Rudra governed 2,219 villages of the Konḍavīḍu country." (!)

---

[1] See Boswell's *Nellore Manual*, *Udayagiri*, p. 424.

[2] As I remarked before, the dates of this history are not accurate, though very nearly so. It is quite possible that about this time the Vijayanagar sovereigns seized the country about Konḍavīḍu, and they may have left members of their family as governors of the territory ; but at present I am not aware of any information which we possess to confirm the fact.

[3] These Gajapati sovereigns belong to the Orissan dynasty (see p. 204). Dr. Hunter gives Kapilendradeva 27 years (A.D. 1452—1479) ; Purushottamadeva 35 years, 1479—1504 ; Pratāpa Rudra 28 years, 1504—1532. The Orissan chronicle credits Purushottama with a conquest of Kāñchīpuram, and Pratāpa Rudra with still more extended conquests.

[4] An inscription at Conjeeveram (*Chingleput District Manual*, 435-6) states that Krishṇadeva Rāya conquered the northern fortresses, including Konḍavīḍu, and defeated several chiefs, amongst whom was Vīrachandra Rāja, son of Pratāpa Rudra Gajapati, and Narahari Rāja, son of Vīrabhadra Gajapati ; while two inscriptions at Udayagiri declare that Krishṇa Rāya gave some lands to temples in Ś.Ś. 1436 (A.D. 1514), after having defeated Pratāpa Rudra Gajapati and taken prisoner his uncle Tirumalappa Rāya. An inscription at Vijayanagar records that Krishṇadeva Rāya returned in triumph to his capital after the completion of the war with Udayagiri in Ś.Ś. 1435 (A.D. 1513). An inscription at Maṅgalagiri (Gunṭūr Taluk, Kistna District) states that Konḍavīḍu was captured by Krishṇadeva Rāya in Ś.Ś. 1437 (A.D. 1515), or rather by his general, Timma.

[5] This is, of course, correct. It took place A.D. 1564.

[6] This would be the king of Vijayanagar, Śrī Raṅga I.

KONGU OR GANGA KINGS,[1] THE—.

As before stated (p. 153), the Chera and Koṅgu dynasties are still far from being clearly worked out. Neither the localities to which their rule was confined nor the dates to which they must be assigned are at all certain. Some writers consider the names as simply interchangeable; some think that the Cheras preceded the Gaṅga kings of the Koṅgu country, while the Rev. Mr. Foulkes (*Salem District Manual*) has entirely separated them. This is not the place to discuss the question, and I shall content myself with a brief summary. We know that in the oldest historical period, from the third century B.C., the ruling powers of the south were called Cheras, Choḷas, and Pāṇḍiyans, the Pāṇḍiyans being in the extreme south and south-east, the Choḷas north of them, and the Cheras partly to the north of the Pāṇḍiyans and partly along the western coast down to the extreme south of the peninsula. The junction of the three kingdoms is by tradition placed at the Karaipōṭṭanār, a small river running into the Kāverī eleven miles east of Karūr, which, in Ptolemy's time, appears to have been the capital of the Cheras (*Κάρουρα, βασιλειον Κηροβόθρου. Geog. Lib. VII, cap. I*, § 86). *Chera* is supposed to be synonymous with *Keraḷa*, and there seems to be little doubt that the supposition is correct. In later times there is some confusion because we have a very definite account of a long dynasty of Gaṅga or Koṅgu kings reigning over at least the northern part of what was formerly called Chera, their territory being called *Koṅgudeśa*. Up to the present, on the authority of the Markāra copper-plates, the dynasty has been believed to have lasted from the beginning of the Christian era down to the year A.D. 894, about which time it was overthrown by the Choḷas. We are now, however, told by Mr. Fleet (*Dynasties of the Kanarese Districts*, pp. 11—14) that the Markāra plates are forgeries, and that so far from being thrown back to the beginning of the Christian era, the brother of the third king (Harivarmā) of the true Gaṅga dynasty (or *Koṅgu*) gave a grant in A.D. 968 (*Ind. Ant.* VII, 101—112). From him down to the last king of the line are seventeen names. We know that the Hoysala Ballāḷas conquered the *Koṅgudeśa* in A.D. 1080, and it is a question, therefore, whether these seventeen kings ruled in the intervening 112 years. If so, the reigns would be short, but this is more easy of credence than that they enjoyed such abnormally long life as must be attributed to them if the Markāra plates and the dates given in the lists already published are to be received.

With this preface I proceed to give a list of the first seven kings of the Koṅgu country, of the solar race, who, it is very possible, we may have hereafter to recognize as true Cheras. The list is taken from Dr. Burgess's paper in the *Indian Antiquary* (I, 360), which followed Professor Dowson's abstract from the *Koṅgudeśa Rājākkaḷ* (J.R.A.S. VIII, pp. 2—6, "*On the Chera Kingdom of Ancient India.*"[2])

Vīra Rāya Chakravarti.
A Raṭṭa born in Skandapura. Sometimes said to be of the Solar, sometimes of the Lunar Race.

|

Govinda Rāya I.

|

Krishṇa Rāya.

|

Kāḷa Vallabha Rāya.

|

Govinda Rāya.
Is mentioned as a conqueror.

A Jaina named Nāganandi was minister to Kāḷa Vallabha Rāya, Govinda Rāya, and his successor Kannaradeva. The relationship of this last to Govinda is doubtful.

Chaturbhuja Kanaradeva Chakravarti.
Wilson (Mack. Coll., p. 199) calls him "Kumāra."

|

Tiru Vikramadeva.

[1] The Markāra and Nāgamaṅgalam Copper-plates (*Ind. Ant.* I, 361—366; II, 155, 271, *note*; III, 152, 262; V, 133) refer to this dynasty. See also the plate published by Mr. Lewis Rice at p. 138 of Dr. Gustav Oppert's issue of the *Madras Journal* for 1878.
[2] See also the translation by Taylor in M.J.L.S., XIV, 1.

He was installed at Skandapura. He is stated, in an inscription, to have conquered "Choḷa, Pāṇḍiya, Keraḷa and Malayāḷam" (the distinction is significant), and to have governed the Karṇāṭaka country as well as *Koṅgudeśa*; but as the inscription, though dated A.D. 178, also adds that the king was converted from the Jaina to the Śaiva faith by Saṅkarāchāryār, its authenticity may well be questioned. The mention of the Śaiva reformer would bring the king's date nearer to us by several centuries; but no theory can be built on an inscription tainted with the suspicion of forgery.

The above seven kings are the earliest known sovereigns of the Koṅgu country. Following them (so far as we know at present) came the kings of the Gaṅga dynasty. They belonged to a different family altogether. According to the Markāra plates, they date from the commencement of our era, but, as above stated, Mr. Fleet has shown strong reason for doubting the authenticity of these plates, and has published (*Ind. Ant.* VII, 101—112) inscriptions at Lakshmeśvara in Dhārwāḍ, from which we gather that the first king Koṅgaṇivarmā must have ruled about the beginning of the tenth century A.D. I therefore omit the dates usually assigned to these kings as being doubtful. The list is taken from Mr. Foulkes' paper in the *Salem District Manual*, with added notes.

1. Koṅgaṇivarmā Rāya I, *or* Mādhava I, *of the Kaṇvāyana family of the Jāhnavī or Gaṅgā race. He was enthroned at Skandapura.*

2. Mādhava II.

- 3. Harivarmā. *Enthroned at Skandapura, but lived at Daḷavanpura in Karṇāṭakadeśa.*
  - 4. Vishṇugopavarmā. *Enthroned at Daḷavanpura. He conquered "the East Country."*
    - (*Adopted*) 5. Mādhava III. *Had to resign his crown in favour of a son subsequently born to Vishṇugopa.*
    - 6. Krishṇavarmā. *Enthroned at Daḷavanpura.*
    - *A daughter.*
      - 8. Koṅgaṇi Mahādhi Rāya II.
        - 9. Dhruvanīti Rāya, Avinīta *or* Duvvinīta. *Ruled over Koṅgudeśa and Karṇāṭakadeśa. Is said to have conquered all the kings of the peninsula. He was called "Dharma Virodhi" or "Punyavirodhi," the "Unjust King."*
- Mārasiṁha, *or* Satyavākya.

Kulatti, *or* Parikulatti Rāya, *of the family of Mādhava III.*
- 7. Dindikara Rāya, *alias* Hariśchandradeva Rāya. *Succeeded Krishṇavarmā, but was deposed by the latter's minister, who raised (8) Koṅgaṇi Mahādhi Rāya II to the throne.*

10. Mushkara Rāya, *or* Brāhmahatya Rāya. *He resumed a number of grants made to Brahmans.*

11. Tiruvikrama, *or* Śrī Vikrama.

12. Bhūvikrama. *Called "Gajapati" from the number of his war elephants.*

- Vallabha, *or* Śrī Vallabhākya, *alias* Viḷanda. *His brother's Commander-in-Chief. Another account makes him younger brother of Koṅgaṇi III.*
- 13. Koṅgaṇi III, *alias* Navakāma. *Made extensive conquests of tributary kingdoms which had withheld payment.*

14. Râja Govinda, *alias* Nandivarmâ. *Lived some time at "Mukundapaṭṭana."*

15. Śivarâma, *or* Śiva Mahârâya I. *Was enthroned at Daḷavanpura, but lived at Mukundapaṭṭana.*

A son.

16. Prithivî Koṅgaṇi, *alias* Śiva Mahârâya II.

Vijayâditya.

17. Malladeva I, *alias* Śiva Mahârâya III.

18. Gaṇḍadeva. *Exacted tribute from the Pallava Râja of Kañchî. Fought with the Choḷa king, but was friendly with the Pâṇḍiyan.*

19. Satyavâkya.

20. Guṇâluttama. *Was enthroned at Daḷavanpura.*

21. Malladeva II. *Dethroned Guṇâluttama, and kept him prisoner at Skandapura. Defeated the Pâṇḍiyan king.*

There is still a good deal of confusion about some of these sovereigns. The above list is from the *Koṅgudeśa Râjâkkaḷ*, but the extant inscriptions "without exception" (*Mr. Foulkes, Salem District Manual*, p. 25), while confirming the pedigree from Koṅgaṇi I, call Mâdhava III son, instead of adopted son, of Vishṇugopa, and state that Koṅgaṇi II was son of Mâdhava III. They ignore the existence of Kṛishṇavarmâ, Dindikara Râya, and Kṛishṇavarmâ's sister. There are other differences also, some of which are pointed out by Mr. Foulkes, who has gone very closely into the question of this dynasty (*id.*, pp. 23—39). I do not propose to devote much space to the subject in consideration of the doubts raised by Mr. Fleet.

Seeing that the conquest by the Hoyśala Ballâḷas in A.D. 1080 seems a well-established fact, and that a Choḷa conquest[1] of the same Koṅgu country previous to that date seems equally certain, we must be very cautious in our dealing with the dates of the dynasty. The Ballâḷa conqueror chose Daḷavanpura (Tâlkâḍ) as his capital.

Mr. Rice considers that the chief who established the Gaṅga line of kings in Orissa in 1132 A.D. was a member of the Koṅgu family, but I think this is far from certain. There was a dynasty of Gaṅgas in Kaliṅgâ who might equally have founded that dynasty or it might have been founded, even, by a Choḷa prince (*see above, p.* 158). The Gaṅga family in Maisûr was by no means exterminated at the time of their overthrow. They remained with some local power, probably as subordinate chieftains, till the complete subversion of the country by the Vijayanagar kings. In the sixteenth century, after the sovereigns of Vijayanagar had been driven from their capital by the Muḥammadans, a Gaṅga Râja rose to power in the south of Maisûr and established a principality at Śivasamudra, the island at the falls of the Kâverî, about twelve miles north-east of Tâlkâḍ. He was succeeded by Nandi Râja, and he by Gaṅga Râja II, with whom the line came to a tragic end early in the seventeenth century under highly romantic circumstances.[2]

The kings of this dynasty are known in their grants by the appellation *Mahâdhi Râya*.

KULBARGA, BÂHMANÎ DYNASTY OF—.

(*See* "Dakhaṇ, Muḥammadan Kings of the—.")

---

[1] Wilson (*Mackenzie MSS.* I, 198) gives the name Âdityavarmâ as that of the Choḷa conqueror. Mr. Rice states that the Gaṅgas were driven out of their country by Râjendra Choḷa. As this king's reign lay between the years A.D. 1064 and 1113, the Choḷa occupation, if it took place in his reign, must have been of very short duration.

[2] Mr. Rice in his "*Mysore Inscriptions*" (p. lxviii) gives an account of this event.

MADURA, SOVEREIGNS OF—.

(*See* the "PĀṆḌIYAN KINGS" and the "NĀYAKKAS OF MADURA.")

MAHRATTAS. THE CHIEF DYNASTY.

- **Bābājī Bhoṅslē.** *Headman of three villages near Poona.*
  - **Mālojī.** *Entered the service of a Chief named Lukhjī Jādu Rāu, who held office under Nizām Shāh. He rose to power.*
    - **Shāhjī.** *Mālojī obtained for his son the hand of Jādu Rāu's daughter, Jījī Bhāy. Shāhjī rose to eminence as a commander, first under Nizām Shāh and then under Ibrahīm 'Ādil Shāh of Bījapur, under whom he governed all the southern conquests. He married also Tūka Bhāy Mohiti. He was born* 1594 *A.D.*
      - (*By Jījī Bhāy*) **Śambujī.** *Killed in a battle.*
      - (*By Jījī Bhāy*) **1. Śivājī.** *The first real sovereign. By* 1673 *he was monarch of the whole of the Koṅkana He seized Kurnool, Ginji, and Vellore in* 1677; *and opposed his brother Ēkojī at Tanjore. Peace was made,* 1678. *He died* 1680.
        - **2. Śambu** *or* **Śambujī,** (1680–1689). *Lost many of his father's possessions. Offended Aurangzīb, by whom he was seized and murdered in* 1689.
          - **Sāhu,** *or* **Shāo,** *or* **Sāhujī,** (1700–1749). *A prisoner in the hands of Aurangzīb from* 1689 *to* 1700. *Sāhu seized Satāra from his cousin Śambu in* 1708. *He led an idle life and the government was carried on by a Pēshwa. Died* 1749.
            - **Rāma Rāja** (*adopted.*)
              - **Sāhu.**
                - **Pratāpa Siṁha.**
                - **Rāma Rāja.**
                - **Shāhjī.**

              (SATĀRA.)
          - **Śambujī.**
        - **Rāma** *or* **Rāja Rām I,** (Regent, 1689–1700). *He ruled for his nephew. Reorganized the Mahratta predatory bands and ravaged the Dakhan. On his death his son seized on Satāra.*
          - **Śivājī.**
            - **Rāma** *or* **Rāja Rām II,** (1749). *He was acknowledged by the Pēshwa, Bālajī Rāu, on Sāhu's death, but had no real power, and was mostly kept in confinement.*
          - **Śambujī.** *Turned out of Satāra by Sāhu. Śambu seized on Kōlhapur, and made it his own rāj. He was aided by his mother Tāra Bhāy. Died without issue.*
            - (*adopted*) **Śivājī.**
              - **Śambujī** *Killed. No issue.*
              - **Shāhjī.**
                - **Śivājī.**
                  - (*adopted*) **Rāja Rām.**
                    - (*adopted*) **Nārāyana Rāu** *alias* **Śivājī.**

                    (KŌLHAPUR.)
                - **Sahu** (*no issue*).
      - (*By Tūka Bhāy*) **Ēkojī.** *Called Veṅkājī by Duff.* (*See the following table.*)
      - (*Illegitimate*) **Santajī.**
  - **Vinājī.**

From 1749 all Mahratta history centres in that of the Pēshwas and the great chiefs, and, as their career is mainly connected with the Bombay and Northern Presidencies, a table of their families is not considered necessary to be given here.

MAHRATTAS. THE DYNASTY OF TANJORE.

- **Bābājī Bhoṅslē.** (*See above.*)
  - **Mālojī.** (*See above.*)
    - **Shāhjī** (*See above.*)
      - (*By his wife Jījī Bhāy*)
        - **Śambujī.** (*See above.*)
        - **Śivājī.** (*See above.*)
      - (*By his wife Tūka Bhāy Mohiti*) **Ēkojī** *or* **Veṅkājī.** *Seized Tanjore in 1674-75 (?)*[1] *from the Nāyakka governor. Was threatened by Śivājī in 1677, but made peace with him in 1678. He was a tyrannous and grasping king, and was perpetually at war with his neighbours.*
        - **Shāhjī,** 1684—1711, (*no issue*).
        - **Sarfōjī,** 1711—1729, (*no issue*).
        - **Tūkajī.** 1729—1736.
          - **Baba Sāheb,** 1736—1737. *Married Sījan Bhāy, who was Regent from 1737 to 1740.*
          - **Sāhujī** *or* **Syājī.** *Being ejected by his brother in 1749, he applied to the English for aid. The fort of Dēvikōṭṭai on the Coleroon was stormed, and given to the English, but Sāhu had no real power.*
          - (*Illegitimate*). **Pratāpa Siṁha.** *Wrested the kingdom from his brother and held it firmly. Died 1765.*
            - **Tuljājī,** 1765—1788. *Was attacked, 1767, by the Navāb of Arcot aided by the English. Tanjore was captured. The Rāja was reinstated afterwards. Died 1788.*
              - (*Adopted*) **Sarfōjī,** 1798—1833. *Placed on throne in 1798 on Amara Siṁha's deposition. In 1799 he handed over the country to the English, receiving a pension.*
                - **Śivājī.** 1833—1855.
                  - **Vijaya Mohana Muktamba Bhāy.** *Present Princess of Tanjore.*
            - **Amara,** *or* **Amīr, Siṁha,** 1788—1798. *Was placed on the throne in 1788 and governed very ill. The English deposed him in 1798.*
      - (*illegitimate*) **Santājī.**
  - **Vīnajī.** (*See above.*)

Tanjore was annexed in 1857.

---

[1] Dr. Burnell (*South Indian Palæography*, page 56, note 4) writes: "The date of the final conquest of Tanjore by Ēkōjī, and the end of the Nayak (Telugu) princes is far from certain. Orme, in the last century, could not be sure about the date though he had all the Madras Government records at his disposal. Anquetil Duperron (*Recherches sur l'Inde*, I, pp. 1—64) has gone into the question very elaborately, and puts the date at 1674-75, which appears to be as near as can be expected."

ÅJAS.

e family of the Rājas of Maisūr is that two young
t of the Vijayanagar kings, having left that court
m an enforced marriage with the chief of Kāruga-
chief of Hadanāḍ. The elder of them, by name
ıus became lord (or *Uḍaiyār*) of Hadanāḍ and

and partly from Mr. Rice's "*Mysore and Coorg,*"

Krishṇa.

these reigns.)

Chama Raja,
Bōl"[2]),
71–1576).
Maisūr in the
[3] *After the*
Vijayanagar in
Maisūr princes
ment of tribute
na Rāja became
independent.

pinadeva.
dest son.

la Deva. (*A son.*) (*A son.*) Kempa Deva Rāja,
(1659–1672).
Assumed the name of Doḍḍa
(*or "Great"*) Deva Rāja.

ka Deva.
2–1704).

ion by
f Bed-
whom
Ranga,
es of
Rrods
of

With Chāma Rāja ends the old line of kings, and a disturbed period of anarchy follows, during which the Muhammadans gradually gained the upper hand, while maintaining a puppet sovereign chosen almost at random from various branches of the royal family. Chikka or Immaḍi Krishṇa Rāja of Keñcheṅgōḍ, a member of a distant branch, was put on the throne in 1734 and died in 1766, being nominally succeeded by his son Chāma Rāja, who died childless in 1775. Chāma Rāja, son of Devarāja Arasu of Ārkōṭār, a member of the Kārugahaḷḷi family, was then selected at random by Ḥaidar, who had usurped the government. He died in 1796. But the real rulers during this period were :—

	A.D.
Ḥaidar 'Alī Khān	1761–1782
Ṭīpū Ṣultān	1782–1799

On the fall of Seringapatam and death of Ṭīpū, the British Government restored the Hindu Rāj, and placed on the throne the son of the last-named Chāma Rāja, since when the line has been continued as follows :—

	A.D.
Krishṇa Rāja Uḍaiyār	1799–1868
Chāma Rājendra Uḍaiyār	1868

The latter was a minor at his accession, and received the reins of government in 1881.

MALAYĀḶAM COUNTRY, RULERS OF—.

Very little is as yet known regarding the rulers of the fertile country west of the Western Ghāts. Its history has yet to be written. There is abundant evidence of a very extensive commerce between the people of the Malabar and Kanarese Coast and the inhabitants of Western Asia and Europe in olden days, but beyond a few isolated facts, no connected story has come down to us. And there is little hope of the tale ever being clearly told, for the few remaining inscriptions in that tract are eminently unhistorical in character. The following sketch is an abstract of the *Keraḷolpati*, or native account of Keraḷa, written by Tuñchattu Rāmānuja, *alias* Rāman Eluthatham.

In ancient days, when the kings of the earth, of the Kshatriya caste, had grieved the majesty of heaven by their violence and wickedness, *Vishṇu* became incarnate as *Paraśu Rāma*, and went about slaying the sinful sovereigns and destroying their dynasties. He determined to create a new country, and recovering *Malayāḷam* (*Malai-āḷa*, "hills and waves") from the sea, he peopled it with Brahmans from other lands. But serpents [1] swarmed in the new tract, and the settlers fled back to their own homes. Then *Paraśu Rāma* brought down the Brahmans of sixty-four villages from the Ārya country in the north and settled them in sixty-four villages along the whole coast. Thirty-six thousand Brahmans [2] belonging to fourteen villages took up arms for the defence of their territory, and amongst them twelve chiefs were appointed. For the propitiation of the serpents, *nāga*-worship was ordained,[3] and temples of the gods were erected.[4] Then the Brahmans who had fled returned, and were called "*Tuḷu-Brahmans*," or "*Payan Tuḷuvas.*" *Paraśu Rāma* instituted charms for the propitiation of devils, portioned out temple services amongst different villages and families, and ordained hereditary descent in the line of the mother.[5] He also introduced Śūdras from neighbouring countries.

After some time, the inhabitants fell out amongst themselves, and required a governor. *Paraśu Rāma*, therefore, selected four villages, and the people consented, first to a joint government of four Brahman chiefs from these four villages, and afterwards to the government of a single chief from one of these four, in turn, each for three years.[6] In those days one-sixth of the produce was paid to the governor. Many years thus passed.

But these governors oppressed the people, and the latter at last determined to dispense altogether with native rulers. They therefore brought in a foreigner, one Kēya Perumāḷ from Kēyapuram [7] and made him ruler for twelve years. "He was named *Chēramān* (or *Keraḷan*) *Perumāḷ*, king of *Malai-nāḍ* just as *Choḷa Perumāḷ* governed *Choḷa*, and *Pāṇḍi* (or *Kulaśekhara*) *Perumāḷ* governed *Pāṇḍya*." [8]

---

[1] "Serpents with human faces." Aborigines?
[2] Called *Vāl-nambis*, "armed half-Brahmans." (*Gundert.*)
[3] It still obtains largely.
[4] Also "gold-dust was scattered in the soil, gold fanams were coined, and treasures were buried in the ground,"
[5] All old customs in the Malayāḷam country are referred back to *Paraśu Rāma*.
[6] Thus originated the Malayāḷam custom of twelve years' rulers.
[7] No clue is given as to the locality of this place.
[8] See Dr. Burgess's note on the Perumāḷs in *Ind. Ant.* IX, 77.

1. Kēya Perumāḷ was thus the first *Chēramān Perumāḷ*. His power was limited, the sixty-four villages constituting a powerful democracy and checking all attempts at independence. His capital was at Allūr. He built a palace at Talayūr. He reigned 12 years.[1]

2. Choḷa Perumāḷ was then appointed.[2] He built a palace called Choḷakkara. He reigned 10 years and 2 months, and retired to Choḷa.

3. Pāṇḍi Perumāḷ was next crowned at Paramba, where he erected a fort. He ruled 9 years, and retired to the Pāṇḍiyan country.

4. Another Choḷa Perumāḷ was brought, who ruled 12 years. After him—

5. Kulaśekhara Perumāḷ, the great Pāṇḍiyan, came to the throne of Keraḷa.

At this point the story seems to break off, and commence again at a period "when the *Kali* age was a little advanced." And we are again brought up to the reign of Kulaśekhara Perumāḷ, but with a totally different set of kings. These confusions are not uncommon in these native legends.

1. "When the *Kali* age was a little advanced" the Brahmans of Malayāḷam brought "from Bāṇapuram in *Para-deśa*" a Perumāḷ named Bāṇa-Perumāḷ. He became a Buddhist, but, after a great disputation in which the Brahmans were victorious, he banished the Buddhists and was reconverted to the Brahman religion. Nevertheless he was excommunicated and "went to Mecca" after reigning for four years.

2. Tuḷuban Perumāḷ, from the north, was the next Perumāḷ. He lived at Kōṭiśvara and named the country about there the *Tuḷu-nāḍ*. He reigned 6 years and died.

3. Indra Perumāḷ succeeded, reigned 12 years at Allūr, and went back to *Para-deśa*.

4. Ārya Perumāḷ was then brought from Āryapuram. He divided Keraḷa into four divisions,[3] *i.e.*:

i. *Tuḷu-rāj*, from Gōkarṇa to the Perum-puṟa[4] river.
ii. *Mūshika*, or *Kupa*, *Rāj* from the Perum-puṟa to Pudu-paṭṭaṇ.[5]
iii. *Keraḷa Rāj*, from Pudu-paṭṭaṇ to Kannetti.[6]
iv. *Kupa*, or *Mūshika Rāj*, from Kannetti to Cape Comorin. He died after a reign of 5 years.

5. Kuṇḍan Perumāḷ was brought from *Para-deśa*. He built a palace near Kannetti, and retired to his own country after a reign of 4 years.

6. Koṭṭi Perumāḷ reigned for a year and died.

7. Māta Perumāḷ reigned 11 years and died. He was succeeded by his younger brother,—

8. Eṟi Perumāḷ, who reigned 12 years and retired after building a fort.

9. Kompen Perumāḷ succeeded. He lived in a tent on the bank of the Neytāra river for 3½ years, and died.

10. Vijayan Perumāḷ came next. He built the fort of Vijayan-Koḷḷam. He reigned 12 years and retired.

11. Vallabha Perumāḷ succeeded. He discovered a *liṅgam*, and built a shrine over it on the banks of the Neytāra river, and a fort. He reigned 11 years and died.

12. Hariśchandra Perumāḷ. He built a fort on the Puṟali Hills and lived therein in solitude, "and was no more heard of."

13. Mallan Perumāḷ succeeded. He reigned 12 years and retired.

"The Perumāḷ who succeeded was Kulaśekhara Perumāḷ" of the Pāṇḍiyan kingdom. His reign is given more in detail, with the reforms he introduced. He introduced some Kshatriyas into the country. He procured two celebrated teachers, on payment, to teach the Brahmans of the country, and established a college at the place now called Tirukaṇṇāpuram. This Perumāḷ reigned 18 years and ascended to heaven "with his body." The year of the *Kali* is given as "*Tiru-vañcha-kuḷam*," and it is said to correspond with A.D. 333.[7]

After this there was a government by a democracy, and, like the government, the so-called "history" lapses into wild confusion for a space. Probably there was a period of anarchy, during which the

---

[1] The commencement of his reign is said to have taken place in A.D. 216. Another version states that he lived only 8 years and 4 months, when he died.

[2] The constant recurrence of Choḷa and Pāṇḍiyan Perumāḷs will be noticed. It will be an interesting subject of inquiry for the future historian to ascertain whether Pāṇḍiyan and Choḷa history corroborates these assertions.

[3] There is a confusion in the different versions as to these divisions.

[4] The river of Paṟayanūr, five miles north by east of Mount D'Eli.

[5] Two miles south-east of Vaḍakarai, a town in Kuṟumbranāḍ Taluk, on the seacoast.

[6] Near Koḷḷam. So *Gundert's* Dictionary. But if so it must be the Southern Koḷḷam now called Quilon, not the northern now called Koilāṇḍi.

[7] According to the former list the date of the close of this Perumāḷ's reign would be A.D. 277. But the dates are probably entirely fictitious and must not be for a moment depended on.

country was split up into factions. The story states that the country was governed by a popular assembly, by whom judges were appointed. At last an assembly took place at which the representatives of the people expressed themselves dissatisfied with the form of government, and they determined to "ask Ānagundi Krishṇa Rāya (!) to send a person to govern them, and he accordingly sent a Kshatriya, Chēramān Perumāḷ, to rule over Keraḷa."

Chēramān Perumāḷ therefore came to the throne. One version says that he succeeded "after the reigns of Âdi-Perumāḷ and Pāṇḍi-Perumāḷ, who were sent, were over." The Brahmans made him an absolute monarch, without restriction, and he governed so well for 12 years that they appointed him ruler for a further similar period, and again for a third. Kṛishṇa Rāya [1] prepared to attack Malayāḷam. The Pāṇḍiyan king also fortified his territory. Chēramān attacked the Rāya's forts but was unsuccessful. A second attack was successful, under the command of two young men, brothers, who led the army.

After this, Śaṅkarāchāryar [2] was born. He wrote the history of Keraḷa, and made fresh improvements in the condition of the Brahmans, making stringent regulations, which are fully detailed. His reforms were promulgated at a great council.

The manuscript here goes back to the time of Chēramān Perumāḷ, and describes the conclusion of his reign. He is said to have given up the throne and gone on a pilgrimage to Mecca "in company with the Bauddhas."[3] The limits of the Malayāḷam country are described, and the neighbouring kingdoms are said to be *Pāṇḍiya, Koṅgu, Tuḷu, Wainaḍ, Punnāḍ.* (The last is a tract of Maisūr, and was ruled by a race of Kshatriyas of whom we have inscriptions.) He divided the Malayāḷam country into eighteen divisions, constituting their chiefs and making regulations. He gave his sword to the ancestor of the present Zamorin of Calicut. (Chēramān Perumāḷ's [4] departure for Mecca is said by some to have occurred in A.D. 350. (*Gundert's Dictionary.*) He sailed from Dharmapaṭṇam, or Calicut. After residing some time at Jeddah he died. Before his death, however, he persuaded an Arab chief to sail for the Malabar Coast with a number of followers in order to establish a Muḥammadan colony and convert the inhabitants to that religion. They did so, and mosques were built. Eleven are named.

After some period had elapsed [5] (duration not mentioned), one of the Malayāḷam chiefs, Kunnala Kōnēttiri, waged war against his neighbour, the Poraḷḷāttiri chief, and defeated him. The Zamorin made Menokki ruler of Poraḷḷātiri and came to terms with the troops and people.

After this follows an account of the founding of the town of Calicut, close to the Zamorin's palace at Taḷi, by a merchant who had amassed a great fortune in trade with Mecca. Afterwards, while Puntura Kōn was Zamorin, one Koya, a foreigner, settled at the town, which was named after him *Koyikkōṭu* (Calicut). Koya assisted the Zamorin in his attainment of increased power.

Shortly after this the Portuguese came to Calicut.

It is unnecessary to continue the sketch further. The *Keraḷolpati* is a very fair specimen of a native attempt at history. It may contain germs of truth, and it certainly embodies a number of scattered traditions, but in the attempt to weave these into a connected story the author is signally unsuccessful.

MĀNYAKHETA RĀJAS.

(*See* Rāshṭrakuṭas, The—.)

MĀTAṄGAS.

That a powerful family of this name existed somewhere in the south in old days is very well known, but very little is known about them. They are mentioned in Saṅskṛit works as mountaineers—barbarians—and the name occurs in some inscriptions.

---

[1] Of course this is an absurd anachronism. It is said by some writers to be an interpolation.

[2] The real date of Śaṅkarāchāryar is about 650 to 700 A.D. (Dr. Burnell's *South Indian Palæography*, p. 37, and note 4. Also his "*Sāmavidhāna Brāhmaṇa*," Vol. I, Pref., p. ii. n.) He flourished 800 years before "Ānagundi Kṛishṇa Rāyar," or Kṛishṇadeva Rāya of Vijayanagar.

[3] Other accounts relate that he died. Pāchu Mutatu, in his *Keraḷa-viśesha-māhātmya*, gives a full account of the fables. He states that Bāṇa Perumāḷ (*see above, 2nd List, No.* 1) was converted to Buddhism by Buddhist priests from China, and that he went with them to China after four years' reign.

[4] The author of the "History of Travancore" states that this last Chēramān Perumāḷ's name was Bhāskara Ravivarma, and that he was one of the sovereigns who signed the grant to the Jews of Cochin. According to Dr. Burnell this would be in the eighth century A.D.

[5] This is generally believed to mark the close of a monarchy and the commencement of government by a Brahmanical aristocracy, the country being divided. The natives call it the period of the Tamburān Rajas.

"The first inscription . . . that gives us any extensive insight into the early history of these parts (the Northern Kanarese Districts and the Western Dakhan) is a stone tablet at the Meguti temple at Aihole, the ancient Ayyâvole or Āryapura in the Kalāḍgi District. It is of the time of the Western Chalukya king Pulikesi II, and is dated *Śaka* 556 (A.D. 634-5).[1] From it we learn that at the time of the advent of the Chalukyas, the dominant families in this part of the country, whom one by one the Chalukyas subjugated and dispossessed, were the Nalas, the Mauryas, the Kadambas, the *Mātangas*, and the Katachchuris . . . . " (Mr. Fleet's "*Dynasties of the Kanarese Districts*," pp. 5, 6.)

They are mentioned in an earlier inscription of Mangalīśa (A.D. 567-8—610). Mr. Fleet writes (*id.*, p. 10): "*Mātanga* means 'a Chāndāla, a man of the lowest caste, an outcaste, a Kirāta mountaineer, a barbarian'; and the Mādigas . . . . usually call themselves *Mātaṅgi-makkaḷu*, *i.e.*, 'the children of Mātaṅgi or Durgā,' who is their goddess. It is probable, therefore, that the Mātaṅgas of this inscription were some aboriginal family of but little real power, and not of sufficient importance to have left any records of themselves."

MAURYAS.

"The Nalas and the Mauryas are mentioned in connection with Kīrttivarmā I, who was the father of Pulikesi II, and whose reign terminated in Śaka 489 (A.D. 567-8). . . . . Of the Mauryas, all the information that we have, furnished in the same inscription, is that they were a reigning family in the Konkana. . . . . It is not at all improbable that their capital was the Puri, or 'the city, the goddess of the fortunes of the western ocean,' which is mentioned in the verse immediately following that in which their subjugation is recorded, and that this is the same town as the Puri which, in the eleventh century A.D., was the capital of the Silāhāras of the Konkana. These Mauryas were perhaps descendants of the Maurya dynasty of Pātaliputra,[2] which was founded by Chandragupta, the Sandrocottus of the Greeks, in the fourth century B.C., and of descendants of which we seem to have some still more recent traces in Western India in the twelfth and thirteenth centuries A.D. in the *Mahāmandalesvaras* or great feudatory nobles of the Gutta family, or the lineage of Chandragupta, whose inscriptions are found at and in the neighbourhood of Chaudadāmpur in the Dhārwād District, and at Halebid in Maisur, and who were feudatories of the Western Chālukya Kings and their successors." (Mr. Fleet's "*Dynasties of the Kanarese Districts*," pp. 6, 7.)

NAḶAS.

(*See above under* MĀTAṄGAS.)

We hear of the Naḷas as a nation or tribe opposed to the Chalukyas in the reign of Kīrttivarmā I, *i.e.*, before A.D. 566; and they are mentioned again in an inscription of Jayasiṁha III (A.D. 1018—1040) of the Western Chālukyas (*Ind. Ant.*, Vol. VIII, 10), but only as a traditional foe of that sovereign's ancestors. Beyond this, nothing, I believe, is known of them. (Mr. Fleet's "*Dynasties of the Kanarese Districts*," p. 6.)

"NAVĀBS OF THE KARṆĀṬAKA" OR "NABOBS OF ARCOT."

1. Zu-l-faqār 'Alī Khān.

Son of Asād Khān. Created Navāb by Aurangzīb, and made subject to the Subahdār of the Dakhaṇ. Governed from A.D. 1692 *to* 1703.

2. Dā'ūd Khān.

Son of Kizar Khān. Was appointed successor to Zu-l-faqār 'Alī and ruled from A.D. 1703 *till* 1710, *when he was made Commander-in-Chief at Delhi.*

---

[1] *Third Archæological Report* Western India, p. 129, and *Indian Antiquary*, Vol. VIII, p. 237.

[2] See above, page 146.

'Agībatti Muḥammad Khān.

- **3. Sa'ādatullāh Khān,** (A.D. 1710–1732), *otherwise called Muhammad Saiyid. He was created successor to Dā'ūd. Adopted his brother's sons, having himself no issue.*
- **Ghulām 'Alī Khān.** *Was made jaghīrdār of Vellore by (3) Sa'adatullāh Khān. Partitioned his estates amongst his four sons.*
  - **4. 'Alī Dost Khān.** (A.D. 1732–1740). *Ghulām Husain, nephew of Sa'ādatullāh's wife, was his Dewān.*
    - **5. Safdar 'Alī Khān,** (A.D. 1740—1742). *Murdered by Murtazā 'Alī.*
      - ———
      - **6. Muḥammad Saiyid,** *alias* Sa'ādatullāh Khān, (A.D 1742—1744). *Murdered at Arcot.*
      - (*A son*), *posthumous.*
    - (*Daughter.*) *Married Murtazā 'Alī.*
    - (*Daughter.*) *Married Taqī Ṣāhib of Wandewash.*
    - (*Daughter.*) *Married Chandā Ṣāhib, a distant relative. Chandā Ṣāhib's daughter by a former wife having married Ghulām Husain, 'Alī Dost's Dewān, Chandā Ṣāhib gained the Dewānship for the time and raised himself to power.*
  - **Bāqir 'Alī.** *Was made governor of Vellore by his adoptive father Sa'ādatullāh in A.D.* 1732.
    - **Ghulām Razā Khān.**
    - **Ghulām Murtazā 'Alī.** *Married a daughter of Alī Dost. He was governor of Vellore.*
  - **Sa'ādat 'Alī Khān.**
  - **Akbar Muḥammad Khān.**

Haji Muḥammad Anwār.

- **7. Muḥammad Anwār-ud-dīn,** (A.D. 1744—1749). *Killed in battle against Chandā Ṣāhib and Muzaffar Jang of Haidarābād.*
  - **Māfūz Khān,** *Was taken prisoner in the battle in which his father was killed, and was shortly afterwards released. He never opposed Muhammad 'Alī, and was by him appointed governor of Madura.*
  - **8. Muḥammad 'Alī,** *alias Navāb Wālājāh,* (A.D. 1749–1795).
    - **9. 'Umdāt-ul Umarā,** (A.D. 1795—1801).
    - **Amīr-ul Umarā.**
      - **10 'Azīm-ud-daulah,** (A.D. 1801—1819).
        - **11. Āzam Jāh Bahādur,** (A.D. 1819—1825).
          - **13. Ghulām Muḥammad Ghaus Khān,** (1842--1855). (*Died without issue.*)
        - **12. 'Azīm Jāh Bahādur,** *Regent* 1825—1842, "*Prince of Arcot*" 1867—1874.
          - **Zahīr-ud-daulah Bahādur,** G.C.S.I. "*Prince of Arcot,*" 1874—1879.
          - **Intizām-ul-mulk Bahādur,** "*Prince of Arcot,*" 1879. (*Present prince*).
          - **Umdāt-ud-daulah Bahādur,** (*Died* 1881).
          - **Mu'azzaz-ud-daulah Bahādur.**
  - **Abd-ul Rahīm.**
  - **Abd-ul Wahāb.**
  - **Najībullāh.**

NĀYAKKAS OF MADURA.

The previous history of the ancient kingdom of the Pāṇḍiyans, of which Madura was the capital, will be found under the head of the "Pāṇḍiyans." Madura fell finally into the hands of the Nāyakka Generals of Vijayanagar in 1559 A.D., who speedily constituted themselves into an independent dynasty, acknowledging, however, the Rājas of Vijayanagar as their suzerains. The following is the genealogy of the family:—

1. Viśvanātha Nāyakka I, (1559-1563). *Governor on behalf of the Vijayanagar sovereigns.*

2. Kumāra Krishṇappa. (1563-1573).

3 Krishṇappa, *or* Periya Vīrappa. ......[*Joint* (1573—1595) *Rulers.*]........ Viśvanātha II.

4. Liṅgayya, *or* Kumāra Krishṇappa. ....[*Joint* (1595—1602) *Rulers.*].... Viśvanātha III, *or* Viśvappa.

5. Muttu Krishṇappa, (1602-1609). "*King of Madura.*"

6. Muttu Vīrappa, (1609-1623.)

7. Tirumala Nāyakka, (1623—1659),

Kumāra Muttu.

(*Illegitimate*)
8. Muttu Arakādri, *or* Muttu Vīrappa, (1659-1660).

9. Chokkanātha, *or* Chokkaliṅgam, *or* Chokkappa. *Married* Maṅgammāḷ. (1660-1682). *He was for one year deprived by his brother,* 1677.

10. Muttuliṅga. (1677).

11. Raṅga Krishṇa Muttu Vīrappa, (1682-1689). *Followed, after his death, by the regency of his father's widow* Maṅgammāḷ. (1689-1704).

12. Vijaya Raṅga Chokkanātha, (1704-1731). *Followed by the reign of his widow* Mīnākshī. (1731-1736).

In 1736 the Musalmāns got possession of the kingdom of Madura.

I now proceed to give a rough sketch of the reigns of these princes. For full particulars Mr. Nelson's "*Madura Country; A Manual*" should be referred to. All that follows is taken from it.

1. Viśvanātha Nāyakka (1559—1563).—Either during or after the government of the three Nāyakkas who ruled Madura after the year 1558 (*see below*, p. 224) a Pāṇḍiyan prince, Chandraśekhara Pāṇḍiyan was placed on the throne, but the Choḷa king of Tanjore, Vīraśekhara, made war and seized the Pāṇḍiyan kingdom. Chandraśekhara fled to Vijayanagar, and the pseudo-Rāya, Rāma Rāja, acting for the real Rāya, Sadāśiva, in captivity, sent a general, by name Kōṭiya Nāgama Nāyakka, to drive

out the Choḷas. He did so and got possession of Madura, but instead of putting the Pāṇḍiyan king on the throne he began to administer the country for himself. The Rāya, indignant, sent an army under Nāgama's own son, Viśvanātha, to reduce the rebel. Viśvanātha defeated Nāgama, took him prisoner, and proceeded to govern the country. Ārya Nāyakka Mudaliyār, *alias* Āryanātha, the builder of the thousand-pillared *maṇḍapam* in Madura, and a justly celebrated man, came to Madura with Viśvanātha and gave him great assistance. Viśvanātha nominally placed Chandraśekhara Pāṇḍiyan on the throne, but really governed for himself. He made Āryanātha his commander-in-chief and prime minister under the title of *Daḷavāy*. The country was wisely governed, fortifications were carried on, temples rebuilt, channels dug, villages erected, and cultivation extended even as far north as the Trichinopoly fort, then belonging to Tanjore. Viśvanātha induced the Tanjore Rāja to exchange Trichinopoly for Vallam, and thus the former became part of the kingdom of Madura. Its rock was fortified, and improved communications were opened.

Soon after this, Āryanātha, who had gone to settle the Tinnevelly country, found himself successfully opposed by five chiefs, who called themselves the "five Pāṇḍavas," and who seem to have possessed considerable power in the south. Viśvanātha, therefore, went south to the aid of his general, but in vain. It is said that Viśvanātha, finding his armies unable to effect the conquest of his enemies, challenged the five chiefs to a personal contest, five to one, on condition that the defeated party should retire from the contest. They accepted, but chivalrously demanded that only one of their number should represent them. In the combat which ensued, Viśvanātha killed his man, and the four survivors honorably carried out their promise and left the country. The Nāyakka was therefore left undisputed chief of the south. He gave *Pāḷaiyams* to seventy-two chiefs by way of settling the country. Viśvanātha died December 1563, and his son succeeded.

2. Kumāra Krishṇappa (1563—1573). The Poligar Dambichchi Nāyakka revolted at a time when Āryanātha was away north looking after some refractory Musalmāns, but the insurrection was quelled and the rebel chief killed.

Āryanātha appears to have been the real ruler of the country. Several new public works were carried out, and some temples and villages were built.

It is alleged—but the story wants proof—that Kumāra Krishṇappa invaded Ceylon and defeated the Kaṇḍian troops; that in a second battle which took place, the king of Kaṇḍi in person led his troops, but was killed and his army defeated; and that Kumāra Krishṇappa then seized Kaṇḍi, and established his own brother-in-law as governor there. He died 1573.

3. Krishṇappa (or Periya Vīrappa) and Viśvanātha II.—Joint rulers (1573—1595). These were sons of Kumāra Krishṇappa. They were enthroned by Āryanātha, and were entirely under his control. A rebellion by a chief styled the "Mahāvilivāna Rāja," probably a Pāṇḍiyan, was quelled. The brothers governed jointly. They strengthened Trichinopoly and Chidambaram. Probably Viśvanātha II died first, for on Krishṇappa's death in 1595 the latter's two sons succeeded.

4. Liṅgayya (or Kumāra Krishṇappa II) and Viśvappa (or Viśvanātha III).—Joint rulers (1595—1602). During the reign of these brothers the country flourished. Āryanātha died 1600. Viśvanātha probably died before his brother. Liṅgayya died 1602.

His uncle, Kastūri Raṅgayya, seized the government, but was murdered after a week, and Liṅgayya's son, Muttu Krishṇappa, obtained the throne.

5. Muttu Krishṇappa (1602—1609).—He re-established the ancient Maṛava dynasty of the Setupati chiefs of Rāmnād (*see below*, p. 227). Christianity spread largely in the country, taught by the great Jesuit Missionaries headed by Robert de Nobilibus, who arrived at Madura in 1606, and proclaimed himself to be a celebrated *Sanyāsi* from Rome. Muttu Krishṇappa died in 1609, leaving three sons, Muttu Vīrappa, Tirumala, and Kumāra Muttu.[1]

6. Muttu Vīrappa (1609—1623).—In his reign there was a small war with Tanjore, and some slight unimportant incursions of predatory bands from Maisūr. The spread of Christianity was checked. He resided at Trichinopoly.

7. Tirumala Nāyakka (1623—1659).—This is the great Tirumala, otherwise called "Mahārāja-Mānya-Rāja-Śrī Tirumala Śēvari Nāyaṇi Āyyalu Gāru." He left Trichinopoly for Madura and took up his permanent residence there. The great temples and palaces at Madura were built. He determined to shake off the Vijayanagar yoke and become independent. An invasion by armies from Maisūr was stopped at Dindigul by the Daḷavāy Rāmappayya, who pursued the enemy into Maisūr and

---

[1] Muḥammad Sharīf Hanafī, who wrote his *Majālisu-s Salāṭīn* in A.D. 1628 (Sir H. Elliot's *History of India*, VII, 139), states that when, on one occasion, he visited Madura, the ruler of that place died after a few days, and all his wives (seven hundred in number) destroyed themselves on his funeral pyre. This was probably Muttu Krishṇappa. He further states that in his day there was "not a single Musalmān" in the Madura country. The statement, however, sounds almost incredible.

stormed one of their principal fortresses. Robert De Nobilibus reappeared at Madura in 1623. Then ensued a war in the Rāmnād country with the Setupati, in which Tirumala was not very successful. In spite of his desires for independence Tirumala had always acknowledged the supremacy of the Rāyas of Vijayanagar, and used to send presents to his suzerain. But in 1657 his want of loyalty seems to have become known, for on the death of the then Rāya, his son declared war against Tirumala. Tirumala was joined by the Nāyakkas of Tanjore and Giñji. The Rāya marched on Giñji, but the Musalmāns, at Tirumala's suggestion, invaded the territories of Vijayanagar, and in the war which ensued greatly extended their conquests. They then turned against the Rāya's southern tributaries, and Tirumala had to flee to Madura. The Muḥammadans invaded him there and the capital was surrendered without a blow. Tirumala then made an alliance with the Muḥammadans of Golkoṇḍa, who ravaged Maisūr and the remaining territories of Vijayanagar. In revenge for his treacherous conduct the Uḍaiyār of Maisūr attacked Tirumala and a vindictive war followed, closing, after varied fortunes, with a victory on the side of Madura in 1659. Tirumala died the same year.

There is a strong probability that he was foully murdered by the Brahmans. Mr. Nelson narrates the various legends of his death (pp. 139, 142).

Tirumala was supposed to have had a strong leaning to Christianity.

Kumāra Muttu, the rightful heir, was some how induced to waive his claims, and the illegitimate son of Tirumala, Muttu Aṛakādri, succeeded.

8. MUTTU AṚAKĀDRI OR MUTTU VĪRAPPA (1659—1660).—He determined to rid the country of the Muḥammadans, and accordingly fortified Trichinopoly very strongly. The Muḥammadans seized Tanjore and other places, and eventually besieged Trichinopoly. But their attack failed and they retired. The Nāyakka died in 1660 and was succeeded by his son,——

9. CHOKKANĀTHA, *alias* CHOKKALIṄGA, *alias* CHOKKAPPA (1660—1677, 1678—1682).—He was sixteen years old when he came to the throne, and unfortunately fell into the hands of unscrupulous ministers who tried to dethrone him, but the young prince outwitted them, himself seized the government, and put himself at the head of his army. The traitors fled to Tanjore. He besieged them there and defeated them. The Tanjore Nāyakka submitted. In 1663-64 another Muḥammadan invasion occurred, signalized by an unsuccessful attack on Trichinopoly and by fearful massacres of innocent villagers. Chokkanātha then marched against the Tanjore Nāyakka Vijaya Rāghava, in revenge for his having assisted the Muḥammadans, and the latter was defeated and reduced to submission. Not long after this Chokkanātha made an unsuccessful attack on his vassal, the Setupati, who had rebelled. In 1674 Tanjore was again invaded, reduced, and Rāja Vijaya Rāghava slain with almost all his family. The romantic story of his gallant death will be found in Mr. Nelson's work, pp. 191, 193. Alagiri Nāyakka was made Governor of Tanjore. In 1675 Chokkanātha married Maṅgammāḷ, who afterwards became famous in history and gave himself up to private enjoyments, living at Trichinopoly and neglecting the government which was carried on by his brother Muttu Aṛakādri. The ministers soon began to intrigue with Aṛakādri at Madura and they at last induced the latter to declare his independence. At the same time, the Muḥammadans in alliance with Ēkōjī (the Mahratta, half brother of the great Śivājī) and with a refugee Tanjore prince, descended on Tanjore and seized it. They then seized almost all the Madura territory, Chokkanātha being quite given up to lethargy. This was in 1676 (?)[1] At last he roused himself and prepared to attack the Muḥammadans in Tanjore. The King of Maisūr also made preparations for an attack on Madura, and Śivājī made a terrible raid to the south, but was stopped by floods in the Coleroon and compelled to return. During his absence the Muḥammadans of Tanjore attacked Śivājī's general, who was left in charge of Giñji and the country around, but were defeated. Chokkanātha then advanced to Tanjore, but either from terror or sheer lethargy remained inactive. Śivājī's armies safely returned to garrison the city and Chokkanātha returned to Trichinopoly. Śivājī fortified Giñji, and settled in Vellore. In 1677 the Rāja of Maisūr invaded Madura, and the ministers dethroned and imprisoned Chokkanātha. They set up in his place his brother—

10. MUTTU LIṄGAPPA (1677).—This prince, however, only reigned a few months when he was deposed and Chokkanātha restored. Chokkanātha remained very subservient to Muḥammadan influence. In 1680 the armies of Maisūr invested Trichinopoly, and other of the Nāyakka's enemies pressed in to attack him, so that at one period no less than four armies surrounded Trichinopoly—(1) Maisūr, (2) the Maṛavas of Rāmnād, (3) the Mahrattas, and (4) the Tanjore Muḥammadans. The Maṛavas and the Muḥammadans remained inactive. The Mahrattas attacked and utterly defeated the troops of Maisūr under the walls of the city, and, flushed with victory, seized the whole country round. In a few days Chokkanātha, bereft of all his possessions except Trichinopoly, died broken hearted. He was succeeded by his son —

[1] Dr. Burnell considers the date doubtful. (*South-Indian Palæography*, p. 56, note 4.)

11. Raṅga Krishṇa Muttu Vīrappa (1682—1689).—The whole country was now in a state of anarchy. Ēkōjī, now chief of Tanjore, seized and sequestered all the temple property and lands. Śivājī was succeeded in Giñji by his son Śambujī, a tyrant. The territories of Madura were split up into fragments and actually shared by five powers—(1) The Nāyakka, (2) Maisūr, (3) The Rāmnād Setupati, (4) Śambujī of Giñji, (5) Ēkōjī of Tanjore. Slowly things got better and the Nāyakka of Madura got more and more free from Maisūr, while he recovered possession of the capital and recovered the lands seized by the Setupati. The other powers were distracted by local dissensions and rebellions. The Nāyakka governed well and energetically. In 1686 the Setupati rebelled against Madura, and his troops, aided by Tanjore, were successful; but the war was not pursued. Shortly afterwards the Nāyakka died of small-pox. His widow, Muttammāḷ, gave birth to a posthumous son, and then killed herself.

Regency of Maṅgammāḷ, Chokkanātha's widow (1688—1704).—Maṅgammāḷ was charitable but unscrupulous. She protected all religions, Christian as well as Hindu. In 1693 the Setupati of Rāmnād tortured and put to death the Jesuit Priest DeBritto. In 1698 Maṅgammāl's army, going to collect tribute from Travancore, was defeated there. It is said that she therefore declared war against Travancore and was victorious, but the statement requires corroboration. The Dutch of Tuticorin, in 1700, acquired the monopoly of the pearl fisheries from the Nāyakka. Desultory war with Tanjore (1700). Bouchet, the priest, was very well received at court. Some Tanjore cavalry being very troublesome, the Madura Daḷavāy Narasappayya defeated them when they were in disorder, and ravaged the territory of Tanjore completely. The Tanjore minister, however, bought off the Madura troops. In 1701 Madura and Tanjore combined against Maisūr, but war was averted. The Daḷavāy Narasappayya was defeated and killed in a battle against the Setupati in 1702. The young Nāyakka prince now came of age (1704 or 1705), and a party being formed against Maṅgammāḷ, she was starved to death.[1]

12. Vijaya Raṅga Chokkanātha (1704—1731).—There was a terrible famine and a fearful flood in 1709, and another famine in 1710. It continued for ten years, only ceasing in 1720. In that year the Pudukōṭṭai Toṇḍamān revolted against his liege lord the Setupati of Rāmnād, who, on the march against his rebellious vassal, died, and a struggle ensued for the Rāmnād musnud. It ended in one of the claimants being killed and the other enthroned (see below, p. 230). He reigned till 1729, and was then defeated, carried to Tanjore, and imprisoned. The territory of Rāmnād was divided, Tanjore taking part and part being given to one of the successful rivals of the late Setupati. This was the Śivagaṅga territory. The remainder was left under his other rival, who became Setupati. The Nāyakka died in 1731 without issue.

Mīnākshī (1731-1736).—Vijaya Raṅga Chokkanātha's widow, Mīnākshī, adopted the son of Vaṅgāru Tirumala, who, however, laid claim to the throne as of right. His faction made an attempt to kill the Rāṇī at Trichinopoly, but were defeated. In 1734 the Muḥammadans under Ṣafdar 'Alī Khān ravaged the country, as well as Tanjore, Travancore, and the Western Coast. Vaṅgāru Tirumala induced Ṣafdar 'Alī to make a fictitious award declaring him king. This was done and Chandā Ṣāḥib was left to enforce it. The Rāṇī was frightened and bought over Chandā Ṣāḥib for an enormous sum to her side, and Vaṅgāru Tirumala retired to Madura. Chandā Ṣāḥib also retired, but returned in 1736, and the Rāṇī placed herself entirely in his hands. He sent troops against Vaṅgāru Tirumala at Dindigul and Madura. They were victorious and entered Madura, Vaṅgāru Tirumala fleeing to Śivagaṅga. Madura now being in the hands of Chandā Ṣāḥib, he seized the sovereignty, and Mīnākshī killed herself in despair.

This event put an end for ever to the Hindu Government of Madura.

Chandā Ṣāḥib remained in possession, and Vaṅgāru Tirumala, too weak to do anything himself, called in the Satāra Mahrattas to his aid. In 1739, therefore, Rāghujī Bhonslē marched with an immense force to Madura. The Muḥammadans were defeated with great slaughter and Dost 'Alī, father of Ṣafdar 'Alī, was killed. The Mahrattas then besieged Trichinopoly, stormed it, and took Chandā Ṣāḥib prisoner to Satāra (1741). The kingdom of Madura was thus left in a state of anarchy.

Concluding Scenes.

Morāri Rāu was left in charge of Trichinopoly by the Mahrattas (1741), while another Mahratta chief administered the State of Madura. In 1743 the whole was yielded up to the Niẓām on his invasion. The Niẓām extended his protection to Vaṅgāru Tirumala, but the latter was shortly afterwards poisoned. His son returned to Madura, but never attempted to regain the throne. In 1748 Muḥammad 'Alī seized

---

[1] Mr. Walhouse gives us a legend connected with the reign of Maṅgammāḷ in *Ind. Ant.* X, 366.

Trichinopoly and proclaimed himself Navāb of Arcot. Chandā Ṣāḥib made war on him with the help of the French, Muḥammad 'Alī making an alliance with the English. Chandā Ṣāḥib was victorious (1751). Muhammad 'Alī attempted to gain possession of Madura, and the English tried to storm the place, but were unsuccessful. The Madura chief, however, sold the city to Maisūr, and the English under Captain Cope returned and took possession. They were driven out by troops from Rāmnād, and the Setupati placed on the throne of Madura the young adopted son of Rāṇi Mīnākshī (1753). There was complete confusion for two years. In 1755 Muḥammad 'Alī sent another expedition against Madura, with the help of some English troops. The city was given up on their arrival, and garrisoned with Europeans, a Muḥammadan being installed as Governor. Much confusion followed, ending in 1758 in the English obtaining permanent possession of Madura. A desultory war with refractory Poḷegars and Kaḷḷans ensued. In 1760 Ḥaidar 'Alī made an attempt on Madura and Tinnevelly, but it was unsuccessful. Muḥammad Yūsuf, the Governor of Madura, exacted tribute from the Poḷegars and from Travancore, and overran Rāmnād and Śivagaṅga. But as he kept all the tribute for himself and paid nothing to the English or to Muḥammad 'Alī, his chief, he was seized and hanged for treason (1763). Another Muḥammadan was placed in charge, with English officers to watch and help him. This went on till 1772. Then ensued the invasion of the Carnatic by Ḥaidar (1780) and the revolt of the Poḷegars. In 1783 Colonel Fullarton marched down, quieted the whole country, and finally subjugated it. It was thereafter administered solely by the English. Mr. McLeod was appointed "Collector of Madura" in 1790, and ever since then the country has remained an English possession.

NIZĀM SHĀHI DYNASTY OF AḤMADNAGAR.

(*See* Dakhaṇ, Muḥammadan Kings of the —.)

NIZĀMS OF HAIDARĀBĀD.

(*See* Haidarābād.)

ORAṄGAL, SOVEREIGNS OF—.

(*See* Gaṇapatis of Oraṅgal.)

ORISSA, KINGS OF—.

The following list is taken *in extenso* from Dr. W. W. Hunter's "Orissa," Appendix vii. The dates must not be relied on, those for the earlier portion at least being purely fabulous, and the whole professedly depending on native chronicles, about the most unsound basis imaginable. I give the list simply as it stands, and because I happen to know of no other. Dr. Hunter himself states that the chronicle, being taken from Hindu sources, does not truly represent the facts of Orissan history after the Musalmān conquest in 1568. The chronicle is based on the palm-leaf records of the Jagannātha temple (Dr. Hunter's "*Orissa,*" Vol. I, p. 199) as digested in the *Purushottama Chandrikā* by Bābu Bhabānīcharan Bandopādhyāya, collated with Mr. Stirling's Essay in the *Asiatic Researches*, Vol. XV (Ed. 1825), and his posthumous paper in the *Bengal Asiatic Society's Journal*, Vol. VI, Part II, 1837. I have not attempted to correct the spelling.

B.C.

"3101—3089. Yudhishthir, a monarch of the *Mahābhārata*, of the lunar race of Delhi. Reigned 12 years. [According to Stirling (*Asiatic Researches*, Vol. XV), 3095—3083 B.C.]

"3089—2358. Parikshit, a monarch of the *Mahābhārata*, of the lunar race of Delhi. Reigned 731 years. (According to Stirling, 3083—2326 B.C.)

"2358—1807. Janmejaya, a monarch of the *Mahābhārata*, and the patron of that work; sprung from the lunar race of Delhi. Reigned 551 years. (According to Stirling, 2326 —1810 B.C.)

B.C.

" 1807—1407. SANKAR DEVA. Reigned 400 years. (According to Stirling, 1810—1400 B.C.)

" 1407—1037. GAUTAM DEVA. Extended the Kingdom of Orissa to the Godāvarī river. Reigned 370 years. (According to Stirling, 1400—1027 B.C.)

" 1037— 822. MAHENDRA DEVA. Founded the town of Rājmahendri (Rajahmundry) as his capital. Reigned 215 years. (According to Stirling, 1027—812 B.C.)

" 822— 688. ISHTA DEVA. Reigned 134 years. (According to Stirling, 812—678 B.C.)

" 688— 538. SEVAK DEVA. Reigned 150 years. (According to Stirling, 678—528 B.C.)

" 538— 421. BAJRA DEVA. In this reign Orissa was invaded by Yavanas from Mārwār, from Delhi, and from Babul Des—the last supposed to be Iran (Persia) and Cabul. According to the palm-leaf chronicle the invaders were repulsed. Reigned 117 years. (According to Stirling, 528—421 B.C.)

" 421— 306. NARSINGH DEVA. Reigned 115 years. Another chief from the far north invaded the country during this reign, but he was defeated, and the Orissa prince reduced a great part of the Delhi Kingdom. The monarch excavated the tank at Dāntan near Jaleswar, which exists at this day. (According to Stirling, this prince was called Sarasankha, and reigned 421—306 B.C.)

" 306— 184. MANKRISHNA DEVA. Reigned 122 years. Yavanas from Kashmīr invaded the country, but were driven back after many battles. (According to Stirling, this king was called Hansa, and reigned 306—184 B.C.)

" 184— 57. BHOJ DEVA; a great prince, who drove back a Yavana invasion, and is said to have subdued all India. Reigned 127 years. (Stirling's date here coincides with that of the palm-leaf record. . . . .)

" B.C. 57 to A.D. 78. Two reigns, that of VIKRAMADITYA and his brother SAKADITYA. Neither the Purūshottama Chandrikā nor Stirling give separate dates for these reigns, but the two extended over 135 years. Vikramaditya made himself master of all India, but was slain by a rebel conqueror from Southern India, named Sālivāhan, identified as his brother Sakāditya, who succeeded him. The current or Sakābda era dates from the end of this reign, 77-78 A.D. During the above fourteen reigns 3179 (or, according to Stirling, 3173) years of the Kali Yug elapsed.

A.D.

" 78— 143. KARMARJIT DEVA; reigned 65 years.

" 143— 194. HATKESWAR DEVA; reigned 51 years.

" 194— 237. BIR BHUVAN DEVA; reigned 43 years. (According to Stirling, the name of this prince was Tribhuvan.)

" 237— 282. NIRMAL DEVA; reigned 45 years.

" 282— 319. BHIM DEVA; reigned 37 years.

" 319— 323. SOBHAN DEVA. During this reign of 4 years, the maritime invasion and conquest of Orissa by the Yavanas under Red-Arm (Rakta Bāhu) took place. The king fled with the sacred image of Jagannāth, and with those of his brother and sister, Balbhadra and Subhadrā, and buried them in a cave at Sonpur. . . . . The lawful prince perished in the jungle, and the Yavanas ruled in his stead. (According to Stirling, the reign commenced 318 A.D.)

" 323— 328. CHANDRA DEVA, who, however, was only a nominal king, as the Yavanas were completely masters of the country. They put him to death in A.D. 328. (Stirling calls this prince Indra Deva.)

" 328— 474. Yavana occupation of Orissa, 146 years. (According to Stirling, these Yavanas were Buddhists.) . . .

" 474— 526. YAYATI KESARI, who expelled the Yavanas and founded the Kesari or Lion dynasty. Reigned 52 years. This prince brought back the image of Jagannāth to Purī, and commenced the temple-city to Śiva at Bhuvaneswar. His capital was at Jājpur. (According to Stirling, he reigned from 473 to 520 A.D.)

" 526— 583. SŪRJYA KESARI; reigned 57 years.

" 583— 623. ANANTA KESARI; reigned 40 years. (According to Stirling, this and the previous reign extended from 520 to 617 A.D.)

A.D.

"623— 677. Alabu Kesari, who completed the temple of Bhuvaneswar, reigned 54 years. (According to Stirling, he was called Lalāt Indra Kesari, and began to reign 617 A.D.)

With the exception of five kings, Stirling does not give the names of the other monarchs of the Kesari dynasty from Lalāt Indra Kesari to the extinction of the line. He merely says that thirty-two uninteresting reigns followed, extending over a period of 455 years. The Palm-Leaf Records, however, give the names of forty princes. Only three of the five kings referred to by Stirling can be identified in the list.

"677— 693. Kanak Kesari; reigned 16 years.
"693— 701. Bir Kesari; reigned 8 years.
"701— 706. Padma Kesari; reigned 5 years.
"706— 715. Briddha Kesari; reigned 9 years.
"715— 726. Bata Kesari; reigned 11 years.
"726— 738. Gaja Kesari; reigned 12 years.
"738— 740. Basanta Kesari; reigned 2 years.
"740— 754. Gandharva Kesari; reigned 14 years.
"754— 763. Janmejaya Kesari; reigned 9 years.
"763— 778. Bharat Kesari; reigned 15 years.
"778— 792. Kali Kesari; reigned 14 years.
"792— 811. Kamal Kesari; reigned 19 years.
"811— 829. Kundal Kesari; reigned 18 years; built the temple of Mārkandeswar in Purī.
"829— 846. Chandra Kesari; reigned 17 years.
"846— 865. Bir Chandra Kesari; reigned 19 years.
"865— 875. Amrita Kesari; reigned 10 years.
"875— 890. Vijaya Kesari; reigned 15 years.
"890— 904. Chandrapal Kesari; reigned 14 years.
"904— 920. Madhusudan Kesari; reigned 16 years.
"920— 930. Dharma Kesari; reigned 10 years.
"930— 941. Jana Kesari; reigned 11 years.
"941— 953. Nripa Kesari. A warlike and ambitious prince, who founded the city of Cattack. Reigned 12 years. (Stirling dates the foundation of Cattack by this prince in 989 A.D.)
"953— 961. Makar Kesari constructed a long and massive stone revetment to protect the city of Cattack from inundation. Reigned 8 years. (Stirling calls this prince Markat Kesari, and places the construction of this work in 1006 A.D.)
"961— 971. Tripura Kesari; reigned 10 years.
"971— 989. Madhav Kesari; (according to Stirling) built the fortress of Sārangarh on the south bank of the Kātjurī river, opposite the city of Cattack; reigned 18 years.
"989— 999. Gobinda Kesari; reigned 10 years.
"999—1013. Nritya Kesari; reigned 14 years.
"1013—1024. Narsinh Kesari; reigned 11 years.
"1024—1034. Kurma Kesari; reigned 10 years.
"1034—1050. Matsya Kesari; built the great bridge across the Athāranālā, at the entrance to Purī, existing to this day; reigned 16 years.
"1050—1065. Baraha Kesari; reigned 15 years.
"1065—1078. Baman Kesari; reigned 13 years.
"1078—1080. Parasu Kesari; reigned 2 years.
"1080—1092. Chandra Kesari; reigned 12 years.
"1092—1099. Sujan Kesari; reigned 7 years.
"1099—1104. Salini Kesari; reigned 5 years. His queen built the Nāt Mandir or Dancing Hall of the temple of Bhuvaneswar.
"1104—1107. Puranjan Kesari; reigned 3 years.
"1107—1119. Vishnu Kesari; reigned 12 years.
"1119—1123. Indra Kesari; reigned 4 years.

A.D.

" 1123—1132. **Suvarna Kesari**; reigned 9 years. The Kesari dynasty ended with this prince, who died childless, and was succeeded by Chorgangā, a king from the south. . . . .Another Palm-Leaf Record, containing a list of the kings of Orissa, and kept by a Brāhman family of Purī, gives a different account of the extinction of the line. It states that Bāsudeva Bāhampati, a powerful officer of the Orissa Court, having been driven from the royal presence, went to the Carnatic, and instigated Chorgangā of that country to invade Orissa, which he did, conquering Cattack, and establishing a new dynasty. (According to Stirling, thirty-six princes of the Kesari line ruled over Orissa, 473—1131 A.D., of whom, however, he only gives the names of nine. One of these, Barujyā Kesari, is said to have quadrupled the land-tax, and another, Surajya Kesari, to have reduced it to the old rate.)

" 1132—1152. **Chorganga**,[1] the founder of the Gangāvansa dynasty; reigned 20 years. His memory is preserved by the name of a quarter in Purī city, called the Churang Sāi, and also by a tank in that town bearing the same name. (Stirling places this reign 1131—1151 A.D.)

" 1152—1166. **Gangeswar**.—His territories are said to have extended from the Ganges to the Godāvarī, and to have included five royal cities, Jājpur, Chaudwār, Amarāvatī, Chatnā, and Birānasī, or Cattack. As a penance for a crime, he excavated a splendid tank called Kausalyā Gangā, between Pippli and Khurdhā. (According to Stirling, he ascended the throne 1151 A.D.)

" 1166—1171. **Ekjatakam Deva**; reigned 5 years.

" 1171—1175. **Madan Mahadeva**; reigned 4 years.

" 1175—1202. **Anang Bhim Deo**, one of the greatest of the Orissa kings. He made a survey of his whole kingdom, measuring it with reeds; and built the present temple of Jagannāth. Reigned 27 years. (According to Stirling, he ascended the throne in 1174 A.D.)

" 1202—1237. **Rajrajeswar Deva**; reigned 35 years. (Stirling places his death in 1236 A.D.)

" 1237—1282. **Languliya Narsinh**; reigned 45 years; built the great Sun Temple at Kanārak on the sea. (The Black Pagoda.)

" 1282—1307. **Kesari Narsinh**; reigned 25 years. This prince filled up the bed of the river Balāgandi, which ran between the temple and the country-house of Jagannāth, and which obstructed the cars that carried the idols at the great festival. Previously a double set of cars had been required for the conveyance of the images. (According to Stirling, this prince was called Kabir Narsingh, and erected the bridge across the Athāranālā at the entrance to Purī; the bridge which the Temple Records ascribe to Matsya Kesari, who reigned 1034—1050.)

" 1307—1327. **Pratab Narsinh**; reigned 20 years.

" 1327—1329. **Gatikanta Narsinh**; reigned 2 years.

" 1329—1330. **Kapil Narsinh**; reigned 1 year.

" 1330—1337. **Sankha Bhasur**; reigned 7 years.

" 1337—1361. **Sankha Basudeva**; reigned 24 years.

" 1361—1382. **Bali Basudeva**; reigned 22 years.

" 1382—1401. **Bir Basudeva**; reigned 19 years.

" 1401—1414. **Kali Basudeva**; reigned 13 years.

" 1414—1429. **Nengatanta Basudeva**; reigned 15 years.

" 1429—1452. **Netra Basudeva**; reigned 23 years.

" 1452—1479. **Kapilendra Deva**, originally a common herd-boy, tending the flocks of his Brāhman master, but afterwards raised to the throne. Reigned 27 years.

---

[1] Who was this Chōrgaṅga? Granting that the dates of this Orissan chronology are not quite certain, a certain liberty may be allowed us in selecting. Nothing can be considered reliable as yet, but we know of a traditionary son of Kulottuṅga I of the Choḷa dynasty, by name Śāraṅgadhara, while Chōrgaṅga of Orissa appears to be known also as *Śāraṅga*, or Chūraṅga. Kulottuṅga I died in A.D. 1113. Two copper-plate inscriptions from the Kaliṅga country (Nos. 213 and 219 of the *List of Copper-plates* given above, pp. 31, 33) mention grants made by "Anantavarmā Choḷa Gaṅgadeva," or "Choḍagaṅga *alias* Anantavarmadeva," whose *abhisheka* took place in A.D. 1077, and who was alive in A.D. 1119. Whoever he was, this Orissan Chōrgaṅga certainly came from the south. Mr. Rice thinks that Chōrgaṅga was one of the Koṅgu line, but I think this is doubtful, or at any rate that as yet there is no proof.

A.D.

" 1479—1504. PURUSHOTTAMA DEVA.[1]—The king of Conjevaram refused to marry his daughter to this prince, on the ground of the Orissa Dynasty holding the office of Sweeper to Jagannāth. Purushōttama accordingly invaded the southern country, defeated the Conjevaram king, and carried off his daughter, whom he swore should be married to a sweeper, in revenge for her father's refusal. The minister to whom he entrusted the execution of his order, brought forth the princess at the next great festival of Jagannāth, as the king himself was publicly performing his lowly office before the god, and presented her in marriage to his master.

" 1504—1532. PRATAB RUDRA DEVA; reigned 28 years. A learned man, deeply versed in the Sāstras. His reign was disturbed by theological discussions as to the merits of the Buddhistic and Brāhmanical religions.[2] Stories are told of how sometimes one, sometimes the other, of these religions obtained supremacy over the mind of the prince, and how the followers of each were persecuted by turns. The great Vishnuvite reformer Chaitanya visited Purī during this reign, and finally converted the king to the Vaidik faith. The temple of Barāha at Jājpur was constructed by this king; and the annalists state that he extended his conquests as far as Cape Comorin, capturing the city of Vizianagaram *en route*. The Afghāns, however, made incursions into Orissa and plundered Purī, the idols being removed and secreted beforehand. (According to Stirling he reigned 1503—1524 A.D.)

" 1532—1533. KALUYA DEVA, son of the last-mentioned king. Reigned one year, when he was murdered by Gobind Bidyādhar, the Prime Minister. (According to Stirling 1524—1529.)

" 1533—1534. KATHARUYA DEVA, THE LAST OF THE GAṄGAVAMSA LINE, brother of the previous king, like him assassinated by Gobind Bidyādhar, who now ascended the throne, after murdering all of the royal blood.

" 1534—1541. GOBIND BIDYADHAR; reigned 7 years. Disputes with the Muhammadans as to the possession of Rājmahendri. (According to Stirling he began to reign 1533 A.D.)

" 1541—1549. CHAKRA PRATAB; reigned 8 years.

" 1549—1550. NARSINH JANA; reigned 1 year.

" 1550—1551. RAGHU RAM CHHOTRA; reigned 1 year.

" 1551—1559. MUKUND DEVA, or Telingā Mukund Deva; reigned 8 years. The last of the independent kings of Orissa, and a man of great courage and ability. He constructed a large landing-place (ghāt) on the Hughli at Tribenī, near the town of Huglī. During his reign Kālāpahār, the general of the Muhammadan king of Bengal, invaded the province with a large force. The Orissa king was defeated and slain in a battle outside the walls of the capital, Jājpur, and the monarchy overthrown, A.D. 1559. (According to Stirling, 1555 A.D.) Kālā Pahār plundered the holy city of Purī. . . .

" 1559—1578, or 1568—1578. An anarchy of 19 years, after which Rām Chandra Deva, the son of the prime minister of the previous reign, was elected to the throne. During the anarchy the Afghān Governor of Orissa, Dāūd Khān, invaded Bengal, but was defeated by the Mughuls under Munim Khān, and the province was annexed to the Mughul Empire. (According to Stirling the anarchy lasted 1558—1579 A.D.)

" 1578—1607. RAM CHANDRA DEVA, the first prince of the present family of Khurdha, reigned 29 years. Rājā Todar Mall, Akbar's general and afterwards prime minister, was deputed to restore order in Orissa. He confirmed the native prince on the throne, but towards the end of this reign the province was disturbed by a rival claimant, who appealed to the Emperor Akbār. Rājā Mān Sinh, another Hindu general of the Mughul Empire, was sent to adjust the quarrel, which he managed amicably by bestowing on the claimant the fort of Al and its dependencies. (According to Stirling the reign lasted 1580—1609 A.D.)

" 1607—1628. PURUSHOTTAMA DEVA; reigned 21 years; was slain in battle. From this period the Orissa kings were merely Rājās of Khurdhā. . . .

[1] Mr. Beames makes the date of Purushottama's accession A.D. 1478 (*Ind. Ant. I*, 355).
[2] All this is most fanciful and reads like a *mélange* of legends relating to sovereigns altogether different.

A.D.

"1628—1653. Narsinh Deva; reigned 25 years. Invasion of Orissa by a Muhammadan general from the south, named Shāhbāz. The king finding himself unable to resist the invaders, was compelled to purchase peace by the payment of a large sum of money. This prince brought the images of the sun and moon from the temple of Kanārak to Purī. (According to Stirling he reigned 1630—1655 A.D.)

"1653—1654. Gangadhar Deva; reigned 1 year. (According to Stirling, 1655—1656 A.D.)

"1654—1662. Balabhadra Deva; reigned 8 years. (According to Stirling, 1656—1664 A.D.)

"1662—1690. Mukund Deva; reigned 28 years. (According to Stirling, 1664—1692 A.D.)

"1690—1713. Drabya Sinh Deva; reigned 23 years. (According to Stirling, 1692—1715 A.D.)

"1713—1718. Krishna Deva; reigned 5 years. (According to Stirling, 1715—1720 A.D.)

"1718—1725. Gopinath Deva; reigned 7 years. (According to Stirling, 1720—1727 A.D.)

"1725—1736. Ram Chandra Deva; reigned 11 years. (According to Stirling, 1727—1743 A.D.)

"1736—1773. Bir Kisor Deva; reigned 37 years. Habib Khān, a Muhammadan officer of the Marhattā army, invaded and wrested the province from this king, but afterwards restored it. In 1753 the Marhattās finally took possession of the province. (Stirling places this reign 1743—1786 A.D.)

"1773—1791. Drabya Sinh Deva; reigned 18 years. (According to Stirling 1786—1798 A.D.)

"1791—1810. Mukund Deva; ruled 19 years. Occupation of Orissa by the British and expulsion of the Marhattās in 1803. In the following year this prince headed a rising of the Khurdhā people, but was defeated and taken prisoner. After being kept in confinement for some time in Cattack and Midnapur he was allowed to retire to Purī.

"1810—1857. Ram Chandra Deva; ruled 47 years.

"1857—1871. Dibya Sinh Deva, the present Rājā of Khurdhā. He is the fifteenth of the line of princes who succeeded in 1575 to the Orissa Kingdom as a fief of the Mughul Empire, after the anarchy which followed the extinction of the Gangavansa dynasty....—W.W.H."

OWK, OR AVUKU,[1] ZEMINDARS OF—.

This table is taken entirely from information supplied to me from private sources. It may or may not be accurate. The family were locally powerful at one period. I insert the pedigree because information regarding any old family is of value when our sources of knowledge are so scanty. The dates are probably more or less accurate, as they tally with those of known historical events. All the Zemindars called themselves Rājas.

1. Bukka,
(A.D. 1473–1481),
obtained the Zemindari from the Rāya of Vijayanagar.

|

2. (?)
(A.D. 1481–1508).

|

3. Timma,
(A.D. 1508–1536).

|

- 4. Nalla Timma, (A.D. 1536–1555). *Gave many gifts to Brahmans.*
  - 5. Raghunātha, (A.D. 1555–1558).
- Yerra Timma.
- Tirunnātha. ⋮ (*See the succession after the 18th Zemindar.*)
- Appala.
- Ōjalapati.

---

[1] *See* Vol. I, p. 100.

6. **Pedda Krishnama,**
(A.D. 1558–1588).
In this Zemindar's life the Râyas of Vijayanagar were overthrown by the Muhammadans, who reduced the size of this Zemindari (1564).

7. **Chinna Krishnama,**
(A.D. 1588–1618).

8. **Ōjalapati,**
(A.D. 1618–1646).

9. **Narasiṁha,**
(A.D. 1646–1668).

10. **Râghava,**
(A.D. 1668–1691).

11. **Pedda Kumâra Râghava,**
(A.D. 1691–1735),
(*Died without issue*).

Dâsama.

12. **Appa Narasiṁha,**
(A.D. 1735–1737).
His widow,
13. **Chellamma,**
held the Zemindari till 1739.

Appa Narasiṁha was succeeded by Narasiṁha, who is described by my informant as great-grandson of Ōjalapati, youngest brother of the fourth Zemindar, Nalla Timma; but this seems impossible on account of the dates. The pedigree is therefore given with the next Zemindar's ancestors printed in italics, as doubtful.

Ōjalapati.

(?)

Narasiṁha.

16. **Ōjalapati,**
(A.D. 1751–1759).

15. **Kichama,**
(A.D. 1743–1751).

Râghava.

Veṅkaṭa Kumâra Râghava.

18. **Veṅkaṭa Narasiṁha,**
(A.D. 1767–1771).

14. **Narasiṁha,**
(A.D. 1739–1743).

17. **Kumâra Râghava,**
(A.D. 1759—1767).

(13) Chellamma, widow of (12) Appa Narasiṁha, being still alive, and the direct line being extinct with (18) Veṅkaṭa Narasiṁha, she was called on to select a successor. She selected Nârâyaṇa of Nandyâla, a descendant of Tirunnâtha, brother of the fourth Zemindar.

19. **Nârâyana,**
(A.D. 1771–1785),
was deposed by Basâlat Jang of Haidarâbâd and removed to Cuddapah. Died at Seringapatam.

20. **Krishṇa,**
(A.D. 1785–1805).
With him the zemindari ceased to exist.

PALLAVAS, THE—.

The Pallavas were at one time the possessors of an extensive kingdom lying mostly along the East Coast of the peninsula, but at one period extending apparently over the whole or almost the whole of the

Dakhaṇ. Their southern boundary was the Choḷa country, and their territory extended far north, at one period at least as far as the Godāvarī river. Their capital was Kañchī or Conjeeveram. As usual with the other kingdoms of ancient India, their possessions greatly varied at different periods. It is abundantly clear that at one time they were very powerful, while we know from the account given by Hiwen-Thsang that, at the beginning of the seventh century, the kingdom then known as *Drāviḍa* was a very small one.

The device of the ruling house was a tiger.[1]

What little is known as yet regarding the Pallavas will be found detailed in Dr. Burnell's *South-Indian Palæography*, pp. 36—39, Mr. Fleet's *Dynasties of the Kanarese Districts*, pp. 14—16, and Mr. Foulkes' Historical Paper in the *Salem District Manual*, pp. 1—11 and App. 349-365. (See also Mr. Foulkes' papers in *Ind. Ant.* VII, 1; and VIII, 1.)

Very few kings can be mentioned by name, and their dates are only to be approximately gathered from the characters used in their inscriptions.

In one inscription which was found near Guṇṭūr, and is "probably the earliest Pallava grant that has as yet come to light," (about the fourth century A.D.—*Burnell*) two kings are mentioned, father and son;—

Vijaya Skandavarmā.
|
Vijaya Buddhavarmā.

The grant is made by the queen-consort of the latter, in the former's reign. The grantor is a Pallava of the *Bhāradvāja gotra*, and is therefore no relation of the Vijayanandivarmā mentioned in the grant published by Dr. Burnell (*South-Ind. Palæography*, p. 135 and plate xxiv) and by Mr. Fleet in *Ind. Ant.* V, 175, who was of the *Śālaṅkāyana gotra*. Yet this latter grant came from the Kōlēr lake, just north of the Kṛishṇā river, *i.e.*, both from the same locality. The latter is referred to the fifth century.[2]

In another, Attivarmā of the family of King Kandara is mentioned. This also was found in the neighbourhood of Guṇṭūr. Some grants of the fifth or sixth century (Dr. Burnell) fix the following genealogy:—

Skandavarmā I.
|
Vīravarmā.
|
Skandavarmā II.
|
(sons:)

- Siṁhavarmā I.
  - Skandavarmā III.
    - Nandivarmā.
- Vishṇugopavarmā.
  - Siṁhavarmā II.

An inscription of this Nandivarmā is published in *Ind. Ant.* VIII, 167. On the back of it is a Tamil endorsement dated in the twenty-sixth year of the reign of Rājendra Kulottuṅga Choḷa, *i.e.*, A.D. 1090. Another of Vishṇugopavarmā is published in *Ind. Ant.* V, 50. It dates from about the fifth century.

It appears that Bādāmi in the Kalādgi District was an ancient Pallava stronghold, and that the Chalukyas wrested it from the Pallavas. Mr. Fleet publishes (*Ind. Ant.* IX, 99) a Pallava inscription on a rock at Bādāmi. It is only a fragment, but in it the Pallavas are mentioned as "the foremost of kings." The date is doubtful, but Mr. Fleet considers it to be older than the oldest Chalukyan inscription at Bādāmi, which is dated A.D. 578. It has in it the name of either *Vishṇu*, *Siṁhavishṇu*, or *Narasiṁhavishṇu*, and it is possible that this may be the Narasiṁhavarmā mentioned as the third of the line of nine sovereigns in the list given below, since that sovereign is stated in Mr. Foulkes' inscription to have been "the crusher of Vātāpi (Bādāmi), who frequently conquered Vallabharāja (the Chalukya ?)..."

This inscription is published by Mr. Foulkes in the *Ind. Ant.* (VIII, 273), and gives the following list of Pallavas, ending with Nandivarmā, who confers a grant in the twenty-first year of his reign. A Tamil endorsement which is appended to the inscription is dated, similarly to the above, in the twenty-sixth year of the reign of Koppara-Keśarivarmā, which, according to present lights, must be Kulottuṅga

[1] Dr. Burnell's *South-Indian Palæography*, p. 106 and note 4.

[2] See below, VENGĪ, p. 239.

Chola I and the date A.D. 1090, but nothing can be gathered from this as to the date of the donor. Mr. Foulkes thinks that the grant dates from the ninth century, but gives no reasons for his opinion.

Siṁhavishṇu.
|
Mahendravarmā I.
|
Narasiṁhavarmā I.
|
Mahendravarmā II.
|
Parameśvaravarmā I.
|
Narasiṁhavarmā II.
|
Parameśvaravarmā II.
|
Nandivarmā.
|
Pallavamalla Nandivarmā.

The Pallavas were perpetually at feud with their neighbours, and are constantly mentioned in inscriptions of other dynasties as having been conquered or checked.

In the later (Choḷa-Chālukya) Eastern Chālukya grants the history of the rise of the Chalukyas is given, but it cannot be depended upon, except as showing that in the early part of the eleventh century the tradition was current that the first Chalukya had gained his hold of that portion of the Dakhaṉ which his family afterwards ruled, by defeating and afterwards intermarrying with the ruling family of the Pallavas who then governed that territory. It is said that a Chalukyan army from the north crossed the Narbadda in the reign of Trilochana Pallava, under the command of the Chalukya, Jayasiṁha *alias* Vijayāditya. The Chalukya king lost his life in battle against the Pallavas, and his widow fled. She gave birth to a posthumous son, who defeated the Pallavas and married a Pallava princess. If true, this would have taken place in the early part of the fourth century A.D. There seems reason to suppose, as Mr. Foulkes has pointed out (*Ind. Ant.* VII, 1) that Fah Hian's "Kingdom of the Dakshiṇa" was a Pallava kingdom. The early Kadamba sovereigns "seem to have established their power originally by defeating either the Gaṅga or Pallava kings, or both combined. Subsequently, Mṛigeśavarmā again conquered both of them, and Ravivarmā (his eldest son) established himself and re-established his family at Palāśikā by overthrowing Chaṇḍadaṇḍa, the Lord of Kañchī, who was undoubtedly of the Pallava dynasty."[1] (*Mr. Fleet.*) Unfortunately the precise date of these Kadambas is not yet definitely fixed, but Mr. Fleet gives reasons for assigning this victory to the close of the fifth century A.D. According to the *Koṅgudēśa Rājākkaḷ*, Durvanīti Rāya, King of the Koṅgu country, conquered *Drāviḍa*, and the fourth king in descent from him, Koṅgaṇi Mahādhirāya III, again conquered it.[2] Early in the seventh century the Pallavas were driven out of their northern possessions, the Kingdom of Veṅgī, by Kubja Vishṇuvardhana, the first of the Eastern Chalukyan dynasty, and about the same time Satyāśraya, or Pulakeśi II of the Western Chalukyas, states that he drove the Pallava sovereign behind the walls of Kañchī.[3] Vikramāditya I, his successor (A.D. 652—680), was, it seems, conquered by the Pallavas, but he afterwards overthrew them and stormed and captured their capital.[4] The commander of his forces appears to have been his son Vinayāditya, who succeeded him. It is to this period that it would seem most reasonable to assign the construction of the great monolithic monuments at Māvalipuram, known as the "Seven Pagodas."[5] In A.D. 640 Hiwen-Thsang visited Kañchī. He declares the city to have been six miles in circumference, and the people to be superior in bravery and piety, as well as in their love of justice and veneration for learning, to many others whom he met with on his travels. Jains were very numerous in his day; Buddhists and Brahmanical worshippers were about equal in strength. About this period (A.D. 650—700) flourished the great Śaiva reformer Śaṅkarāchāryār (Dr. Burnell's *South Indian Palæography*, p. 37, note 4), who, it is said, preached at Kañchī. It appears from Chalukyan records that, immediately after his coronation, the Western Chalukya king Vikramāditya II (A.D. 733 to 747)

---

1 *Dynasties of the Kanarese Districts*, 9.
2 His elder brother, Śrī Vallabhakya, *alias* Viḻanda was his commander-in-chief.
3 *Indian Antiquary* V, 67.
4 *Indian Antiquary* VI, 75—85. See above, p. 150.
5 *Volume* I, *pp.* 189, 190.

made war on the Pallava king Nandi Potavarmā, killed him, and entered his capital Kañchī in triumph (*see above*, p. 151). Wilson states that in A.D. 788 the Buddhists were finally expelled from the neighbourhood of Kañchī to Ceylon by Prince Hemasitala, who became a Jain (*Mackenzie Collection* I, lxv). King Dhruva of the dynasty of the Rāshṭrakūṭas, is recorded to have "humbled the pride" of the Pallavas; while his successor, Govinda III, in an inscription dated A.D. 803-4, boasts of having conquered Dantiga, the ruler of Kañchī.[1] And somewhat later than that, the Koṅgu king, Gaṇḍadeva Mahārāya, claims to have subverted the Pallavas again, but states that he afterwards made an alliance with them. It is about to this period that Mr. Foulkes assigns the grant of Pallavamalla Nandivarmā mentioned above (*Indian Antiquary* VIII, 273—284), whose three wars with Udayana, King of the *Śabaras* (probably *Sauras*), "Prithivīvyāghra," King of Nishāda (on the slopes of the Vindhya Mountains) and the Pāṇḍiyan king are mentioned therein. In the eleventh century occurred, according to tradition, the conquest of the Pallavas by Ādoṇḍai, son of the great Choḷa sovereign Rājendra Kulottuṅga I. Ādoṇḍai is said to have utterly defeated them, crushed for ever their power, and annexed the whole of their territories to the Choḷa kingdom. He is stated to have "founded" the city of Kañchī, and it seems quite possible that he improved it. Kañchī then became the capital of the Choḷa province called *Toṇḍaimaṇḍalam* or *Toṇḍaināḍu*. A number of Pallava sculptures are still to be seen in the old city.

PĀṆḌIYANS, THE—.

The following lists of seventy-four and forty-one kings of the Pāṇḍiyan country [2] can in no sense be considered historically reliable. They are taken from Mr. Nelson's "*Manual of the Madura District*," and in a work of that class the author was no doubt right to publish everything on record regarding the Pāṇḍiyan dynasty, whether authentic or mythological. But in such a work as the present it may well be argued that unauthenticated lists ought to find no place. On the other hand it must be remembered that the present compilation is not intended to record the results of a completed archæological survey so much as to precede such a survey. And, therefore, though the lists may be absolutely useless for historical purposes, they will be of interest, first, as showing the beliefs of native writers regarding the Pāṇḍiyan dynasty, and, secondly, because I think there is reason to believe that the *names* may possibly be more or less authentic. They differ much from those in use amongst the Choḷas, and the list of names alone may, therefore, sometimes serve as a guide when in doubt. I have, therefore, determined to reprint the lists and at the same time to prefix to them the following extract from the latest work of Bishop Caldwell (*History of Tinnevelly*, pp. 26, 27):—

"The existence of a Pāṇḍya kingdom and dynasty can be traced back . . . . . several centuries before the Christian era by means of the Asoka inscriptions and the notices contained in the Mahā-wanso, the Mahā-bhārata, and the writings of Megasthenes. The existence of the dynasty, however, is all that can be concluded with certainty from these notices; no name of any king has survived. We learn from the Greek geographers who wrote after the Christian era that the Pāṇḍya dynasty not only survived till their time, but rose to special importance amongst the Indian States, but still no name of any Pāṇḍya king appears. The next authentic reference to the Pāṇḍyas after the visit of the Greeks and before the composition of the Mahā-wanso, is that which is contained in the Brihat-samhitā, one of the astronomical, or rather astrological, works of Varāha-mihira, an Indian astronomer who lived in A.D. 404 [3] . . . . . He mentions incidentally "the Pāṇḍya king," the river Tāmraparnī, and the chank and pearl fisheries. When the Dravidas are mentioned as distinct from the Chōḷas, as they sometimes are in the Mahābhārata and the Purāṇas, the Pāṇḍyas must be meant. I should be delighted to be able to supplement the deficiencies of the Greeks and the early Indian authorities by supplying a list of the Pāṇḍya kings

---

[1] Mr. Fleet's *Kanarese Dynasties*, p. 34; *Indian Antiquary* VI, 63; XI, 126.

[2] For notices of the Pāṇḍiyan Kingdom see the following:—"*Historical Sketch*" by H. H. Wilson, in J.R.A.S. III, 199—242, with its annexed list of manuscripts consulted; Taylor's remarks on the above in M.J.L.S. VI, 142—176; Nelson's "*Madura Country, A Manual*," Part III; Caldwell's "*Dravidian Grammar*" and his "*History of Tinnevelly*;" Wilson's Introduction to the *Descriptive Catalogue of the Mackenzie MSS.*, p. 36. Prinsep's List ("*Useful Tables*," in Thomas' Edition, II, 280) is of little use. As to the name, Bishop Caldwell derives it from *Pāṇḍu*, the father of the Pāṇḍavas, and considers "*Pāṇḍiyan*" to be a Tamil corruption. Dr. Burnell, however, thinks that *Pāṇḍiyan* was the original, and *Pāṇḍya* a Saṅskṛitic perversion. (For notes on this subject and others akin, see *Ind. Ant. VIII*, 146, 148, and *note*.)

[3] The Bishop has wrongly quoted this date, which should be A.D. 504. The date is not yet certainly fixed. Kern, quoted by the Bishop, thinks that possibly A.D. 504 was the *birth-year* of Varāha-mihira (see Weber's *History of Indian Literature*, Trübner's 8vo. edition of 1878, Oriental Series, No. III, p. 261, note 293). The year of his death is given by Amaraja, a scholiast on Brahmagupta, as Ś.Ś. 509 (A.D. 587), and this is generally received as accurate.

from Pāṇḍyan sources, but I regret to say that I can place no confidence whatever in the lists of Pāṇḍya kings furnished by local poets and panegyrists. I should be happy to avail myself of any information respecting the Pāṇḍyas and their affairs coming from the outside, but I believe it is the greatest possible error to trust to home-made lists of kings, in the absence of reliable contemporary information from coins and inscriptions . . . . It seems better, therefore, that I should leave those lists for the present unnoticed. One name only in those lists has hitherto, so far as I am aware, been authenticated by a coin; that is Samara Kolāhala (din of war, a title, rather than a name), which I found on a coin belonging to Sir Walter Elliot. The date, however, is unknown; this is a department of research in which very little has yet been done."

While entirely concurring in the learned Bishop's remarks, I may point to his last statement as furnishing an example to justify the present publication of the traditionary lists. It is possible that other coins or inscriptions may be found from which light may be thrown on the subject, and the student should have the lists before him to refer to in case of need.[1]

The capital of the Pāṇḍiyan kingdom was at Madura. The device of their house was the fish.

The following list of kings, with the exception of the seventy-fourth, is taken from the Madura *Sthala Purāṇa*. The notes under the kings' names are compiled mostly from Mr. Nelson's work. I do not insert them as my own, or because I believe them to be authentic. They consist mainly of assertions made by native authors.

i. Kulaśekhara.
Of the Lunar Race, the founder of Madura.

|

ii. Malaya Dhvaja.
Married Kāñchanamālā, daughter of Śūrasena, a Choḷa Rāja.

|

(No sons.)
iii. (*Daughter*) Tatātakai.
Married, according to legend, Śiva under the name of Sundara. Mr. Nelson suggests that this may be the Pāṇḍiyan princess whom Vijaya of Ceylon married (see the Mahāwanso). She and her husband were deified under the names "Sundara" and "Mīnākshī," and are still worshipped at Madura.

|

iv. Ugra Pāṇḍiyan.
("Hāra-dhāri"), married Kāntimatī, daughter of Somaśekhara, the Choḷa king of Kāñchipura(!) The Pāṇḍiyan, Choḷa, and Chera kings were on friendly terms.

|

v. Vīra Pāṇḍiyan.

|

vi. Abhisheka Pāṇḍiyan.

|

vii Vikrama Pāṇḍiyan.
Attack on Madura by Choḷas, who had been converted to Jainism.

|

viii. Rājaśekhara Pāṇḍiyan.
A literary king; lived to a great age.

|

ix. Kulottuṅga Pāṇḍiyan.
No. 1 of Prinsep's List ("Useful Tables," p. 280).

|

x. Anantaguṇa Pāṇḍiyan.
Another attack on Madura by Jains. In this reign the legends say that Rāma marched southwards, past Madura, to conquer Rāvaṇa.

|

[1] Mr. Scott of Madura was so good as to give me a few coins from his fine collection, which supply the names of *Kachchi Varaṅgum Perumāḷ*, "the king who made a present of Kañchi," or the king who conquered the Pallavas (or Choḷas) and gave back the capital to its sovereign; *Korkai Āṇḍār*, "the prince of Korkai," a little common, Mr Scott thinks, to the Pāṇḍiyan "Yuvarājas" or crown princes; *Sundara Pāṇḍiyan*; *Bhuvanēka Vīra*; *Kōnēri Rāyan*; and *Samara Kolāhala*.

xi. Kulabhūshaṇa Pāṇḍiyan.

"Kālabhūshana" (Prinsep). Threatened attack on Madura by a huntsman king of the "Chēdi" country. He is killed by a "lion" and the siege raised. In this reign the Choḷas were Śaivas, but not on good terms with the Pāṇḍiyans. They, however, made friends.

Rājasiṁha.

Married a Choḷa princess, deceiving his brother.

xii. Rājendra Pāṇḍiyan.

The Choḷas and Pāṇḍiyans were closely allied. But a feud arose when the Pāṇḍiyan king was cheated out of his alliance with the Choḷa king's daughter by Rājasiṁha, and the Choḷa king made war on the Pāṇḍiyan. Choḷa was defeated.

xiii. Rājeśa Pāṇḍiyan.

"Rājeswara" (Prinsep).

xiv. Rāja Gambhīra Pāṇḍiyan.

"Gambhira" (Prinsep).

xv. Pāṇḍiyavaṁśa Pradīpa Pāṇḍiyan.

"Vansapradipaka" (Prinsep).

xvi. Puruhuta Pāṇḍiyan.

"Puruhutajit" (Prinsep).

xvii. Pāṇḍiyavaṁśa Paṭāka Pāṇḍiyan.

"Pandya Vamsapātākā" (Prinsep).

xviii. Sundarēśvara Pādaśekhara Pāṇḍiyan.

Built many temples and shrines; was attacked by Choḷas, who drove the Pāṇḍiyan behind the walls of Madura, when the Choḷa king was drowned in the fort ditch and his army retired.

"Padasekhara."

This sovereign's name is inserted here by Prinsep.

xix. Varaguṇa Pāṇḍiyan.

Prinsep's list states that he united Choḷa and Toṇḍa to Madura. Bhadra, the great musician, flourished. Choḷa was about to attack the Pāṇḍiyan, but Varaguṇa made a counter attack and drove him far into his own country. Bhadra was sent to the Chera king, who was directed to give him valuable presents, which was done; implying that Chera was subsidiary to the Pāṇḍiyan.

xx. Rājarāja Pāṇḍiyan.

"Rājendra" (Prinsep).

xxi. Suguṇa Pāṇḍiyan.

xxii. Chitravrata Pāṇḍiyan.

"Chitraratha" (Prinsep).

xxiii. Chitrabhūshaṇa Pāṇḍiyan.

xxiv. Chitradhvaja Pāṇḍiyan.

xxv. Chitravarmā Pāṇḍiyan.

xxvi. Chitrasēna Pāṇḍiyan.

xxvii. Chitravikrama Pāṇḍiyan.

xxviii. Rāja Mārtāṇḍa Pāṇḍiyan.
" *Udanta* " (*Prinsep*).

xxix. Rāja Chūḍāmaṇi Pāṇḍiyan.
" *Rāja Charāmani* " (*Prinsep*).

xxx. Rāja Śārdūla Pāṇḍiyan.
" *Rāja Śārdula* " (*Prinsep*).

xxxi. Dvija Rāja Kulottuṅga Pāṇḍiyan.

xxxii. Āyudha-pravīṇa Pāṇḍiyan.
" *Yodhana pravīra* " (*Prinsep*).

xxxiii. Rāja Kuñjara Pāṇḍiyan.

xxxiv. Pararāja Bhayaṅkara Pāṇḍiyan.

xxxv. Ugrasena Pāṇḍiyan.

xxxvi. Mahāsena Pāṇḍiyan.

xxxvii. Satruñjaya Pāṇḍiyan.

xxxviii. Bhīmaratha Pāṇḍiyan.

xxxix. Bhīmaparākrama Pāṇḍiyan.

xl. Pratāpa Mārtāṇḍa Pāṇḍiyan.

xli. Vikrama Kañchaka Pāṇḍiyan.
" *Vikrama Kunjaka* " (*Prinsep*).

xlii. Yuddha Kolāhala Pāṇḍiyan.

xliii. Atula Vikrama Pāṇḍiyan.

xliv. Atula Kīrti Pāṇḍiyan.

xlv. Kīrtti-vibhūshaṇa Pāṇḍiyan.
A deluge is said to have taken place which swept away the population. After this Śiva re-created all castes and nations just as before, and the new created king of Madurā was of the race of the Moon and in all respects corresponding. Probably this is the commencement of a new dynasty, which, to establish itself, claimed to belong to the old one.

xlvi. Vaṁśaśekhara Pāṇḍiyan.
Fortified Madura and enlarged the city. The Choḷa king Vikrama invaded the country and was driven back with loss. The Tamiḻ College of Poets was established.

|

xlvii. Vaṁśa-chūḍāmaṇi Pāṇḍiyan.
("Champaka") "*Vamsachurāmani*" (*Prinsep*).
This is the last of Prinsep's list.

|

xlviii. Pratāpa Śūrasena Pāṇḍiyan.

|

xlix. Vaṁśa-dhvaja Pāṇḍiyan.

|

l. Ripumardana Pāṇḍiyan.

|

li. Choḷa-vaṁśāntaka Pāṇḍiyan.

|

lii. Chera-vaṁśāntaka Pāṇḍiyan.

|

liii. Pāṇḍiya-vaṁśeśa Pāṇḍiyan.

|

liv. Vaṁśa-chūḍāmaṇi Pāṇḍiyan.

|

lv. Pāṇḍyeśvara Pāṇḍiyan.

|

lvi. Kula-dhvaja Pāṇḍiyan.

|

lvii. Vaṁśa-vibhūshaṇa Pāṇḍiyan.

|

lviii. Soma-chūḍāmaṇi Pāṇḍiyan.

|

lix. Kula-chūḍāmaṇi Pāṇḍiyan.

|

lx. Rāja-chūḍāmaṇi Pāṇḍiyan.

|

lxi. Bhūpa-chūḍāmaṇi Pāṇḍiyan.

|

lxii. Kuleśa Pāṇḍiyan.
A very learned but very conceited king.

|

lxiii. Arimardana Pāṇḍiyan.
The king's minister, a clever Brahman, Māṇikya-vāchaka, confuted the Jains "who came from a certain island." The Choḷa (?) king of Kāñchī, a Jain, was converted by him, and he crushed the Choḷa Jains in oil-presses.

|

lxiv. Jagannātha Pāṇḍiyan.
It seems uncertain whether this persecution of Jains took place in his or his father's reign.

|

lxv. Vīrabāhu Pāṇḍiyan.

|

lxvi. Vikrama Pāṇḍiyan.

|

lxvii. Surabhi Pāṇḍiyan.

|

xviii. Kuṅkuma Pāṇḍiyan.

|

lxix. Karpūra Pāṇḍiyan.

|

lxx. Kāruṇya Pāṇḍiyan.

lxxi. Purushottama Pāṇḍiyan.

lxxii. Satruśāsana Pāṇḍiyan.

lxxiii. Kubja, or Sundara, Pāṇḍiyan.

Known in Tamil as "Kūn" or "Kūna Pāṇḍiyan." Conquered the Choḷa king and married his daughter, Vanitēśvarī. Appointed the Choḷa minister Prime Minister of Madura. He became a Jain, but his queen summoned Jñānasambandhamūrti, the celebrated Priest of Śiva, and he cured the king of his illness as well as his heresy. The Jains were all put to death. He is said to have destroyed Choḷa and burnt Tanjore and Uraiyūr. He made the Choḷa's son a Pāṇḍiyan by title; but the son seems to have fled and gone north on a raid. There were "Arabs" at Madura in his day.

lxxiv. Vīra Pāṇḍiya-Choḷa.

Kūn Pāṇḍiyan had a son, Vīra Pāṇḍiya-Choḷa, who reigned in Choḷa. He is the seventy-fourth and last of the Pāṇḍiyans of the old line.

Almost every writer on the Pāṇḍiyan dynasty varies in his estimates of the date of Kūn or Sundara Pāṇḍiyan, and it is not within the scope of the present summary to enter into a detailed criticism on the various theories raised. I shall content myself, therefore, with one or two remarks. There were several sovereigns known as "Sundara Pāṇḍiyan," and it is as unsafe to jump to conclusions regarding the date of a sovereign known by that name, purely by reason of his bearing it, as it would be for an uneducated student to assign a date to "King Henry" of England without any information as to which Henry is referred to. For instance, it is certain that Rājendra Kulottuṅga Choḷa's younger brother assumed the name of "Sundara Pāṇḍiyan," and lived at the close of the eleventh and beginning of the twelfth century A.D., while the Muḥammadan writers, Amīr Khusrū and others, speak of a "Sundara Pāṇḍiyan" at Madura in A.D. 1311. Several other monarchs seem have been known by that name, and we know of one being on the throne at the date of Marco Polo's voyage. I am not, therefore, inclined to assume that the "Sender Bundi" of the latter author was necessarily identical with the Kūn, *alias* Sundara, Pāṇḍiyan abovementioned. It would seem more probable that Kūn Pāṇḍiyan was the father of the Vīra Pāṇḍiyan who was conquered by Rājendra Kulottuṅga Choḷa in 1064 A.D., and therefore that he bore another name, "Vikrama," by which he was known to the writer of the inscription at Chidambaram mentioned by Dr. Burnell. (*South Indian Palæography*, p. 45, n.) According to that inscription, Rājendra, *alias* Koppara Keśarivarmā,[1] established his younger brother Gaṅgaikoṇḍān Choḷa on the throne of the conquered country, naming him "Sundara Pāṇḍiya-Choḷa." This would seem far more likely than that the real king of Madura should confer on a conquered Choḷa the name of "Pāṇḍiyan" as boastfully stated in the inscription quoted by Mr. Nelson at p. 56, &c. of his work. If it be so, the entire subversion of the old line of Pāṇḍiyans is at once accounted for. But, as before stated, at present all theories are dangerous.

After the last king's death without legitimate issue, it is said that his illegitimate sons fought with one another for the supremacy, and each reigned where he could and as long as he could.

Mr. Nelson gives the following list of forty-one princes. A comparison of the "*Śri-Tāla*" book with Taylor's *Supplementary Manuscripts* would seem to show that the first twenty-four and the last may be accurately given, the intermediate ones, Nos. 25 to 40, being doubtful. The notes under the kings' names are from Taylor's Manuscript, but as he does not give the names, but only the consecutive number of the reign, it is possible that there may be errors. And it must be clearly understood that the whole line may be purely apocryphal. The evidence of the few inscriptions yet known to me does not serve to corroborate the list.

---

[1] That Rājendra, *alias* Kulottuṅga I, was also called "Koppākeśari" or "Kopparakeśari" is proved by a number of inscriptions at different places (*see* the list, pp 102—109 above).

1. Somaśekhara Pāṇḍiyan.
(*About* 1100 *A.D.* ?)
All agree that this was the prince who at last secured the throne.
Reigned 20 *years.*

|

2. Karpūra Sundara Pāṇḍiyan.

|

3. Kumāra-śekhara Pāṇḍiyan.

|

4. Kumāra Sundara Pāṇḍiyan.

|

5. Sundara Rāja Pāṇḍiyan.

|

6. Shaṇmukha Rāja Pāṇḍiyan.

|

7. Meru Sundara Pāṇḍiyan.
This king is said to have ruled over Choḷa and Chera as well as the Pāṇḍiyan Kingdom.

|

8. Indravarmā Pāṇḍiyan.
Son of the last. He is declared to have released the Choḷa king from imprisonment, placed him on the Choḷa throne, and married his daughter.

|

9. Chandrakula Dīpa Pāṇḍiyan.

|

10. Mīna-ketana Pāṇḍiyan.

|

11. Mīna-dhvaja Pāṇḍiyan.
Taylor's Manuscript says that he married the daughter of the Choḷa king, and, as the Choḷa had no issue, this king's younger son ruled over Choḷa.

|

12. Makara-dhvaja Pāṇḍiyan.
Taylor's Manuscript states he was a great conqueror.

|

13. Mārtāṇḍa Pāṇḍiyan.

|

14. Kuvalayānanda Pāṇḍiyan.
He carried on commerce by sea to a considerable extent. Reigned four years, and amassed much wealth. Was drowned at sea in a storm. (*Taylor's Manuscript.*)

|

(*A daughter*)
married
15. Kuṇḍala Pāṇḍiyan.
"*He grieved much and would not reign in Madura.*"
(*Taylor.*)

|

16. Śatru Bhīkara Pāṇḍiyan.

|

17. Śatru Saṁhāra Pāṇḍiyan.

|

18. Vîravarmā Pāṇḍiyan.
He conquered the Malayāḷa country. (*Taylor.*)

19. Vîrabāhu Pāṇḍiyan.

20. Makuṭavardhana Pāṇḍiyan.
He was killed in battle against the Choḷa. (*Taylor.*)

21. Vajra-siṁha Pāṇḍiyan.

22. Varma Kulottuṅga Pāṇḍiyan.
He conquered the Choḷas. (*Taylor.*)

23. Ati Vîra Rāma Pāṇḍiyan.
Taylor's Manuscript makes him a close ally of the Choḷas, with whose aid he conquered many countries.

24. Kula-vardhana Pāṇḍiyan.

25. Soma-śekhara Pāṇḍiyan.

26. Soma-sundara Pāṇḍiyan.

27. Rājarāja Pāṇḍiyan.

28. Rāja-kuñjara Pāṇḍiyan.

29. Rāja-śekhara Pāṇḍiyan.

30. Rājavarmā Pāṇḍiyan.

31. Rāmavarmā Pāṇḍiyan.

32. Varadarāja Pāṇḍiyan.

33. Kumārasiṁha Pāṇḍiyan.

34. Vîrasena Pāṇḍiyan.

35. Pratāpa Rāja Pāṇḍiyan.

36. Vîraguṇa Rāja Pāṇḍiyan.

37. Kumāra Chandra Pāṇḍiyan.

38. Varatuṅga Pāṇḍiyan.

39. Chandraśekhara Pāṇḍiyan.

40. Somaśekhara Pāṇḍiyan.

41. Parākrama Pāṇḍiyan.
This king is said to have obtained the throne by fighting against and driving out "some foreigners." Before him there was a period of anarchy. He was driven out by the Musalmān chief "Ādi Sultān Malik Nēmi" or Malik Nāib (= Malik Kāfur).

As to this last list of forty-one kings, it will suffice to say that it may possibly not be entirely inaccurate. On the arbitrary assumption that the last king of the original line was ejected by Kulottuṅga Choḷa in A.D. 1064, and that the forty-first king of the second line, whatever his name may have been, was subverted by Malik Kāfur in A.D. 1311, the question arises whether it is possible for the interval between the two dates to be covered by the reign of forty-one sovereigns. The interval consists of 246 years, or six years to a reign, and therefore there is no reason for discrediting *primâ facie* the assertion that a dynasty of forty-one kings succeeded him whom the Choḷa conquered, though, if their reigns only occupied a period of 246 years, each could not have been the son of his predecessor.

Turning now from these doubtful and possibly fanciful lists, let us direct our attention to the more solid basis of inscriptions and contemporary records.

The earliest notice of the Pāṇḍiyan kingdom as yet extant is to be found in the writings of Megasthenes (B.C. 302) who speaks of a country called *Pandaia*; the next is in one of Aśoka's inscriptions (B.C. 250) in Northern India. Pliny (A.D. 77) mentions both the country and the city. Bishop Caldwell thinks that the Indian king who sent an embassy to Augustus at Rome was the then Pāṇḍiyan sovereign. "The name, as written by Eusebius, appears in the Chronographia of Georgius Syncellus (A.D. 800), whose work has been used to restore or complete the Greek text of the Chronicon, and who says, under the head of the 185th olympiad, 'Pandian, King of the Indians, sends an embassy to Augustus, desiring to become his friend and ally.'" (Bishop Caldwell's *History of Tinnevelly*, p. 17) In the *Periplus Maris Erythræi* (third century A.D.)[1] its capital Madura (*Μόδουρα*) is mentioned, and the king is called *ὁ Πανδίων*. It seems probable that there was at one time a Roman colony settled at Madura, as Roman copper coins in considerable numbers have been found in the sandy bed of the river there. Silver or gold coins would simply indicate commerce, but copper coins seem to imply the residence of the traders. However this may be, there is abundant evidence of an extensive trade between Rome and the western coast (at least) of the peninsula of India in those days. Kolkai ("*Kolkhoi Emporium*") was one of the principal trading cities of the Pāṇḍiyans.

The great age of the Pāṇḍiyan kingdom is amply attested by the Singhalese epic, the *Mahāwanso*, which professes to be a historical record, and the first part of which was written by Mahānāma between the years A.D. 459 and 477. According to that poem (*Turnour's translation, pp.* 47—53) Vijaya, first King of Ceylon, who landed in that island at the date of Buddha's *Nirvāṇa* (B.C. 477 ?), married the daughter of the Pāṇḍiyan king. If this story proves nothing else, it proves that the Singhalese, in the fifth century A.D., believed that the Pāṇḍiyan kingdom was older than their own.

According to Singhalese chronicles the Pāṇḍiyan king about the year A.D. 840 attacked the capital of Ceylon, and was bought off with a large ransom, while a little later the Singhalese king invaded the Pāṇḍiyan country to aid the Pāṇḍiyan king's son in an insurrection against his father. Madura was then captured and plundered.

During the reigns of the Choḷa kings Rājarāja (1023—1064) and Rājendra Kulottuṅga I (1064—1113), the Singhalese were constantly at war with the Choḷas, and the silence of the Singhalese chronicles regarding the Pāṇḍiyans at that period affords additional proof of the complete subversion of the latter kingdom by the conquering Choḷa. As before stated, this (A.D. 1064) is the date to which some writers have assigned the last Pāṇḍiyan sovereign of the old stock. Whatever be the truth regarding the date of Kūn, or Sundara, Pāṇḍiyan, there seems little doubt that the name of the Pāṇḍiyan conquered by Rājendra Choḷa was Vīra, son of Vikrama Paṇḍiyan, for there is an inscription extant to that effect at Chidambaram,[2] wherein Rājendra is known by his name "Kopparakeśari" (or "Koppākeśari"). The Choḷa's son, Gaṅgaikoṇḍān Choḷa, was placed on the throne under the name of "Sundara Pāṇḍiya-Choḷa" (*Inscription at Karuvūr*).[3] A number of inscriptions of Rājendra's reign are extant, even to the furthest confines of the Pāṇḍiyan country, in an old temple near Cape Comorin,[4] proving how complete was his conquest.

The affairs of Ceylon[5] had been for some years previous to Rājendra's date in a very confused state. Mihindu 4th ascended the throne at his capital, Anurādhapura, in A.D. 1023, the year of the accession of Rājarāja to the throne of the Choḷas. The immigrants from the continent had become so numerous that in 1033 they acquired the ascendancy, and Mihindu fled. Twenty-six years later, *i.e.*, in A.D. 1059, the Choḷas captured King Mihindu, carried him prisoner to the mainland, and placed a Choḷa viceroy to govern the island. The Pāṇḍiyan kingdom was, as stated above, conquered by Rājarāja's successor,

---

[1] Reinaud's date for the *Periplus* is A.D. 246 or 247 (*Ind. Ant.* VIII, 331, 334, 337. Translation, notes and commentary were published by Mr. McCrindle in *Ind. Ant.* VIII, 107—151.)

[2] Dr. Burnell's *South Indian Palæography*, p. 45, note 1.

[3] Bishop Caldwell's *History of Tinnevelly*, p. 27 *et seq.*

[4] Bishop Caldwell's *History of Tinnevelly*, p. 28.

[5] Turnour's *Mahāwanso*, Introd., lxiv.

Rājendra, in A.D. 1064, and in 1071 the ancient kingdom of Ceylon was restored in the person of Vijaya Bāhu, who succeeded, though with great difficulty, in driving out the Choḷa usurpers after an anarchical interregnum of twelve years. During this period we find three names of Pāṇḍiyan princes as governing in Ceylon, "Vikrama Pāṇḍiyan," "Jagat Pāṇḍiyan," and "Parākrama Pāṇḍiyan." The statement needs explanation.

Rājendra Choḷa died in A.D. 1113 and was succeeded by Vikrama Choḷa (1113—1128). Kulottuṅga II succeeded in 1128. The length of his reign is not yet accurately known, but it was more than 30, and Bishop Caldwell thinks at least 44, years (*History of Tinnevelly*, p. 29). All these ruled over the Pāṇḍiyan country.

"The Chōla or Chōḷa-Pāṇḍiya kings that followed appear to have been Karikāla Chōḷa, Vīra Chōḷa, Vikrama Chōḷa. Each of these is in some inscriptions styled Chōḷa-Pāṇḍiya." (*Id.*) This latter statement needs proof.

The next allusion to Pāṇḍiyan affairs that I can trace is to be found in the Singhalese annals of the reign of Parākrama Bāhu I (1153—1186 A.D.). After recording an expedition "in the sixteenth year of his reign" against another king (*i.e.*, in 1169), the summary given in Turnour's *Mahāwanso* (p. lxvi) goes on to say that the king next turned his attention to the chastisement of Kulaśekhara, the Pāṇḍiyan king, "for the countenance and aid he had always afforded to all invaders of Ceylon." An expedition was despatched, Rāmeśvaram was captured, and six neighbouring provinces; the Pāṇḍiyan was driven from his throne, and his son Vīra Pāṇḍiyan installed in his place. The names of the chiefs are given. Kulaśekhara, aided by the Choḷa king, made three attempts to recover his throne, but in vain. He was defeated at all points and surrendered. The invaders restored him to his kingdom, and Vīra Pāṇḍiyan was solaced for this reversal of his fortunes by the gift as a principality of a portion of the Choḷa country which had been captured by the Singhalese. This affair is generally placed in the year A.D. 1171 or 1173. The account is confirmed by an inscription at Dambula in Ceylon (*Ind. Ant.* I, 196), which states that Parākrama Bāhu built a temple at Rāmeśvaram dedicated to *Nissaṅkeśvara*, and resided in that city.

Dr. Burgess has lately made a most valuable discovery in the shape of several inscriptions at Vikramaṅgalam, in the Tirumaṅgalam Taluk of the Madura District, which may perhaps fix the fact of a king named "Kulaśekhara" having ascended the Pāṇḍiyan throne about A.D. 1200 and ruled till at least 1213. If the dates given above for the period of Parākrama Bāhu of Ceylon are accurate, this Kulaśekhara must have been a successor of the king of the same name who was conquered and then restored by Parākrama.

In 1292 A.D. we have the account given by Marco Polo, the traveller, of the kingdom of Madura being ruled over by "Sundara Pāṇdyadeva," one of five brothers; and by the evidence of the Muhammadan historian Wassaf it would appear that this Sundara Pāṇḍiyan died A.D. 1293. Wassaf and Amīr Khusrū, writing of the capture of Madura by Malik Kāfur the general of 'Alā-ud-dīn Khilji of Delhi in A.D. 1311, both speak of the king of Madura at that date as being "Sundara Pāṇḍiyan," and they detail his adventures, his expulsion at the hands of his half-brother (illegitimate) "Tīra" or "Vīra" Pāṇḍiyan, and his flight to Delhi. I do not see any necessity for supposing that Wassaf is in error in relating the death of Sundara Pāṇḍiyan in 1293, or that there was not a successor of his of the same name at the date of the Muhammadan conquest in 1310-11. As to the identity of either of these with the Kūn or Sundara Pāṇḍiyan whose name closes the first list of seventy-three Pāṇḍiyan kings, the discussion is summarized in Mr. Lewis Moore's *Manual of the Trichinopoly District* (pp. 116, 120). My own impression is that Kūn Pāṇḍiyan belongs altogether to an earlier date than the period 1292—1311 A.D.

According to Wassaf ("*Tazjiyatu-l amsār va Tajriyatu-l āsār*," Sir Henry Elliot's *History of India* III, 49—54) and Amīr Khusrū (*Id.* 91) we have for the last real Pāṇḍiyan sovereigns, (1) "Kales Dēvar" (Kulaśekharadeva ?), who lived a prosperous life, ruled for 40 odd years, and was murdered (1310) by his own son Sundara; (2) Sundara, the parricide, who gained the throne in 1310, defeated his brother Vīra (*Tīra*) at first, but was afterwards defeated by him by the help of "Manār Barmūl," son of the daughter of "Kales Dēvar," and fled to Delhi; and (3) Vīra, who succeeded and was firmly established on the throne when he was attacked, defeated, and the city of Madura sacked by the Muhammadans under Malik Kāfur. Sundara gave up the country of '*Arīkanna* (?) to the Muhammadans.

There can be no doubt of the fact that this invasion of the Muhammadans actually, if not nominally, effected the entire subversion of the ancient kingdom of the Pāṇḍiyans. It convulsed the whole of Southern India. The Choḷa kingdom went to pieces at the same time, and all over the peninsula there was a period of anarchy and confusion till the rise of Vijayanagar a few years later. During this period it seems that there was a succession of Muhammadan chiefs ruling over their Pāṇḍiyan conquests. Mr

Nelson gives a list of eight of these, who governed Madura for forty-eight years from A.D. 1310. Their names are—

			A.D.
Malik Nāib Kāfur	... ...	3 years,	1310—1313
'Alā-ud-dīn Khān	... ...	6 „	1313—1319
Uttum-ud-dīn Khān	... ...	3 „	1319—1322
(His son-in-law) Quṭb-ud-dīn Khān	... ...	5 „	1322—1327
Nakal-ud-dīn Khān	... ...	7 „	1327—1334
Savāda Malik, Ahad Malik	together	12 „	1334—1346
Fandahk Malik	... ...	12 „	1346—1358

Mr. Nelson then gives us the usurpation of Kampaṇa Uḍaiyār, which he dates about the year 1372. (He does not bridge the fourteen years' interval). From the evidence of the inscriptions at Conjeeveram it would appear that this conqueror quitted that place or neighbourhood in order to fight the Musalmāns at Madura. He may have been an agent of Bukka Rāya of Vijayanagar (1350—1379).[1] From this time (1370) forward, till about the year A.D. 1623, we have conflicting Pāṇḍiyan inscriptions, clashing, from an historical point of view, with the various usurping rulers, who will now be mentioned in order as given by Mr. Nelson. The contemporary Pāṇḍiyan line is noted afterwards.

Mr. Nelson mentions the Uḍaiyārs of Madura as being (1) Kampaṇa, (2) Embaṇa his son, (3) the latter's brother-in-law Porkāsa (Prakāsa?), who ceased to reign in A.D. 1404. The Conjeeveram and other inscriptions give us a different list (see the list as given under the Choḷa Kings, *supra*, p. 160)

After this comes the first mention of any "Nāyakka." This is :—

		A.D.
Lakkana Nāyakka	jointly.	1404—1451
Mattanan Nāyakka		

In 1451 one Lakkana Nāyakka brought four persons to Madura as belonging to the old Pāṇḍiyan stock. The first was son of a dancing-girl "by a (or the) Pāṇḍiya Rāja." They were crowned, and ruled for 48 years. Their names are—

	A.D.
Sundara Tōḷ Mahā Vilivānāthi Rāyar	1451—1499
Kālaiyār Somanār	
Anjāda Perumāḷ	
Muttarasa Tirumalai Mahā Vilivānāthi Rāyar	

Mr. Nelson thinks that it is possible that these were the kings who rebuilt the four lofty *gopuras* which had been destroyed by the Musalmāns, and which, by tradition, were built "by the Pāṇḍiyans"? The chronicles appear to be silent regarding the great progress in the acquirement of power by the Vijayanagar sovereign Narasiṁha at this period, who is stated to have extended his conquests over the Pāṇḍiyan and Choḷa countries. He reigned from A.D. 1487—1509. After these 48 years a Nāyakka came and "got possession."

	A.D.
Narasa Nāyakka	1499—1500
Tenna Nāyakka	1500—1515
Narasa Piḷḷai	1515—1519

Inscriptions call this chief "Narasa Ayyar," "Narasa Piḷḷai," or "Narasa Nāyakka." It is not known how he became king. Two inscriptions have been found of 1515 and 1516. Both of these call him a servant of the Rāyar of Vijayanagara, *i.e.*, the great Kṛishṇadeva Rāya. He was succeeded according to Mr. Nelson by—

	A.D.
Kuru Kuru Timmappa Nāyakkan	1519—1524
Kattiyama Kāmaiya Nāyakkan	1524—1526
Chinnappa Nāyakkan	1526—1530
Ayyakārai Veyyappa Nāyakkan	1530—1535

[1] The idea of his having been a relative of the "then king of Mysore" is probably apocryphal, arising simply from the coincidence of the title *Uḍaiyār* with that of the more modern Maisūr dynasty. In those days there was no "King of Maisūr," and what *Uḍaiyārs* there were were petty chiefs, lords of twenty or thirty villages. Kampaṇa may have been one of the latter.

	A.D.
Viśvanātha Nāyakkan Ayyar	1535—1544
Varadappa Nāyakkan	1544—1545
Dumbichchi Nāyakkan	1545—1546
Viśvanātha Nāyakkan	1546—1547
Viṭṭhala Rāja	1547—1558

This last Mr. Nelson believes to have been Rāma Rāja of Vijayanagar. A Madura inscription calls him "Rāma Rāja Viṭṭhala-deva Mahārāyar."

After this the names of three Nāyakkas are given as rulers, but a Pāṇḍiyan also was crowned, and the Rāja of Tanjore drove him out, while a Vijayanagar general drove out the Tanjore conqueror. All this took place in a very short time. The Vijayanagar general's son, after defeating his father's army, assumed the sovereignty. This was the great Viśvanātha Nāyakka, A.D. 1559.[1] (For subsequent history of the dynasty founded by him, see the NĀYAKKAS OF MADURA, *supra*, p. 199.)

I have stated above that, contemporary with the above list of rulers of Madura, we have from inscriptions a list of Pāṇḍiyan kings or chiefs from A.D. 1365 to 1623 (about), and I now proceed to give their names and dates as given by Bishop Caldwell,[2] to whom we are indebted for the information. It is quite possible that the Pāṇḍiyans really held the country, or it may be only the south, while the usurpers occupied the city and neighbourhood of Madura. On the other hand, it is equally possible that the inscriptions may record the names of the descendants of the ancient Pāṇḍiyans, living, but entirely devoid of any real sovereignty, in the period in question. Time and study of the existing inscriptions will alone settle these doubtful points. The line is as follows:—

PARĀKRAMA PĀṆḌIYAN commenced to reign in A.D. 1365. An inscription at Kōṭṭār in South Travancore, in the fifth year of his reign, is dated in the *Śaka* year corresponding to A.D. 1370. Bishop Caldwell notes the conquest of Kampaṇa Uḍaiyār, referred to above, in A.D. 1372, and a statement by Muhammadans (authority not quoted) that in A.D. 1374 Mujāhid Shāh of the Bāhmanī dynasty "over-ran the countries between Vijayanagara and Cape Comorin, and advanced, like Malik Kāfur, to Rāmēśvaram." This was, the Bishop thinks, probably a "mere plundering expedition."

From 1374 to 1431 Dr. Caldwell is unable to assist us, but I may point to an inscription at Tiruttarakōśamaṅgai near Rāmnād (*Vol. I*, p. 302), which, if the copy sent to me be accurate, gives us a VĪRA PĀṆḌIYAN reigning in A.D. 1383; and to the inscription at Karivalam Vandanallūr in the Śaṅkaranainār Taluk of the Tinnevelly District, which mentions a Kulaśekhara Pāṇḍiyan as ruling in A.D. 1402 (*Vol. I*, p. 306).

PONNAN PERUMĀḶ PARĀKRAMA PĀṆḌIYAN began to reign A.D. 1431. (Inscription at Teṅkāśi in Tinnevelly.) Local tradition asserts that this Pāṇḍiyan was preceded by his father KĀŚI KAṆḌA PARĀKRAMA PĀṆḌIYAN. This may help to bridge the interval.[3]

VĪRA PĀṆḌIYAN began to reign A.D. 1437. (Two inscriptions at Śrīvaikuṇṭam in Tinnevelly.)

VĪRA PĀṆḌIYAN. Began to reign, according to the Mackenzie MSS., in 1475. He is mentioned in an inscription as reigning in 1490.

PARĀKRAMA PĀṆḌIYAN began to reign in A.D. 1516. (Inscription at Kuttālam.)

VIKRAMA PĀṆḌIYAN began to reign in 1543 (authority not given).

Dr. Caldwell thinks that no interval elapsed between this king and Ati Vīra Rāma, but Mr. Nelson (*Madura Country*, p. 95) mentions an inscription at Śrīvilliputtūr (*see Vol. I*, p. 305), which records a grant in A.D. 1546 by a PARĀKRAMA PĀṆḌIYAN.

VALLABHA DEVA *alias* ATI VĪRA RĀMA PĀṆḌIYAN began to reign A.D. 1565. (Inscription at Kuttālam, dated in his fortieth year, A.D. 1605.) An inscription of his in Teṅkāśi gives the date of the commencement of the reign as 1562. Dr. Burnell informed Bishop Caldwell that he had seen a copper-plate grant belonging to "a maṭha in the Tanjore District" (it would be of great assistance if

[1] According to the Nāyakka History of Madura we have an anarchy following the decease, or at least the close of the reign, of a Viṭṭhala Rāja in 1557 A.D., and a Chandraśekhara (Bishop Caldwell thinks the name "quite uncertain") gaining the crown in 1558 or thereabouts, only to be ejected by a Tanjore Rāja, who, in his turn, was overthrown by the Vijayanagar general Kōṭiya Nāgama Nāyakka in 1559. The latter seized the country for himself and threw off his allegiance to his sovereign, but Viśvanātha Nāyakka, Nāgama's own son, being sent to chastise the rebel, fought him and defeated him. This Viśvanātha founded the Nāyakka dynasty, but seems all his life to have acknowledged as his own sovereign the Rāyar of Vijayanagar (all the Nāyakkas did so), and, as lord of the country he was governing, the Pāṇḍiyan king.

[2] *Comparative Grammar*, Introd., 145; *History of Tinnevelly*, pp. 52 *et seq.*

[3] According to the information given me there is at Teṅkāśi an inscription on a stone (I, 309) which mentions the name of Kāśi Kaṇḍa Parākrama Pāṇḍiyan and is dated in A.D. 1248. It is probable that the date has been wrongly quoted, or else that no king of that name reigned in the fifteenth century, as it is difficult to believe that the title *Kāśi Kaṇḍa* would have been prefixed to two sovereigns named *Parākrama*.

the Bishop could tell us which), by which it is clear that Ati Vīra Rāma died in A.D. 1610 and was succeeded by a SUNDARA PĀṆḌIYAN, of whom Dr. Burnell possessed a grant dated in his thirteenth year (A.D. 1623). Ati Vīra Rāma's name is one of those best known in the south of India, especially amongst the Tamiḻ races. He has immortalized himself as the greatest patron of Tamiḻ learning that ever lived, and his own poems are much quoted and admired.

Clashing with the above account, if the dates given me are accurate, are some inscriptions at Karivalam Vandanallūr (*see above*), whereby grants are recorded of VARATUṄGA RĀMA VĪRA PĀṆḌIYAN in A.D. 1578, 1589, and 1595 (Vol. I, p. 306).

According to a copper-plate inscription sent to me by the Collector of Madura (*see above*, p. 81, *No.* 211), which records a grant by one of the early Nāyakkas in A.D. 1596, Ati Vīra Rāma Pāṇḍiyan had a son RĀMĀBHI RĀMA.

Dr. Burnell's grant quoted above, however, mentions a son SUNDARA PĀṆḌIYAN as succeeding his father in A.D. 1610, and ruling till at least 1623.

It remains to be seen whether Pāṇḍiyan history can be continued further than this date. It would seem improbable, because the last semblance of royalty must have passed away from the ancient dynasty in the time of Tirumala Nāyakka of Madura (1623–1659) and his successors. But a great deal remains to be done, and for this purpose all the inscriptions must be examined and recorded with the most scientific exactitude. We do not yet know, for instance, whether the names above quoted refer to a continuous dynasty, or to chiefs claiming in various parts of the country as Pāṇḍiyans of the old stock, and possibly maintaining their local authority precariously by internecine struggles amongst themselves.

PUDUKŌṬṬAI, THE TOṆḌAMĀN MAHĀRĀJAS OF—

This State was created by Raghunātha Kilavan Setupati of Rāmnād (1673–1708 A.D.). He fell in love with a girl of the Kaḷḷan caste, married her, and appointed her brother chief of the district of Pudukōṭṭai, with the title of Raghunātha Toṇḍamān, in lieu of one Pallavarāyan Toṇḍamān, the former chief, who had attempted to transfer the estate from the Rāmnād territories to those of Tanjore. Pallavarāyan's predecessor was Śērvai. (Mr. Nelson's *Madura Country*, p. 206.) The following pedigree was kindly supplied to me by the Honorable A. Śeshayya Śāstrī, C.S.I., who says that he cannot guarantee the accuracy of the earlier portion. I give it for what it is worth.

Tirumala Toṇḍamān.
Namana Toṇḍamān.
Pachchai Toṇḍamān.
Tāṇḍaka Toṇḍamān.
Namana Toṇḍamān.
Tirumala Toṇḍamān.
Namana Toṇḍamān.
Pachchai Toṇḍamān.
Namana Toṇḍamān.
Pachchai Toṇḍamān.
Kiṅkiṇi Toṇḍamān.
Tāṇḍaka Toṇḍamān.
Tirumala Toṇḍamān.
Pachchai Toṇḍamān.
Rāya Toṇḍamān (*Pallava Rāya* ?).
Raghunātha Rāya Toṇḍamān,
(*about* 1680—1730 *A.D.*)
|
A son.
|

Vijaya Raghunātha Toṇḍamān, (1730—1767).	....
|	|
Rāya Raghunātha Toṇḍamān, (1767—1789).	**Rāya Vijaya Raghunātha,** "Rai Bahādur," (1789—1807).

Vijaya Raghunātha, "Rai Bahādur," (1807—1825).

Raghunātha Toṇḍamān, (1825—1839).

Rāmachandra Toṇḍamān, (*succeeded* 1839. *The present Mahārāja*).

PUṄGANŪR ZEMINDĀRI, THE—.

The following slight sketch of this family is taken from the *North Arcot District Manual*, by Mr. A. F. Cox, pages 235-6 :—

The earliest known member of the family was one Sītappa Gaunivāru, who, in the thirteenth century, settled in this part of the country and acquired large estates. In A.D. 1249 he built the town and fort of Suṅgatūr. In 1479 the head of the family, Timmappa Gaunivāru, built the town and fort of Kōlār. His son Immaḍi Timmayya succeeded, and, under Krishṇadeva Rāya of Vijayanagar, fought against the 'Ādil Shāhi Muḥammadans. In 1510 he built three more forts. His son was Chikkarāya Timmayya. He was honored by his sovereign and extended his possessions. He built Puṅganūr. His son Chikkarāya Basava was an infant when he succeeded. In 1639 the Muḥammadans captured the estate and seized a portion of it, but confirmed the Zemindar in the possession of the remainder, and gave him a sanad. His son Vīra Chikka Rāya was well-treated by the Muḥammadans, but the next Zemindar, Immaḍi Chikkarāya, was deprived of part of his estate for arrears of tribute. His son fought, under his liege lord the Navāb of Cuddapah, against the Mahrattas and was killed in battle. This was in 1757. The Mahrattas were victorious, and the zemindari passed into their hands. In 1775 it fell under Ḥaidar 'Alī. In 1780 the Zemindar fought on the side of his new sovereign, but died during the campaign. His son succeeded, but fled on being unable to pay his tribute. He then sided with the English, and proved of great assistance to them in their war against Tīpū Ṣultān. He and his successors were allowed, after Tīpū's fall, to hold their ancestral estate, but only as lessees. In 1832 the Zemindar died, and was succeeded by his brother, whose son is the present Zemindar.

PUNNĀḌU, RĀJAS OF—.

In his paper on a Rāshṭrakūṭa grant from Maisūr, published in *Indian Antiquary* XII, 11, Mr. Rice notices the mention, in the Markāra Plates, of the "Pūnāḍ Ten Thousand," forming part of the Rāshṭrakūṭa dominions. He writes as follows :—

"With regard to the Pūnāḍu Ten Thousand, it may be pointed out that it corresponds with the Padi-nāḍ, or Ten Nāḍ country of the sixteenth century (*Mysore Inscriptions, Yelandur Inscription, No.* 175). The name survives in the existing Hadināḍu, now corrupted into Hadināru, a village on the Kabbani river not far from its junction with the Kāverī, and the scene of the romantic adventure to which the royal family of Maisūr trace their origin. (*Wilks*; also *Mysore Gazetteer*, Vol. I, p. 239.)

"Pūnāḍu, Punnāḍu or Punnāṭa, as it is variously written, seems also to be indicated by the Pannuta in Lassen's Map of Ancient India according to Ptolemy (*Indische Alterthumskunde*, Vol. III) ; and by the Pannata of Colonel Yule's Map of Ancient India, '*ubi beryllus.*' (*Dr. Smith's Atlas of Ancient Geography.*)[1]

"Since writing the above, I have through the kindness of Mr. R. Sewell seen a grant of the Punnāṭa Rājas, which must belong to early in the sixth century. In it their succession is thus given :—

1. Kāśyappa Rāshṭravarmma.
2. Nāgadatta, his son.
3. Siṅga Varmma, son of the last.
4. His son, not named.
5. Skandāvarmma, son of the last.
6. Ravidatta, his son.

"The addition to the first name may point to a suzerainty of the Rāshṭrakūṭas. But from other inscriptions (*Indian Antiquary*, Vol. V, p. 140, Vol. VII, p. 175; *Mysore Inscriptions*, pp. 292, 295) we

---

[1] See Vol. I of this publication, p. 220, *s.v.* PADIYŪR.

know that in the time of Skandavarmma the Punnāḍ kingdom was annexed to the Gaṅga dominions by Avinīta, who married the king's daughter."

QUTB SHĀHI DYNASTY OF GOLKONḌA.

(*See* DAKHAṆ, Muḥammadan Kings of the—.)

RĀMNĀD,[1] SETUPATIS OF—.

The Setupatis claim to belong to the ancient Maṛava race and to have been rulers of the whole of the south of India before the immigration of the Kuṛumbas, by whom the Maṛavas were defeated and driven back to the extreme south. Their chiefs lost all semblance of power, till the descendant of the old ruling family was, in the seventeenth century, reinstated in a portion of his ancient patrimony by Muttu Kṛishṇappa, the Nāyakka of Madura, and installed at Rāmnād. Mr. Nelson (*Madura Country*, pp. 110—115) discusses the former history of the Setupatis, and his remarks should be studied. He concludes that there were certainly lords of Rāmnād from a very remote period, and that the Setupati created by Muttu Kṛishṇappa was probably grandson of the last Setupati, who had been murdered by "one of the last of the Pāṇḍiyas, who preceded Viśvanātha Nāyakkan." I have Dr. Burgess' authority for the statement that there was an Uḍaiyān Setupati in Ś.Ś. 1336 (A.D. 1414-15), who built the shrines of the inner temples at Rāmeśvaram and gave four villages in the Tinnevelly District to the temple there; also a Chinna Uḍaiyān Setupati, who in Ś.Ś. 1411 (A.D. 1489-90) made additions to the temple; and a Tirumala Setupati, who in Ś.Ś. 1422 (A.D. 1500-1) built part of the second *prākāra* and had a son named Raghunātha Tirumala, who was alive in Ś.Ś. 1461 (A.D. 1539-40).

Pharoah's *Gazetteer*, published in 1855, contains (pp. 392—396) an account of the later dynasty of Setupatis, varying in some degree from what follows, but I do not detail the differences, since the whole needs thorough examination.

Abandoning all attempt to trace their earlier history, the following genealogy gives a sketch of the family from the Setupati who was first created chief of Rāmnād by the Nāyakka of Madura in A.D. 1604. It is taken from various sources, principally from information given to other writers by native officials of the zemindari, and needs authentication.

The Setupatis had a coinage of their own.

---

[1] For an account of the province of Rāmnād, see *Madras Journal* V, 371.

.vay Setupati,
.
Madura on his
s adopted son
his successor.
y Tambi Tēvar

(*Illegitimate*).
"Tambi" Tēvar.
In Pharoah's Gazetteer this man is called "Bettana Naiker, generally called Tumbi."

(?)

Setuvattāyi Nāchchiyār, (*daughter*).

utta Tēvar, *alias* āra Muttu Vijaya .unātha Setupati. (1728—1734).
principality was dis-
vered, Śivagaṅgai and
country north of the
ār being split off.

i. Muttu Kumāra unātha Setupati, (1734—1747).
is death without issue,
second cousin Rākka
r was installed.

Āyi Piḷḷai Nāchchiyār, (*daughter*).

Pachchai Piḷḷai Nāchchiyār, (*daughter*).

xii. Rākka Tēvar Setupati. (1747—1748).
Deposed by the Dala-

Taṇḍar Tēvar.

Taṇḍar Tēvar, *married* Kuḷandai Nāchchiyār, sister of Kūtta Tēvar.

viii. Taṇḍar Tēvar Setupati, (1723—1724).
Was attacked by

I append extracts from the notes on the Setupatis, kindly sent to me by the manager of the estate, T. Rāja Rāma Rāu Avargaḷ. Mr. Nelson, in writing his "Madura Country," was indebted, it seems, to another native in high official position in Rāmnād for the statements he makes. And it must, therefore, be strongly pointed out that this list should be accepted with reservation. I do not know the authority on which my informant rests his assertions, nor does Mr. Nelson supply this vital deficiency. Dr. Burgess, who is at work at the inscriptions in the Rāmnād country, tells me that he believes the dates to be erroneous.

"It is observed that at the beginning of the sixteenth century there was no Setupati in existence. The cultivation had become very limited. Thick jungles had sprung up in every direction. The roads were infested with gangs of robbers. Every village was under a petty ruler, who acted with free independence and oppressed and harassed the pilgrims who resorted to Rāmēśvaram. Muttu Krishṇappa, the then ruler of Madura, was earnestly exhorted by the pilgrims to appoint a ruler, whose authority could conduce to their safe travel to and from Rāmēśvaram. Further, there was also the cessation of revenue collection from these petty chiefs to be attended to. Muttu Krishṇappa therefore thought it expedient to re-establish the ancient Marava dynasty of the Setupatis or the Guardians of Rāmēśvaram.[1] Accordingly he had Śaḍayaka Tēvar, a descendant of the ancient Setupati, crowned at Pogaḷūr, a village ten miles to the west of Rāmnād, in the year 1604. He was further created chief of the seventy-two Poḷegars. It is from this period that we have got some authentic history of the Setupatis."

1. Śaḍayaka Tēvar Uḍaiyān Setupati (1604—1621).—"He amply satisfied the expectations of Muttu Krishṇappa, to whom an annual tribute was sent. Peace was restored to the country. Cultivation was encouraged. The towns of Rāmnād and Pogaḷūr were fortified and improved. He further made some conquests by subduing the important villages of Vaḍakku-vaṭṭagai, Kāḷaiyārkōvil and Pattamaṅgalam. After a useful reign of seventeen years this prince died in 1621. His son, Kūttan Setupati, succeeded him."

2. Kūttan Setupati (1621—1635).—"This prince quietly enjoyed the fruits of his father's labour. The country was prosperous and peaceful during the fourteen years that he ruled over it. He died in 1635, leaving his brother Śaḍayaka Tēvar to succeed him. He left a sister named Gaṅgai Nāchchiyār." (*Mr. Nelson's "Madura Country,"* p. 128.)

3. Saḍayaka Tēvar *alias* Daḷavāy Setupati (1635—1645).—"Nothing of importance transpired during the first three years of this prince's reign. But in the fourth year the prince announced his intention of appointing his adopted son, Raghunātha Tēvar, as his successor. This disclosure enraged his illegitimate brother, Tambi Tēvar, who ruled over Kāḷaiyārkōvil as governor. Tambi was not inactive. He gained over to his side the King of Madura, who, besides creating him "Tambi Setupati," supplied him with funds and forces to dethrone the prince. Rāmnād fell into the hands of the King of Madura's forces, and the Daḷavāy Setupati retreated to Pāmban, where he was finally defeated and taken captive. He was sent to Madura and thrown into a dungeon.

"Tambi had now a very difficult task before him. The Daḷavāy Setupati's nephews, Raghunātha Tēvar and Nārāyaṇa Tēvar, were in arms against him, and at last, finding no one to befriend him among the relatives of the Setupati, Tambi was obliged to flee to the court of Madura." Tirumalai Nāyakka, however, now discovered his mistake, and in order to quiet the country released the Daḷavāy Setupati and restored him.

"The Setupati was set at liberty to the satisfaction of all parties in 1640. After his restoration he reigned for four or five years in peace, when he was murdered in cold blood by Tambi Tēvar in 1645.

"Then followed anarchy and confusion at Rāmnād. The principal Marava chiefs were preparing for war: but this was opportunely averted by the interference of Tirumalai Nāyakka, who partitioned the Rāmnād kingdom into three portions in 1646. Raghunātha Tēvar, the nephew of the Daḷavāy Setupati, was placed on the hereditary throne of the Rāmnād Setupati. His brothers, Tanaka Tēvar and Nārāyaṇa Tēvar, were made to rule jointly at Tiruvāḍānai. Śivagaṅgai was placed under the sovereignty of Tambi Tēvar."

4. Raghunātha Setupati *alias* Tirumalai Setupati (1645—1670).—"This Setupati's reign was remarkable for territorial aggrandisement. The partitioned countries became again incorporated owing to the early deaths of Tanaka Tēvar and Tambi Tēvar. When Tambi Tēvar was alive, the Setupati, in alliance with him, defeated the forces of Tanjore in a pitched battle, and the Setupati annexed the towns of Mannārkōvil, Paṭṭukkōṭṭai, Devakoṭṭai, Arundāṅgi and Tiruvāḷūr.

"At this time the King of Maisūr invaded Madura, and, at the request of the King of Madura, the Setupati went in command of a large army and defeated the enemy in two very severely contested

[1] Mr. Nelson's account ("*Madura Country*," 109-110) is similar to this.

engagements. The King of Madura, in gratitude for the services rendered, ceded to the Setupati the villages of Tiruppūvanam, Tiruchuḷai and Paḷḷimaḍai. On the whole this Setupati became very powerful. It was he who introduced the celebration of the Navarātrī festival at Rāmnād. After a quiet and beneficent reign of thirty years he died in 1670, leaving his nephew Rāja Sūrya Tēvar to succeed him."

Mr. Rāja Rāma Rāu omits to notice that this Setupati refused to aid his suzerain against the Muḥammadan invasion, and that, consequently, the Nāyakka invaded his territories to punish him for treason (*op. cit.* p. 187). The war was conducted with varying fortunes and seems to have died a natural death. The Setupati joined in the war, which ended in the downfall of the Nāyakkas of Tanjore and the sack of the city, but according to Mr. Nelson, the Maṛava army was little more than a marauding mob.

5. Sūrya Tēvar (1670).—This Setupati compromised himself in some way in the Tanjore war, and was seized shortly after his accession by Veṅkaṭa Krishṇappa, the Madura Daḷavāy, and was imprisoned at Trichinopoly, where he was secretly put to death.

"Sūrya Tēvar left no immediate heir to succeed him. Consequently the task of nominating a successor devolved on the principal Maṛava chiefs, who came to no definite understanding. For a time the country was without a Setupati, but Attana, and after him Chandrappa Śērvaikāran, managed the affairs of the kingdom. Finally Raghunātha Tēvar Kiḷavan, illegitimate son of the last Setupati, was installed."

6. Raghunātha Tēvar Kiḷavan Setupati (1673—1708).—"The reign of this ruler was very remarkable for several important events. The commencement of his reign was marked by his assassination of the two principal men who had assisted him in coming to the throne. His whole reign was further remarkable for the way in which he persecuted the Christians." The revolting circumstances attending the murder of the Missionary John DeBritto—a murder consummated under the express orders of the Setupati—are fully narrated by Mr. Nelson (*id.*, p. 217—224). "He appointed his brother-in-law Raghunātha (belonging to the Kaḷḷa family), whose sister Kattāri he had married, Toṇḍamān of Pudukōṭṭai.

"It was in this reign that the capital of the territory was removed from Pogaḷūr to Rāmnād, the present seat of Government. This prince was also famous for his bravery in war. He rescued the Nāyakka of Madura from the tyranny of Rustam-Khān, and successfully prosecuted a war against the King of Tanjore, who was obliged to cede all the territories south of the Āmbūri river."

Intrigues seem to have been the order of the day during this reign, and the history is a succession of plots and rebellions, resulting in constant disturbance and warfare. There was a desultory war with Tanjore in A.D. 1700, and in 1702 on one occasion an army from Madura, aided by a force from Tanjore, was defeated by the Setupati and driven back. Another signal victory was obtained over Tanjore in 1709, a year which was also signalized by a most appalling famine, aggravated by a desolating flood. "Raghunātha Tēvar Kiḷavan Setupati breathed his last in 1708 and his numerous wives burned themselves alive with the dead body of their husband. He was succeeded by his adopted son[1] Tiruvuḍaiya Tēvar *alias* Vijaya Raghunātha Tēvar, son of Kadamba Tēvar."

7. Vijaya Raghunātha Tēvar *alias* Tiruvuḍaiya Tēvar (1709—1723).—"The King of Tanjore was not inactive during this reign He gained over the Rāja of Pudukōṭṭai to his side, and declared war against the Setupati, who went out to meet the allied forces at Arundāṅgi. Some indecisive actions were fought. An epidemic broke out in the camp of the Setupati which carried off many of his sons and wives, and he himself contracted the disease, which proved fatal shortly after he was brought to Rāmnād. He nominated one Tāṇḍar Tēvar, a great grandson of the father of the late Kiḷavan Setupati, to be his successor."

8. Tāṇḍa Tēvar (1723-1724).—"The accession of this Setupati to the throne was contested by Bhavānī Śaṅkara Tēvar, an illegitimate son of Kiḷavan Setupati. He got the assistance of the King of Tanjore by promising to cede him some territory, and invaded Rāmnād with the Tanjore forces within four months of the accession of the Setupati. The allied forces of the Setupati, Toṇḍamān and the King of Madura were unable to arrest the advance of the Tanjore army, which finally captured Rāmnād and took the Setupati prisoner. He was shortly after put to death and Bhavānī Śaṅkara Tēvar proclaimed himself Setupati."

9. Bhavānī Śaṅkara Setupati (1724—1728).—"He was very injudicious in his treatment of the Poligars under him. One Śaśivarṇa Periya Uḍaiya Tēvar was deprived of his *Pāḷaiyam*. He therefore fled to the court of Tanjore. Śaśivarṇa gained the favour of the King of Tanjore by the extraordinary bravery he showed in fighting with a large tiger. Kūtta Tēvar,[2] the maternal uncle of the late Setupati and the legal heir, who had escaped from Rāmnād at the time of its capture by Bhavānī

[1] The relationship is somewhat doubtful (*Madura Country*, p. 247).

[2] Mr. Nelson calls him "Kattayadeva" (*Madura Country*, p. 249.)

Śaṅkara, was also at this time at Tanjore. Kūtta and Śaśivarṇa became close friends, and by their joint inducement got the King of Tanjore to entrust them with a large force, with which they defeated the Setupati at a battle fought at Uṛaiyūr in which the Setupati was taken prisoner. After this success Kūtta Tēvar was proclaimed Setupati."

10. KŪTTA TĒVAR, *alias* KUMĀRA MUTTU VIJAYA RAGHUNĀTHA SETUPATI (1728—1734).—"Kūtta Tēvar was not destined to rule over the extensive territories of Rāmnād. For it was arranged, before the success which gained him the throne, that the territory should be parcelled out between the confederates. Accordingly the King of Tanjore took all the lands north of the Pāmbār. The remainder was divided into five parts, of which two went to the share of Rāja Muttu Vijaya Raghunātha Periya Uḍaiya Tēvar, who made Śivagaṅgai his capital. (He married Akhilāṇḍiśvarī Nāchchiyār, the illegitimate daughter of the Setupati. His territory is also called *Śinnavāḍagai*). Over the remaining three parts called *Periyavāḍagai*, which form the present Rāmnād territory, the Setupati Kūtta Tēvar ruled. He was succeeded by his son Muttu Kumāra Vijaya Raghunātha Tēvar."[1]

11. MUTTU KUMĀRA VIJAYA RAGHUNĀTHA SETUPATI (1734—1747).—"During the reign of this prince the Daḷavāy was all-powerful. The prince dying in the prime of his life without any issue, the Daḷavāy nominated Rākka Tēvar, a cousin of the deceased Kūtta Tēvar, to the rule."

12. RĀKKA TĒVAR SETUPATI (1747-1748).—"This reign was remarkable for the repulsion of an invasion by the Rāja of Tanjore by the Daḷavāy Veḷḷaiyan Śērvaikāran, who also commanded several military expeditions and subjugated several insubordinate Poḷegars in the Tinnevelly District. The Setupati grew afraid of the Daḷavāy's power and recalled him from Tinnevelly. This step proved fatal to him. On his return the Daḷavāy openly rebelled, and the Setupati was therefore obliged to flee for his safety to Pāmban. Thither he was pursued and taken prisoner and was deposed. One Śella Tēvar, *alias* Vijaya Raghunātha Tēvar, a member of the Kiḷavan family, was placed on the throne by the Daḷavāy."

13. ŚELLA TĒVAR, *alias* VIJAYA RAGHUNĀTHA SETUPATI (1748—1760).—"This prince ruled for twelve years, during which another invasion by the Tanjore Rāja was firmly met with and defeated by the Daḷavāy. Śella Tēvar died in 1760 and was succeeded by his sister's son Muttu Rāmaliṅga Tēvar, a child two months' old."

Dr. Burgess informs me, on the authority of the best informed men at Rāmeśvaram, that Śella Tēvar's sister Muttu Tiruvāy Nāchchiyār, married Neriñji Tēvar of Yelambāḍu, and had a son born in Ś.Ś. 1647 (A.D. 1725-6). He adds that she is stated to have ruled from Ś.Ś. 1643 (A.D. 1721-2).

14. MUTTU RĀMALIṄGA SETUPATI (1760—1772, 1780—1794).—"Veḷḷaiyan Śērvaikāran, the powerful Daḷavāy, died at the commencement of this reign. He was succeeded by Dāmōdaram Piḷḷai in his Daḷavāyship. Muttu Tiruvāy Nāchchiyār, the mother of the infant prince, acted as regent."

Mr. Nelson adds, "In 1770 the Rāja of Tanjore was again defeated, this time most decisively, by an army under the command of Thomōtharam (*Dāmōdaram*) Piḷḷai: and this was the last occasion on which the troops of Rāmnād were permitted to distinguish themselves."

"In the year 1773 the army of the Setupati was defeated by an English force under general Joseph Smith, who subdued the territory on behalf of the Navāb of Trichinopoly. The infant Setupati, his mother Muttu Tiruvāy Nāchchiyār and his sister Maṅgaliśvari Nāchchiyār were removed from Rāmnād and kept at Trichinopoly under surveillance."

"The territory was for a period of eight years, *i.e.*, from 1773—1780, under the direct management of the Navāb.

"The petty chiefs who had respected the power of the Setupati raised an army and threatened to capture Rāmnād and drive away the Navāb's managers. This circumstance alarmed the Navāb, who deemed it prudent to set the Setupati at liberty and to despatch him to Rāmnād at the head of an army: this arrangement had the desired effect. The country became tranquil and the chiefs were defeated.

"The Setupati resumed again the reins of government. He continued to rule for fourteen years until 1794. His acts at the end of this period became very suspicious, verging on rebellion, so that at the instance of Maṅgaḷiśvarī Nāchchiyār, the sister, the Setupati was deposed and carried away as prisoner to Trichinopoly under the orders of the Navāb.

"The English at this time became the virtual rulers of the Carnatic, and they sent the Setupati to Madras as a State prisoner. The Rāmnād territory was taken under the British rule and continued for seven years up to 1802. In 1803 the English Government placed Rāṇī Maṅgaḷīśvarī Nāchahiyār, the sister of the Setupati, on the throne."

---

[1] Mr. Nelson gives different dates for the death of Kūtta Tēvar and the reigns of his successors. According to him Kūtta Tēvar died in 1752, his son died after a reign of a few days or weeks, and Rākka Tēvar succeeded.

15. Maṅgaliśvarī Nāchchiyār (1803—1812).—"In the year 1803 the permanent settlement was made, by which the Rāṇī Setupati bound herself and her successors to pay to the English Government the annual pēshkash of Rs. 3,24,387-1-2. She ruled the estate for ten years. She was called the Istimrāri Zamīndārṇī in remembrance of the settlement. This reign is particularly remarkable for the charitable endowments she made out of the permanently settled villages of the estate. Her adopted son, Aṇṇāsvāmi Setupati, *alias* Muttu Vijaya Raghunātha Setupati, succeeded her."

16. Aṇṇāsvāmi Setupati, *alias* Muttu Vijaya Raghunātha Setupati (1812—1815).—"This prince was a minor when his adoptive mother died. Pradhāni Tyāga Rāja Piḷḷai carried on the administration of the country. This prince's title, in other words the adoption, was not undisputed. Śivakāmī Nāchchiyār, the daughter of Muttu Rāmaliṅga Setupati, sued in the Company's courts to have her claim to become Rāṇī Setupati in preference to Aṇṇāsvāmi recognised. She succeeded in her suit and was legally appointed the ruler of the estate in the room of Aṇṇāsvāmi in the year 1815."

17. Śivakāmī Nāchchiyār (1815—1829).—"This princess enjoyed the kingdom for one full year while she allowed the pēshkash to fall in arrears. The estate, therefore, was placed under the management of the Court of the Sadar Adālat for fourteen years on her behalf. In the interval the law suit between the Rāṇī Zemindar and Aṇṇāsvāmi Setupati was prosecuted with the utmost vigour in the Appellate Court, which finally directed the restoration of the estate to Aṇṇāsvāmi Setupati. This prince having died in the meanwhile, his widow Muttu Vīrāyi Nāchchiyār, who successfully conducted the suit to the end, had adopted one Rāmasvāmi Tēvar as her son, in whose favour she resigned her right to become Setupati."

18. Rāmasvāmi Tēvar, *alias* Vijaya Raghunātha Rāmasvāmi Setupati (1829).—"This prince died in the same year in which he commenced to reign and was succeeded by his infant daughter Maṅgaliśvarī Nāchchiyār."

19. Maṅgaliśvarī Nāchchiyār (1829—1838).—"Muttu Vīrāyi Nāchchiyār, the Rāṇī's grandmother, and Muttu Śella Tēvar managed the affairs of the State on behalf of the Rāṇī Setupati, who met with an early death. She was succeeded by her infant sister Dorai Rāja Nāchchiyār."

20. Dorai Rāja Nāchchiyār (1838—1845).—"Muttu Śella continued to act as manager, but his management was not approved by the East India Company, to whom several charges against the manager were preferred. The estate was placed under the Court of Wards, and although the manager was declared innocent after a thorough inquiry, he was not entrusted with the control of the estate, which continued under the management of the Court of Wards. Dorai Rāja Nāchchiyār died in 1845. Even after the death of the Rāṇī the Court of Wards continued to govern the estate until Parvatavardhinī Nāchchiyār, the wife of Rāmasvāmi Setupati, was declared to be the lawful proprietress to the estate."

21. Parvatavardhinī Nāchchiyār (1845—1868.)—"She assumed the management of the estate in 1846. She died in 1868, leaving her adopted son, Muttu Rāmaliṅga Setupati, to succeed her. During her management there were several protracted litigations which necessarily involved the estate in heavy debt. Even the pēshkash fell into arrears and accumulated. Ponnusvāmi Tēvar, the son of the adopted Setupati, managed the estate."

22. Muttu Rāmaliṅga Setupati (1868—1873).—"When this prince assumed the management of the estate, he found the debts of the estate had alarmingly increased. But he could devise no means to get himself out of it. The estate was in danger. The English Government, therefore, was compelled to interfere. The estate was placed under the attachment of a Special Assistant Collector. In the year 1873 the Setupati died suddenly, leaving two minor sons, Bhāskara Setupati and Dinakarasvāmi Tevar. The former in now recognised as the proprietor of the estate."

23. Bhāskara Setupati (1873).—This prince being a minor, the estate is under the management of the Court of Wards.

RÂSHṬRAKÛṬAS,[1] THE—.

The latest and best account of this dynasty yet published is by Mr. Fleet at pages 31—38 of his *Dynasties of the Kanarese District*. From it I extract most of what follows. Dr. Bühler (see especially *Ind. Ant.* VI, p. 59, &c.) has carefully studied the records of this family; and Dr. Burgess gives an account of them in his Third Archæological Report for Bombay, published in 1878. A paper by Professor Shaṅkar Pandurang Paṇḍit published in *Ind. Ant.* I, 205, may be studied with advantage.

The Rāshṭrakūṭas, coming from the north, subverted the older dynasty of the Chalukyas in the Kanarese districts of the Bombay Presidency in the early part or middle of the eighth century A.D.

[1] Sometimes called "*Yādavas of Mānyakheta*" (*Ind. Ant.* I, 205).

The kings of this dynasty did not come much into contact with those of the south, but, as they are occasionally met with, the genealogy of the family is here given :—

1. Dantivarmā I.

2. Indra I.

3. Govinda I,
about A.D. 660.

4. Karka I *or* Kakka I,
about A.D. 685.

5. Indra II,
about A.D. 710.

6. Dantidurga[1]
or Dantivarmā II,
A.D. 753-4.

7. Kṛishṇa I,[2]
about A.D. 756.

8. Govinda II,[3]
about A.D. 765.
(*Dethroned by Dhruva*).

9. Dhruva,
Dhora, Nirupama I, *or* Dhārāvarsha,
A.D. 770.

10. Govinda III,[4]
Prabhūtavarsha,
Jagattuṅga I,
or Vallabhanarendra I,
A.D. 803-4 *and* 807-8.

1. Indra III,
(*King of Gujarāt*).

2. Karka II,
(Kakka II), *or*
Suvarṇavarsha I,
A.D. 812-3.
(*In Gujarāt*).

3. Govinda IV,
or Prabhūta-
varsha II,
A.D. 827.
(*In Gujarāt*).

11. Amoghavarsha I,
A.D. 851-2 *and* 877-8.
(*Dr. Burgess says A.D.* 810.)

12. Kṛishṇa II, *or* Akālavarsha,
A.D. 875 *and* 911.
(*Dr. Burgess says A.D.* 835.)
Married Mahādevī, daughter of Kokkala,
of the family of the Kaḷachuris of Tripura.

13. Jagattuṅga II,
married Lakshmī, daughter of
Raṇavigraha, son of Kokkala.

By his wife Lakshmī.
14. Indra IV,
or Nityavarsha,
married Dvijāmbā, daughter of
Ammana, son of Arjuna, son of
the same Kokkala.

(*Not named.*)

15. Govinda V,
Suvarṇavarsha II, *or*
Vallabhanarendra II,
A.D. 933-4.

By his wife Govindāmbā.

16. Kṛishṇa III.[5]

17. Amoghavarsha II,[5]
Married Kundakadevī, daughter
of Yuvarāja of the family of the
Kaḷachuris of Tripura.

18. Koṭṭiga, *or* Khoṭṭiga,
or Nityavarsha II.[5]

19. Kṛishṇa IV, Kannara,
Nirupama II, *or*
Akālavarsha II,
A.D. 945-6 *and* 956-7.

---

[1] Called "Vairamegha" in an inscription published by Mr. Lewis Rice in *Ind. Ant.* XII, 11.
[2] Called "Akalavarsha" and "Kannesvara" in the same. [3] Called "Prabhūtavarsha" in the same.
[4] He was reigning in *Śaka* 735 (A.D. 813-4) according to the same inscription.
[5] Mr. Fleet is doubtful whether these three persons ever came to the throne, because the interval between Govinda V and Krishna IV is so small. But a succession of three kings in a very short space of time is not an unusual occurrence in Indian history.

20. Kakka III,
(Karka III), Kakkala, Karkara,
Amoghavarsha III,
or Vallabhanarendra III,
A.D. 972-3.

(*Daughter*)
21. Jākabbe
or Jākalādevī,
(*married to the Western Chālukya king, Taila II*).

Dantivarmā II is said to have conquered, amongst other kings and countries, the kings of Kañchī and Kaliṅgā, and the Śrīśaila country (*Ind. Ant.* XI, 111).

King Dhruva is said to have humbled the pride of the Pallavas.

His successor, Govinda III, in an inscription of A.D. 803-4, boasts of having conquered Dantiga, the ruler of Kañchī (Conjeeveram). The boast is repeated in other inscriptions, "which tell us also that the ruler of Veṅgī, *i.e.*, his contemporary of the Eastern Chālukya family, was one of his vassals, and was employed to build for him the high walls of a town or fortress." The Chālukyan sovereign would seem to be Vijayāditya, *alias* "Narendra Mṛigarāja." The inscription of A.D. 803-4 contains the earliest known instance of the use of the cycle of 60 years, which grew into common use from the fourteenth century downwards. The inscription is dated in the year *Subhānu.*

The twentieth sovereign Kakka III claims to have subdued the Chola and Pāṇḍiyan kings, but this is probably mere empty boasting, as in A.D. 973-4 he himself was defeated and probably slain by Taila II of the Western Chālukyas. The Rāshṭrakūṭa dynasty ceased with him.

RAṬṬAS, THE—.

The Raṭṭa *Mahāmaṇḍaleśvaras*, or great feudatory lords, are often alluded to in inscriptions of the Kanarese districts of the Bombay Presidency, but do not appear to have come much in contact with the southern chiefs. Their capital was first Saundatti, then called *Sugandharvarti* in the Belgaum District, and afterwards *Venugrāma* or *Velugrāma*, the modern Belgaum itself. They were at first feudatories of the Rāshṭrakūṭas, but afterwards raised themselves into the condition of independent chiefs. They were of the Jain religion. Grants of the family are found dated between the years A.D. 875-6 and A.D. 1228-9. They seem to have succumbed to the rising power of the Yādavas of Devagiri, as recorded in the Behatti grant of Kṛishṇa of that dynasty, dated Ś.Ś. 1175 (A.D. 1253–4). (For genealogy and account of the family, see Mr. J. F. Fleet's *Dynasties of the Kanarese Districts*, pp. 79—83, and Dr. Burgess' Second Bombay Archæological Report, 1876, *Kāṭhiāwāḍ and Kachh*, p. 232.)

REḌḌI, THE — DYNASTY OF KOṆḌAVĪḌU.

(*See* Koṇḍavīḍu.)

ŚĀLAṄKĀYANA, THE — DYNASTY OF VEṄGĪ.

(*See* Veṅgī.)

SAṄGA, THE — DYNASTY.

(*See* the Andhra Dynasty.)

THE ŚĀNTARA KINGS IN MAISŪR.

This was a family of chiefs, apparently feudatories of the Chālukyas, who lived at Hombucha or Humcha (*Paṭṭi Pombuchchapura*) in the Nagar Country of Maisūr. They were Jains. Mr. Lewis Rice gives the following list in his "*Mysore Inscriptions*" (*Introduction*, p. lxix):—

Śāntara, Śāntarēśvara, *several kings of this name.*
Kāmana.
Siṅgideva.
Taila.
Kāma (married Bijjalādevī. Her sister Chaṭṭalādevī was married to Vijayādityadeva of the Kādamba family of Goa).
Jagadeva, Jagaddeva, Tribhuvana Malla (*son*), A.D. 1149.
Siṅgideva, *his brother.*
Bammarasa, *his son.*

An inscription of A.D. 1162-3 at Anumakoṇḍa, close to Oraṅgal, of the Gaṇapati sovereign Kākatīya Rudradeva, records that in the time of the Gaṇapati sovereign Prōlē, Jagaddeva besieged that place, but was repulsed and put to flight. Mr. Fleet (*Ind. Ant.* XI, 10) thinks that this is evidently the Śāntara king Jagaddeva, and that it was as a feudatory of Taila of the Western Chālukyas that he laid siege to Anumakoṇḍa.

SENDRAKAS, THE—.

"One of the Kadamba inscriptions mentions incidentally" the dynasty of the Sendrakas, "the representative of which in the time of the Kadamba King Harivarmā,[1] was Bhānuśakti. But all else that we at present know for certain about this dynasty is that, in the time of the Western Chalukya king Vikramāditya I, the representative of it was Devaśakti, who seems to have been a feudatory of the Chalukya monarch;[2] and that in the time of Vinayāditya, the son of Vikramāditya I, the representative of it was Pogilli, who again appears to have been a feudatory of the Chalukyas."[3] (Mr. Fleet's *Dynasties of the Kanarese Districts*, p. 10.)

The dates of these Sendraka kings would be about the close of the fifth century and the close of the sixth century.

SETUPATIS OF RĀMNĀD, THE—.

(*See* Rāmnād.)

THE ŚILĀHĀRAS OF KOLHĀPUR.

From Mr. Fleet's sketch of the history of this family (*Dynasties of the Kanarese Districts*, pp. 98—106) I do not gather that, so far as is yet known, they ever came in contact with the powers in the south; but as it is quite possible that they may have done so, and that some reference to them may yet be discovered in some inscriptions of the Southern Dakhaṇ, I give the genealogy as given by Mr. Fleet. His work should be consulted for a fuller notice of the family and an able discussion as to the site of the ancient city of *Tagara* mentioned in Ptolemy and the *Periplus*. (See also *Ind. Ant.* V, 276.)

Jatiga I.
|
Nāyivarmā
or Nayimma.
|
Chandrarāja.
|
Jatiga II.
|

---

[1] His date is not yet conclusively settled (see above, p. 179).
[2] *Ind Ant.*, Vol. X, p. 244, "No. 12." See also above, p. 16, No. 100, Copper-plate Grant from Kurnool.
[3] *Pali, Sanskṛit and Old Canarese Inscriptions*, No. 152.

Goṅka, Goṅkala, Gokala, *or* Gokalla. — Guvala I *or* Guhala. — Kīrttirāja. — Chandrāditya.

Goṅka, Goṅkala, Gokala, *or* Gokalla.
- Mārasiṁha, (*A.D.* 1058).
  - Guvala II.
  - Gaṅgadeva.
  - Bhoja I, (*about A.D.* 1098).
  - Ballāḷa.
  - Gandarāditya, (*A.D.* 1109 *and* 1135).
    - Vijayāditya *or* Vijayārka, (*A.D.* 1142 *and* 1153).
      - Bhoja II, (*A.D.* 1178 *and* 1209).

SINDAS OF ERAMBARAGE, THE—.

The information which follows is also taken from Mr. Fleet's *Dynasties of the Kanarese Districts*, (pp. 95—97).

Inscriptions of the Sinda dynasty are found in the Kalāḍgi and Dhārwāḍ Districts. Their capital was Erambarage or Erambarige, probably 'Yelburga' in the Nizam's Dominions. Their territory embraced a small portion of the country in that neighbourhood.

The following is the genealogy of the dynasty :—

(*Not named.*)
- Āchugi I.
  - Bamma.
  - Siṅga II.
    - Āchugi II, (*A.D.* 1098? *and* 1122.)
      - Permādi I, (*A.D.* 1104 *and* 1144).
      - Chavunda II *or* Chāvunda II, (*A.D.* 1162).
        - *By his wife Demaladevī.*
          - Āchugi III, (*A.D.* 1162).
          - Permādi II.
        - *By his wife Siriyādevī.*
          - Bijjala. (*A.D.* 1169).
          - Vikrama, *or* Vikramāditya, (*A.D.* 1169 *and* 1180).
- Nāka.
- Siṅga I *or* Siṁha.
- Dāsa.
- Dāma *or* Dāva.
- Chavunda I, Chāvunda I *or* Chaunda.
- Chāva.

Āchugi II made war on the Hoysala Ballāḷas under orders of his suzerain, Vikramāditya VI of the Western Chālukyas. He was victorious and took Goa ("Gove"). He "caused the Pāṇḍyas to retreat, dispersed the Malapas, or people of the Western Ghauts, and seized upon the Konkana." He burnt Goa and "Uppinakatti" (? Uppinaṅgaḍi in South Canara).

Permāḍi I is recorded to have "pursued Jayakesi, who must be the second of that name of the family of the Kādambas of Goa, and seized upon the royal power of the Hoysalas." He seems to have defeated King Bittiga or Vishṇuvardhana of the latter dynasty, and besieged his capital city, Dvārasamudra.

ŚIVAGAṄGAI ZEMINDARS.

The Śivagaṅgai Zemindari was originally part and parcel of the territories of the Setupatis of Rāmnād, for a sketch of whose dynasty see above (p. 227). It will there be found that in the reign of Kūtta Tēvar, *alias* Kumāra Muttu Vijaya Raghunātha Setupati (1728—1734), the territories of Rāmnād were divided into five parts, two of which went to Śaśivarṇa, *alias* Muttu Vijaya Raghunātha Periya Uḍaiyār Tēvar. This became the Śivagaṅgai Zemindari. It is called the *Śinna Vāḍagai* by the natives, and the "Lesser Maṛavar" by some European writers.

The zemindari being quite of modern origin, it is useless to give a sketch of its ruling family here. Readers are referred for information to pages 423—427 of "Pharoah's Gazetteer."

TANJORE, THE MAHRATTA DYNASTY OF—.

(*See* MAHRATTAS.)

TRAVANCORE (TIRUVARAṄKŌḌU), RĀJAS OF—.

(The following list is taken mostly from Mr. P. Shungoonny Menon's "*History of Travancore.*")

The family are said to be descendants of the old Chera Rājas, who owned the south and west of the peninsula. Other accounts make them descendants of Chēramān Perumāḷ.

Mr. Shungoonny Menon's history traces the family from a Chera king, Bhānu Vikrama, whom the mythological *Paraśu Rāma* placed on the throne of South Keraḷa after it had been recovered from the sea.[1] *Paraśu Rāma* is said to have crowned Bhānu Vikrama's nephew, Āditya Vikrama, in succession to his uncle, and to have made Uḍaiyavarmā king of North Keraḷa. This was in the *Tretāyuga.* In the *Kaliyuga* a list of forty-eight kings is given who reigned over South Keraḷa during the first ten centuries, *i.e.,* up to 2102 B.C. Mention is made of a sovereign, by name Kulaśekhara Āṛvār, in *Kaliyuga* 1860 (1242 B.C.), who became an ascetic, and has since been worshipped as a saint; and coming to comparatively modern times, Vīravarmā Pāṇḍiyan of Madura is said to have conquered and ruled over the Chera country at the time of the reign of Śālivāhana (A.D. 78). The Chera country was afterwards overrun by the Koṅgu chiefs [2] and the Chera royal family retired to their original home in Travancore (South Keraḷa), giving up their extensive acquisitions in Madura and Tinnevelly.

The Perumāḷs ruled over most of the Keraḷa country for about 200 years, during which period the Syrian Christians and Jews settled in Cochin. The last Perumāḷ is said to have disappeared from his residence after having handed over his insignia of office to two dependents, whom he constituted respectively Rāja of Cochin and Zamorin of Calicut. (*See above*, p. 197.)

All the above is purely traditionary. Now commences a list, seemingly more reliable, but requiring proof.

(?)

Vīra Mārtāṇḍavarmā, *was alive in A.D.* 731. — ~~~~~~

~~~~~~ *Died in A.D.* 800. — ~~~~~~ Uḍaiya Mārtāṇḍavarmā, (A.D. 800–830). *Established the Kollam era in A.D.* 824.

Little more is known for five centuries, and the author's remarks, as he attempts to bridge the interval, show a lamentable want of historical knowledge. A king named Ādityavarmā is mentioned as living in A.D. 1189, and another of the same name in A.D. 1330.

---

[1] Probably the Bāṇa Perumāḷ of the *Keraḷolpati* (see above, p. 196).

[2] All Chera grants of any age commence with the phrase "*Śrī Vīra Keraḷa Chakravarti*" or "*Chēra Maṛavan Tribhuvana Chakravarti,*" while the Koṅgu grants commence "*Śrī Vīra Rāya Chakravarti.*" (*History of Travancore*, 31.)
~~~~~~

Then come the following, belonging to a branch of the family :—

(?)

- **Vīra Rāma Mārtāṇḍa**, (A.D. 1335–1376). *Built Trevandrum palace and fort.*
- ~~~~~
  - **Keraḷa Varmā**, (A.D. 1382). *Died after three months. He was called "Kulaśekhara Perumāḷ."*
  - **Chera Uḍaiya Mārtāṇḍavarmā**, *twin brother of Keraḷavarmā*, (1382–1444). *Resided at Chēra-mā-dēvī (Shermadevi), where an inscription of his, in 1439, exists.*
- **Eravivarmā**, (A.D. 1376–1382).

Now follows a list of kings, without any relationship given :—

	A.D.
Vanavanāḍ Mūtta Rāja	1444—1458
Vīra Mārtāṇḍavarmā	1458—1471
Ādityavarmā	1471—1478
Eravivarmā	1478—1504
Mārtāṇḍavarmā	1504
Vīra Eravivarmā	1504—1528
Mārtāṇḍavarmā	1528—1537
Uḍaiya Mārtāṇḍavarmā	1537—1560
Keraḷavarmā	1560—1563
Ādityavarmā	1563—1567
Uḍaiya Mārtāṇḍavarmā	1567—1594
Vīra Eravivarmā	1594—1604
Vīravarmā	1604—1606
Ravivarmā	1606—1619
Unni Keraḷavarmā	1619—1625
Ravivarmā	1625—1631
Unni Keraḷavarmā	1631—1661
Ādityavarmā	1661—1677

The last Ādityavarmā and his male relatives were murdered, and his niece Umayamma Rāṇī became regent in 1677 A.D. In 1680 occurred a Muḥammadan inroad and their leader established himself at Trevandrum, but was driven out and killed by the regent's general, Keraḷavarmā, a member of the royal house. The regent's son, attaining his majority, was crowned A.D. 1684.

Umayamma Rāṇī, *Regent*, (1677–1684).

- **Ravivarmā**, (1684–1718). *Adopted the Rāja of Kolatnāḍ's relatives, two brothers, viz.* :—
  - **Unni Keraḷavarmā**, (1718–1724).
  - **Rāmavarmā**, (1724–1728). *Acknowledged the Madura Nāyakka as his suzerain in* 1726.

This chief was succeeded by Mārtāṇḍavarmā, the son of a Rāṇī of Kolatnāḍ, adopted into the Travancore family by Ravivarmā.

Mārtāṇḍavarmā,
(1728–1758).
War with the Dutch East India Company and treaty with them. Also with the Muhammadan Navāb at Trichinopoly.

Rāmavarmā,
(1758–1798).
War with Māphuz Khān and with Tīpu Sultān, and alliance with English against the latter.

Balarāmavarmā,
(1798–1810).
A British Resident appointed. Constant disturbances.

Two sisters were adopted, viz.:—

Rāṇī Gauri Lakshmī Bhāy,
(1810–1815).

Gauri Pārvatī Bhāy,
Regent,
(1815–1829).

Rāmavarmā,
Minor (1815–1829).
Ruled 1829–1847.

Mārtāṇḍavarmā,
(1847–1860).

Rukmaṇī Bhāy.

Rāmavarmā,
(1860–1880).

Rāmavarmā.
The present Rāja, from 17th June 1880.

The succession in this family takes place entirely in the female line.

TONḌAMĀN, THE—FAMILY.

(See PUDUKŌṬṬAI.)

UḌAIYĀRS OF THE CHOḶA COUNTRY.

(See CHOḶA.)

VARAṄGAL, SOVEREIGNS OF—.

(See the GAṆAPATIS of Oraṅgal.)

VEṄGĪ, KINGS OF THE—COUNTRY.

The Veṅgī kingdom, that is the country lying between the Krishṇā and Godāvarī rivers and extending from the sea to a distance inland at present not known but apparently not very great, was ruled by the Pallavas (*see* p. 212) till the dynasty was subverted by Kubja Vishṇuvardhana of the Chālukya family about the year A.D. 605. It is not yet quite certain whether the Veṅgī kingdom was independent or merely a province of the kingdom of Kañchī, but the evidence would seem to show that the latter was the case. We find the Pallava sovereign of Kañchī, Siṁhavarmā II, about the fifth or sixth century,[1] granting in his eighth year the village of Māṅgaḍūr in Veṅgorāshṭra (the Veṅgī province) to a Brāhman.[2]

The capital of the Veṅgī country seems to have been Vēgi or Pedda Vēgi, a few miles north of Ellore in the Godāvarī District.[3] Dr. Burnell speaks of Veṅgī as an independent kingdom, governed by a dynasty of Śālaṅkāyanas, and attributes a grant published by Mr. Fleet [4] and containing the

---

1 He was one of the last of a family ascribed by Dr. Burnell on palæographic evidence to "the fifth or sixth century."
2 *Indian Antiquary* V, 154.
3 *South-Indian Palæography*, p. 16, *note* 1.
4 *Indian Antiquary* V, 175, &c.; *South-Indian Palæography*, pp. 14—16, and plate xxiv.

names of the sovereign, Vijaya Chaṇḍavarmā, and his son Vijaya Nandivarmā, to the fifth century A.D. He thinks that the origin of the kingdom "does not probably go back beyond the second century A.D." Mr. Fleet mentions a second inscription examined by him, which contains the names apparently of the same Vijaya Nandivarmā and his son "Vijaya Tuṅgavarmā" or "Vijaya Buddhavarmā."

Shortly after the Chālukyas had subverted the Veṅgī dynasty the country was visited by Hiwen-Thsang, who calls the kingdom "An-ta-lo" (Andhra), and the capital city "Ping-ki-lo," which Dr. Burnell ingeniously translated into "Veṅgī" with the Telugu suffix *lō* added to it by mistake on the part of the traveller.

A grant of Govinda III of the Rāshṭrakūṭa dynasty [1] speaks of the Eastern Chalukya sovereign in A.D. 807 as "Lord of Veṅgī" and states that he came and worked for the Rāshṭrakūṭa king as a servant.

An inscription of a later date on a pillar at Amarāvatī, unfortunately mutilated, gives a number of names of kings which may be those of a Veṅgī dynasty, but the context is doubtful. The names are "Siṁhavarmā," "Siṁhavishṇu," "Nandivarmā," "Siṁhavarmā II," "Arkavarmā," "Ugravarmā," "Mahendravarmā." The names also of "Sūra" and "Pallava" occur.

VEṄKAṬAGIRI.

The present estate of Veṅkaṭagiri lies in the district of Nellore. I am unable as yet to give any reliable dates, but the following table is compiled from a pamphlet published in Madras in 1875 by T. Rāma Rāu Avargal, a Vakeel of the High Court.

Chavvi Reḍḍi.
A Vellama of Anamagallu; discovered an immense buried treasure. Was patronized by Kākatīya Gaṇapati Rāja of Oraṅgal, who died A.D. 1257? *Chavvi Reḍḍi was also called Bhētāla Nāyuḍu.*

- Dāma Nāyuḍu. *Was granted the family device of the Gaṇḍa-bheruṇḍa by the Oraṅgal king. Married Jayamādevī.*
  - Vennama Nāyuḍu. *Married Pāchamādēvī.*
    - Yerra Dācha Nāyuḍu. *Fought with Immaḍi Rāja of Kuṇtlur at Gollapalle and defeated him. Was sent by Pratāpa Rudra II of Oraṅgal (A.D.* 1292—1323) *against the Pāṇḍiyans, who had conquered Conjeeveram, and was successful. Upheld the kingdom of "Tirukkala Rāja."*
      - Siṅgam Nāyuḍu. *A bold warrior; was protected by Pratāpa Rudra II.*
      - Vennama Nāyuḍu.
      - Yāchama Nāyuḍu.
  - Sabbi Nāyuḍu.
- Prasāditya Nāyuḍu. *Became powerful at the Court of Oraṅgal, and, on the death of Gaṇapati Rāja* (1257 *A.D.*?), *raised Rudramma to the throne of the Gaṇapatis, himself having chief power.*
- Rudra Nāyuḍu.

---

[1] *Indian Antiquary* XI, 126.

Anapōta Nāyuḍu.
Defeated a combination of "Chalukya kings," i.e., *Reḍḍi Poḷegars and others of that caste. Won a great battle against* 101 *chiefs in the year Śārvari, which the author asserts to be A.D.* 1300. *This seems impossible; more probably* 1360 *if the story is true.*

Māda Nāyuḍu.
Made additions to the Śrīśailam temple. Killed Anapōtā Reḍḍi, a relative of Anavēma Reḍḍi of Koṇḍavīḍu (1339—1369 *A.D.*)

Pedda Vedagiri Nāyuḍu.
Defeated Satyakadeva, Kaṅkaladeva, and Kannaḍadeva, chiefs of the north. Also "Chālukya Dora," or "the Chālukya chief." (This line failed in the fourth generation from him.)

Pedda Siṅgama Nāyuḍu.

Dharma Nāyuḍu.

Timma Nāyuḍu.

Annamma Nāyuḍu.
Killed at Gundikōṭa. No issue.

Chinna Siṅgama Nāyuḍu.
(This line failed after two generations.)

Dharma Nāyuḍu.
(Line failed.)

Chitti Dāsa Nāyuḍu.

Anapōtā Nāyuḍu.
His relative in the elder line, Siṅgama Nāyuḍu, grandson of Chinna Siṅgama Nāyuḍu, was contemporary with Prauḍhadeva of Vijayanagar (1456-1477?).

Pedda Māda Nāyuḍu.
(Line failed with his son.)

Chinna Māda Nāyuḍu.

Yerra Sūra Nāyuḍu.

Mādhava or Māda Nāyuḍu.
(No issue.)

Yāchama Nāyudu.

Chinna Siṅgama Nāyuḍu.

Nirvāṇa Rāyappa Nāyuḍu, *or* **Pedda Rāyappa Nāyuḍu.**

Siṅgama Nāyuḍu.
(Line failed after four generations. Little is known of them.)

Kumāra Timma Nāyuḍu.
Lived at Velugōḍu.

Pedda Koṇḍappa Nāyuḍu.

Tirumala Nāyuḍu.
Lived at Velugōḍu in reign of Krishnadeva Rāya of Vijayanagar. Died without issue.

Gani Timma Nāyuḍu,
Was sent by Achyutadeva Rāya (?) *of Vijayanagar to destroy a confederation of robber chiefs who harassed the Palnāḍ country and territory south of the Krishṇā; was successful. Also defeated a combination of Krishṇā chiefs at Mallapuram in A.D.* 1530. *Was killed in battle soon after. Line failed after three generations. His son fought with Musalmān chiefs.*

Koṇḍappa Nāyuḍu.

(Two sons). *Line of elder failed fater two generations. The second had no issue.*

Pedda Kondappa Nāyudu.

(Two sons). *The line of the elder failed after four generations. The younger died without issue.*

Yāchama Nāyudu.

(Four sons.)

Chennappa Nāyudu. *Defeated the Muhammadans at Gandikōta and drove them out. Died without issue, as did his two brothers.*

Kastūri Rangappa Nāyudu. *Conquered Muhammadans of Golkonda and the chiefs of Kondavīdu and Vinukonda. Fought for the Vijayanagar sovereign, and defeated a confederation of chiefs in A.D.* 1579.

Ākuvīti Timma Nāyudu. *Died without issue.*

(A son). *Died without issue.*

Pedda Yāchama Nāyudu, *alias* Yācha Sūrudu. *Lived at Madrāntakam in Chingleput. Received as a gift from Venkatapati Rāya of Vijayanagar, then at Chandragiri, the Permādi country. Defeated a neighbouring chief in A.D.* 1602. *He recovered Venkatagiri, which had been lost.*

A son.

(Five sons), *of whom nothing is known.*

Kumāra Yāchama Nāyudu. *Fought a successful battle with the Maisūr king and was rewarded by the Emperor of Delhi.*

(Two sons), *of whom nothing is known.*

Bangāru Yāchama Nāyudu. *Built an agrahāram in A.D.* 1639 *or* 1699.[1] *He was murdered by Zu-l-faqār Khan, the Chief of Vellore, in the reign of Aurangzīb of Delhi* (1658—1707).

Sarvaghna Kumāra Yāchama Nāyudu. *Confirmed as chief by Aurangzīb in A.D.* 1695. *Sanad granted. Fought with Vellore A.D.* 1700, *with Maisūr* 1712, *and with Ginji* 1714. *Died* 1747.

Kumāra Nāyudu.

Bangāru Yāchama Nāyudu. *Joined with Navāb of the Carnatic against the Nizam and the French. Built a temple at Venkatagiri* 1760. *Ruled* 1747 *to* 1776.

Pedda Yāchama Nāyudu.

[1] 1579 says the writer, and on the next page chronicles a successful battle fought by this chief in A.D. 1683 ! ! But he only goes by the cyclic year "Siddharti," and I have no hesitation in placing the date 60 or 120 years later.

(*Adopted*).
Kumāra Yāchama Nāyuḍu.
A.D. 1776—1804. *Veṅkaṭagiri was sacked and destroyed by Haidar. The Rāja sided with the English. Sanad by Lord Clive in* 1802.

(*Adopted*).
Baṅgāru Yāchama Nāyuḍu.
(1802—1847).

Kumāra Yāchama Nāyuḍu,
(*the present Rāja*).

Mr. Boswell gives a history of this family in the *Nellore District Manual* (712—724), which slightly differs from the above and should be consulted.

VIJAYANAGAR DYNASTY, THE—.

It is a matter for great regret that the genealogy of the dynasties that successively ruled the countries forming the Vijayanagar kingdom have been found so difficult to work out and so confusing. But it is a fact that great confusion exists in the various contemporary records as to the relationships of the sovereigns, and a large number of inscriptions will have to be very carefully collated before absolute certainty can be arrived at. More harm than good is done by attempts to harmonize the lists given by native poets or interested informants, most of whom had some object in view when they wrote.

The information given below is almost entirely obtained from inscriptions, and as a basis to work on Dr. Burnell's table, given in his *South Indian Palæography* (pages 54, 55) has been taken. This was compiled mostly from the Villappākkam Plates, which are published in *Indian Antiquary* II, 371.

On pages 125—128 above will be found sixty-seven inscriptions noted, belonging to the older dynasty that preceded the powerful dynasty founded by Narasiṁha. Of a number of these I have only had rough notes sent to me, but some have been fully examined by other writers, as well as by myself, with the aid of my fellow-worker, Paṇḍit Nateśa Śāstrī.

I put forward the following table of the genealogy of the first dynasty, tentatively, premising that it may be found necessary to alter it by the light of other inscriptions hereafter.

Bukka,
married Meṅgāmbā.

Saṅgama,
married Mālāmbikā,
alias *Śāradā.*

1. Harihara I. (A.D. 1336—1350).[2]	Kampa *or* Kampa Mahīpati. — Saṅgama.	2. Bukka *or* Bukka Mahīpati, *alias* Rājendra, *married Gaurāmbikā and Kāmākshī*, (A.D. 1350—1379).	Mārapati *or* Mārappa.	Uddhati *or* Muddappa.

Children of 2. Bukka:

(*By Kāmākshī*) 3. Harihara II. (A.D. 1379—1401), *married Mallādevī, daughter of Rāmadeva.*	Bhāskara Bhūpati (?)

4. **Deva Râya I,** *or*
Vîra Prauḍhadêva,
married Padmâmbâ and Mallayavve or Mallâmbâ,
(A.D. 1406, 1409, 1410, 1412).

Virûpâksha.

5. **Vijaya Bhûpati,**
married Nârâyaṇîdevî,
(A.D. 1418).

Vîra Mallanna Uḍaiyâr.

6. **Deva Râya II,** *or*
Vîradeva.
(A.D. 1422, 1424, 1426, 1427, 1429, 1430, 1431, 1436, 1437, 1438, 1445, 1447).

The earliest Vijayanagar grant I have yet seen is noted as No. 79 of the List of Copper-plate Grants given above.[1] I am inclined to look on it with some suspicion, since, while professing to date from the year A.D. 1336—the date, that is, of the first real sovereign of the dynasty—it gives a genealogy traced roughly downwards through a few mythological names from *Chandra.* Such mythological pedigrees are, as a rule, to be found only in the later grants of a dynasty, after it has become firmly established, and when the sovereigns have acquired sufficient power to attract to their courts a number of sycophantic poets and poetasters.

Other inscriptions seem to be more reliable. One, of Harihara I, dated Ś.Ś. 1261 (A.D. 1339), is peculiarly interesting, as it styles him merely *Mahâmaṇḍaleśvara ;* and this is followed by inscriptions of Bukka, his younger brother, who bears the same inferior title. (Mr. Fleet's *Pâli, Sanskṛit and Old Canarese Inscriptions,* Nos. 149, 150.) Harihara II was, in Ś.Ś. 1310 (A.D. 1388), entitled *Mahârâjâdhirâja.* An inscription of Bukka, dated A.D. 1354-5 (published by Mr. Rice)[2] gives us only the names of Saṅgama and Kampa, and so does a grant published by Mr. Fleet,[3] which is dated in the same year (Ś.Ś. 1276 expired, *Vijaya*). Bukka's inscription of A.D. 1355-6 (Ś.Ś. 1277 current, *Manmatha*), noted by Mr. Fleet,[4] shows that he had then made "Hôsapaṭṭaṇa in the Hoyisaṇa country" his capital. No. 58 of my List of Copper-plate Grants (*supra*, p. 8) is a grant by Saṅgama son of Kampa[5] in A.D. 1356-7 (Ś.Ś. 1278 current, *Durmukhi*), and gives the genealogy of the earlier kings. We have yet to learn why Kampa or his son Saṅgama did not succeed to Harihara and how they were ousted by Bukka. From the grants of 1355-6 and 1356-7 (Ś.Ś. 1277 current, *Manmatha*, and Ś.Ś. 1278 current, *Durmukhi*) published by Mr. Rice,[6] we find that the name of the commander-in-chief of Bukka's armies was Naḍegonta Mallinâtha, son of N. Sâyyana. His boast that he commanded the "*Turaka* army, the *Sevana* army, the *Teluṅga* army, the powerful Pâṇḍiya army, and the Hoyśaṇa army" must be accepted with reservation.[7] In 1364 A.D. occurred the first conflict between the Muḥammadans and the troops of Vijayanagar. An inscription of A.D. 1368 (Ś.Ś. 1290 current, *Kîlaka*)[8] states that Bukka lived at Hastinâvatîpura, and mentions his prime minister Mâdhavâṅka, *i.e.*, the celebrated priest of Śiva, Mâdhavâchârya-Vidyâraṇya, abbot of the monastery at Śriṅgêri. An inscription at Porumâmilla in the Cuddapah District[9] mentions Bukka's son Bhâskara Bhûpati as reigning or governing in Udayagiri in A.D. 1369, but this inscription requires examination, because it would seem probable that the Reḍḍis held Udayagiri at that period.

The genealogy given in the inscription published by Mr. Fleet in the J.B.B.R.A.S. (XII 338, 372) confirms that given above as far as Harihara II, in whose reign (A.D. 1379, Ś.Ś. 1301 current,

---

[1] Pages 11, 12.
[2] *Mysore Inscriptions*, p. 234, No. 131.
[3] J.B.B.R.A.S. XII, pp. 337, 349.
[4] J.B.B.R.A.S. XII, p. 329.
[5] *Asiatic Researches* XX, 5 ; J.B.B.R.A.S. XII, 336 ; *Indian Antiquary* IV, 206 ; *note* §
[6] *Mysore Inscriptions*, p. 2, No. 1 ; p. 4, No. 2.
[7] Another inscription of Ś.Ś. 1278 is noticed by Mr. Fleet in J.B.B.R.A.S. XII, p. 340.
[8] J.B.B.R.A.S. XII, p. 340 ; *Indian Antiquary* IV, p. 206.
[9] *Above*, Vol. I, 126.

Siddhārti) it was executed. The glorification attached to the name of Saṅgama coincides with that ascribed in a subsequent grant of Narasa to the then sovereign, and it was probably a formula.[1] It states that he worshipped at Rāmeśvaram, built a bridge over the Kāverī, crossed it, defeated his enemy, and captured Śrīraṅgam; also that he defeated the armies of Chēra, Choḷa, Pāṇḍiya, the Turushka, the Gajapati, and others. The same grant shows that Harihara I and Bukka did not reign jointly, or, at any rate, that Bukka succeeded Harihara; and that the capital was then at Vijayanagara. Harihara II gave many gifts to the great southern temples. He also endowed some Jain temples, as is apparent from the inscription on the *dhvajastambha* of a Jaina shrine at Vijayanagar (Vol. I, 106; *Asiatic Researches* XX, p. 20), which records a grant by that monarch, mentioning his minister, Chaicha Daṇḍanāyaka, whose son's name was Iruga. The minister of Harihara II was, as we learn from inscriptions at Harihara and Bēlūr in Maisūr,[2] named Mudda Daṇḍādhipa, or Daṇḍeśa, in the years A.D. 1379 and 1382. Another powerful minister, by name Guṇḍa Daṇḍādhipa, is mentioned[3] as living in the reign of Harihara, but the date is not certain. In 1380 A.D. Harihara expelled the Muhammadans from Goa, Madhavāchārya being his minister (J.B.B.R.A.S. IX, 227). A grant of Virūpāksha, son of Harihara son of Bukka, quoted by Mr. Garstin in his *South Arcot Manual* (p. 2), dated in A.D. 1383-4, gives us the name of "Mallādevī, daughter of Rāmadeva," as that of his mother, and "Kāmākshī" as that of his grandmother. An inscription of A.D. 1399 (Ś.Ś. 1321 current, *Pramādhi*, noticed by Mr. Fleet)[4] states that a minister named Bāchaṇṇa Uḍaiyār (or *Voḍeya*) was then in charge of the government of Goa.

Dr. Burnell gives the date 1401 as the last of the reign of Harihara, and names as his successor his son Bukka II (1401–1418), who married Tippāmbā. He also gives us the elder son of Bukka II, "Devarāja, Vīradeva, or Vīrabhūpati," as reigning 1418—1434, and notes the name of his brother Krishṇarāja. He states that Devarāja married Padmāmbā and Mallāmbā, and was succeeded by the following sovereigns:—

Vijaya	(? 1434—1454) and others ?
Prauḍha Deva	(? 1456—1477)
Mallikārjuna	(1481—1487)
Rāmachandra	(1487)
Virūpāksha	(1488—1490)

In opposition to this table, I may point to the thirty-five dated inscriptions noted in my list[5] as between the years 1406 and 1487 (or 1497 ?), all of which combine to show that Harihara II was succeeded(?) by Deva Rāya I in or before the year 1406, that the latter had a son Vijaya Bhūpati, who was living in A.D. 1418, and that his son Deva Rāya II reigned from A.D. 1422 (about) till at least the year 1447 A.D. My inscriptions then give the names of Mallikārjuna (1459), Virūpāksha (1470 and 1473), and Prauḍhadeva (1476). I am not certain as to the accuracy of the single inscription at Āvūr in South Arcot,[6] which gives us a Narasiṁha as reigning in A.D. 1470-1, and prefer that it should be further examined.

The inscription at Hasan in Maisūr[7] gives the coronation of Deva Rāya as having taken place in A.D. 1406 (Ś.Ś. 1328 *current*, year *Vyaya*), and I have seven other inscriptions of that reign dated 1409, 1410, and 1412 A.D.[8] Inscriptions Nos. 87, 89, and 138 of my List of Copper-plate Grants[9] give the genealogy of Deva Rāya II, son of Vijaya Bhūpati, son of Deva Rāya I, son of Harihara II. This is confirmed by the inscription published in the *Asiatic Researches* (XX, p. 22), dated in Ś.Ś. 1348 (A.D. 1426-7), in which the same genealogy is given, and in which Deva Rāya II, or Vīradeva Rāya, is expressly termed "*Abhinava*," or the "young" Deva Rāya. 'Abdu-r Razzāk also speaks of him as "exceedingly young" in A.D. 1444, so that he must have been a mere child at his accession. (*Matla'us*

---

[1] J.B.B.R.A.S. XII, 343.
[2] *Mysore Inscriptions* (Mr. Rice), pp. 55, 267.
[3] *Ibid*, p. 226.
[4] J.B.B.R.A.S. XII, 340.
[5] Above, pp. 126—128.
[6] Above, Vol. I, p. 205. The inscription, however, mentions the year *Vikṛiti*, which corresponds with A.D. 1470.
[7] Mr. Rice's *Mysore Inscriptions*, p. 279, No. 150.
[8] One dated 1412 A.D. mentions that Sāvanna, son of the Daṇḍanāyaka, Nāganna, was then Viceroy of Goa, under Vijayanagar; while another at Vijayanagar (*Asiatic Researches* XX, 31) states that one Krishṇa was minister to king Deva Rāya. Krishṇa came from a family of ministers. Dharmadarasu and Suvena, brothers, were ministers. They had a sister named Siṅgambā, who married Rāmarasu, and had five sons, the eldest of whom was the minister Krishṇa.
[9] Above, pp. 13, 14, 21, 22.

Sa'dain, in Sir H. Elliot's *History of India* IV, 121.)[1] A stone inscription, however, at Tiruvaṇṇāmalai[2] seems to mention Vijaya Bhūpati as reigning in 1418. After that date till 1447 my nineteen inscriptions give me no name but that of Deva Rāya II. His minister was Nāganna Dhaṇṇāyaka.[3]

We now come to the second or Narasiṁha dynasty, whose scions became more powerful than any monarchs who had ever reigned over the south of India. Dr. Burnell fixes A.D. 1490 as the initial date of Narasiṁha's reign, and at present no inscription that I can be sure of appears to overthrow that statement. I observe, however, that Bishop Caldwell, in his *History of Tinnevelly* (p. 48), fixes the date of the beginning of "Narasiṁha, or Vīra Narasiṁha's" reign as A.D. 1487, and I have been told of an inscription at Conjeeveram (which should be examined) dated in that same year, in which Narasiṁha is mentioned. Narasiṁha's family name was *Sāḷuva*.[4] We have yet to learn the history of his acquiring the sovereignty of Vijayanagar and ousting the older dynasty.

From the grant (No. III) published by Mr. Fleet in Vol. XII of the J.B.B.R.A.S. (pp. 342 *et seq.*) and from others similar we learn that Kṛishṇadeva was son of Narasa, Nṛisiṁha or Narasiṁha, who had a wife Tippājī. Kṛishṇa's mother was Nāgaladevī or Nāgāmbikā, and some inscriptions expressly state that she was not the wife of the sovereign, but merely a favourite dancing girl. Narasa was son of Īśvara, whose queen was Bukkammā; Īśvara was son of Timma who married Devakī.

Before going into the question of the inscriptions of the second dynasty, I have determined to give a sketch of the period from Ferishta's History; for though this seems at variance with the evidence of the inscriptions, it is reasonable to suppose that it is trustworthy. From Ferishta we learn that in A.D. 1489, "Heemraaje" (*Scott's Edit., I*, 210), Minister of Vijayanagar, had in that year usurped the sovereignty, "leaving the Roies (*Rāyas*) only nominal power"; that in 1492 (*id.*, p. 212-13), after a battle on the Kṛishṇā against the 'Ādil Shāhi Muḥammadans, the "young roy" (*name not given*) died of his wounds, the usurping minister fleeing to Vijayanagar; and that "Heemraaje" then seized on the government of the country. Further on (p. 228) we read that "Heemraaje was the first usurper. He had poisoned the "young Rāja of Beejanuggur (*Vijayanagar*), son of Sheoroy (*Siva Rāya ?*), and made his infant brother a "tool to his designs; by degrees overthrowing the ancient nobility, and at length establishing his own "authority over the kingdom." This is narrated as showing the state of Vijayanagar previous to the commencement of the reign of 'Ismā'īl 'Ādil Shāh of Vijayapura (Bijapur), *i.e.*, about the year A.D. 1511. When 'Ismā'īl began to assume for himself the reins of government, "Heemraaje" was at Raichūr, which fortress had been surrendered to Vijayanagar (*id.*, p. 236). In 1520 'Ismā'īl made an unsuccessful attempt to recover territory from Vijayanagar. In 1530 another expedition against Vijayanagar was undertaken, "the affairs of Beejanuggur being in confusion owing to the death of "Heemraaje, who was newly succeeded by his son Ramraaje, against whom rebellions had arisen by

---

[1] 'Abdu-r Razzāk landed at Calicut on an embassy from Samarkand in June (?) 1442, and gives a graphic description of Calicut and Vijayanagar, with his journeys to and from the latter place. He experienced kind treatment at the hands of the Zamorin, and notices that all vessels were equally received in the port of Calicut, whereas in other ports strange ships were often plundered. Men and women both went about with their bodies bare from the waist upwards. Polyandry prevailed. Calicut was not then under the power of Vijayanagar, but the Zamorin was much afraid of the power of his great neighbour. The ambassador journeyed to Vijayanagar by way of Mangalore, Mūdabidri, and Bednūr (Bidrūr). He describes the temple at Mūdabidri as being all of brass and the statue made of gold, while he launches out in admiration of the sculptures of the temples at Bidrūr. He describes Vijayanagar as a magnificent city, with seven fortified walls, and, outside these, *chevaux de frise*, 50 yards broad, of lofty stones set on end. The palace stood in the centre with four bazaars round it, at the head of each of which was a lofty mandapam. The palace was loftier than all. Water flowed along the streets in cut-stone troughs. To the right of the palace was the minister's office, called the *Diwán Khána*, very large, and with a *mandapam* in front. Behind the king's palace was that of the *Danaik*. To the left of the palace was the mint, where "*varāhas*, *partābs*, and *fanams*" were coined. All the people in the streets wore golden jewels. Behind the mint was a bazaar 300 yards long and 20 broad, furnished with stone seats. The name of the king was "Deva Raya." He was exceedingly young, with an olive complexion, of spare body, but tall. Before the ambassador's arrival, and while he was still at Calicut, a desperate attempt had been made on the sovereign's life by his (the king's) brother. All the nobles were treacherously assassinated, and the king was stabbed by his brother. But the attempt was frustrated and the traitors slain. 'Abdu-r Razzāk gives a glowing account of the splendours of the *Mahānavami* festival at Vijayanagar. While he was there the *Danaik* went on an expedition against Kūlbarga, the king of which country, 'Ala-ud-dīn Aḥmad Shāh Bahmanī, having heard of the attempted murder of the Vijayanagar Raya, thought the opportunity an admirable one for making demands on the latter. A number of battles took place (1443-4) and great devastation followed. Shortly after the *Danaik's* return, the author left and returned to Hormūz. He arrived at Mangalore in January 1444. (Sir H. Elliot's *History of India* IV, 96-126). Ferishta mentions this war (Scott's Edition, I, 119).

[2] Vol. I, p. 207, No. 8. The note to this inscription probably needs correction.

[3] Mr. Rice's *Mysore Inscriptions*, p. 39, No. 23.

[4] *Sāḷuva* (Telugu) = hawk. It is possible that Narasiṁha may have belonged to a family of *Mahāmaṇḍaleśvaras* who had attained to power under the Yādavas of Devagiri. We find (Mr. Fleet's *Kanarese Dynasties*, p. 74) in A.D. 1277-8 (Ś.Ś. 1199) a feudatory of Rāmachandra of Devagiri (1271—1309 A.D.) by name Saḷuva Tikkamma, a *Mahāmaṇḍaleśvara*, making a successful raid against the Hoysala Ballāḷas as far south as Harihara in Maisūr, and receiving the titles of "establisher of the Kadamba kings" and "overthrower of the Hoysala kings." It is noticeable, too, that five years earlier, Rāmachandra's prime minister was Achyuta *Nāyakka*, the chief officials under the Vijayanagar kings being always termed *Nāyakkas*.

"several roies." This time Mudkal and Raichūr were retaken by 'Ismā'īl (*id.*, 252). Later on we read that at the accession of Ibrahīm 'Ādil Shāh I in 1535, "Ramraaje of Beejanuggur" took 3,000 foreign troops into his pay. Ferishta then gives a sketch of later Vijayanagar history which rather conflicts with his former account. He states that, at the death of "Seoroy," the latter's son, a minor, succeeded, but, dying shortly after, was succeeded by his younger brother. He too died, and, the rightful sovereign being an infant only three months' old, Heemraaje, one of the ministers, became regent, "and was cheer-"fully obeyed by all the nobility and vassals of the kingdom for forty years; though, on the arrival of the "young king at the age of manhood, he had poisoned him and put an infant of his family on the throne, "in order to have a pretence for keeping the regency in his own hands. Heemraaje, at his death, was "succeeded in office by his son Ramraaje, who, having married a daughter of the son of Seoroy, by that "alliance greatly added to his dignity and power" (*id.*, p. 262). Designing to raise himself to the throne by the total extirpation of the legitimate line, Rāma Rāja found himself opposed by a number of the nobles, and therefore he "placed on the throne an infant of the female line, and committed his person to "the care of his uncle, Hoje Termul Roy, who was not without a cast of insanity in his mind, and from "whose weakness he apprehended no danger of competition" (*id.*, p. 263). Rāma Rāja, after five or six years, rid himself by treacherous means of the nobles who opposed him, and then reduced several rājas in Malabar. Being absent on an expedition against a rāja who lived to the south of the capital, a slave in whom Rāma Rāja trusted seized the opportunity of liberating the young monarch, "and having "procured Hoje Termul Roy to embrace his interest, assumed the office of minister and began to levy "troops. Several tributary roies, who were disgusted with Ramraaje, flew with speed to Beejanuggur to "obey their lawful king; and in a short time thirty thousand horse and vast hosts of foot were assembled "under his standard at the city" (*id.*, p. 263). Rāma Rāja at once returned, but finding resistance hopeless, retired to his own estates. The young Rāja had not long to live in peace, for he was soon strangled by "Hoje Termul," who then seized the throne. His government proving oppressive and distasteful to the nobles, they invited Rāma Rāja to return and take upon himself the administration of affairs (*id.*, 264). The king, stricken with terror, made overtures to Ibrahīm 'Ādil Shāh for assistance, promising to become tributary to Vijayapura (Bijapur). The Muḥammadans accordingly took the field and marched into Vijayanagar in A.D. 1535, whereupon Rāma Rāja and his allies submitted, and entreated that the Muḥammadans might be sent out of the capital. The king accordingly dismissed his allies, but no sooner had they crossed the Kṛishṇā than Rāma Rāja marched on the capital. The king in despair destroyed all that he could of the royal property and then killed himself. "Rāma Rāja now "became Roy of Beejanuggur without a rival" (*id.*, 265). Ibrahīm 'Ādil at once despatched an army against Adoni, "which was on the point of surrender when Negtaderee (Veṅkaṭādri), the younger "brother of Ramraaje, marched from Beejanuggur with a great army to relieve it." A battle ensued, and in the end a peace was concluded (*id.*, 266). In 1543 the princes of the Muḥammadan States of the Dakhaṇ quarrelled amongst themselves, and Bijapur was simultaneously attacked by several armies, one of which was that of "Negtaderee," brother of Rāma Rāja. Peace was speedily concluded with Vijayanagar, and the Hindu army retired (*id.*, 271). In 1551 an agreement was made between Rāma Rāja and the Niẓām Shāhi Musalmāns, which resulted in Mudkal and Raichūr being captured from Ibrahīm 'Ādil. Six years later Rāma Rāja was called to the assistance of Ibrahīm and sent his brother Veṅkaṭādri with a large army to aid him. Veṅkaṭādri was successful (*id.*, 284). Ibrahīm died in 1557 and was succeeded by 'Alī 'Ādil, one of whose first actions was to affect a warm friendship for, and interest in, Rāma Rāja, who had just lost a son (*id*, 289) In 1558 these two monarchs, now allied, fought against the armies of Huṣain Niẓām Shāh, in which expedition the Muḥammadan historian accuses the Hindu soldiers of being guilty of gross barbarities and excesses (*id.*, 291). Rāma Rāja then insulted the Musalmān sovereigns by his arrogance and haughtiness, and the result was the grand Muḥammadan league which overthrew utterly the power of Vijayanagar. In 1564 the four princes met on the plains of Bijapur and marched to Talikōṭa on the Kṛishṇā. Rāma Rāja sent his "youngest brother Eeltumraaje" to block the passages of the river, while he himself, preceded by an army under his brother Veṅkaṭādri, marched to the attack of the allies. Ferishta gives a graphic description of the battle (*id.*, p. 295–298). The Hindus were utterly defeated, Rāma Rāja was captured by the soldiers of Niẓām Shāh, who promptly decapitated him; and the Muḥammadans, entering Vijayanagar in triumph, "razed the chief buildings, and committed all manner of excess." "The "raaje of Beejanuggur since this battle has never recovered its ancient splendour, and the city itself "has been so destroyed that it is now totally in ruins and uninhabited" (*i.e.*, in A.D. 1593–1606, the period of the composition of Ferishta's History).

Leaving Ferishta, we will now revert to the inscriptional evidence as to the chief kings of the

Narasiṁha dynasty down to the destruction of the kingdom. A number of inscriptions combine to give the following genealogy :—

Timma,
married Devakī.

|

Īśvara,[1]
married Bukkamma.

|

Narasa,
Narasa Avanipāla, Narasiṁha, *or*
Nṛisiṁha. (A.D. ?—1509).
Married Tippājīdevī, and Nāgalādevī, or
Nāgāmbikā (? a dancing girl).

(*By Tippājīdevī*)[2]
Vīra Narasiṁha *or* Vīra
Nṛisiṁhendra (A.D. 1509).

(*By Nāgalādevī*)
Kṛishṇadeva Rāya or "Vīra Narasiṁha Kṛishṇadeva Mahārāya,"
(1509—1530).
Married Chinnadevī and Tirumalādevī.
One of these was daughter of the King of
Orissa.

(*By Chinnadevī*).
A daughter—married Tirumala Rāya.

(*By Tirumalādevī*),
Tirumalāmbā (?)—*married*
"Aḷiya" Rāma Rāya.

An inscription, noted as No. 107 of my List of Copper-plate Grants (*supra*, p. 16), states that Kṛishṇa's successor, Achyuta, was younger brother of Kṛishṇa, while that noted similarly as No. 207 (*id.*, p. 30) gives this relationship still more clearly and minutely. It relates that Kṛishṇa's father, Narasa, besides his wife, Tippājīdevī, and Nāgalā, the mother of Kṛishṇa, had a wife Ōbāṁbikā, and that to each of the ladies was born a son, Achyuta being son of Ōbāṁbikā. On the other hand, the two inscriptions noted as Nos. 25 and 26 of the same list (*id.*, pp. 4, 5), both from the same place, Pūṇḍi in North Arcot, state that Achyuta, or Achyutendra, was *son* of Kṛishṇadeva. Achyuta reigned from A.D. 1530—1542.

The relationship of Achyuta's successor, Sadāśiva, who succeeded as an infant in 1542 and was kept entirely under the control of his ministers, is equally doubtful with that of Achyuta. An inscription of A.D. 1532 at Conjeeveram (*Vol. I, p.* 182, *No.* 115) mentions that Achyuta had a wife named Varadādevī, and a son Veṅkaṭādri, while a copper-plate grant from the banks of the Kṛishṇā (*No.* 81 *of my list above, p.* 12) mentions the name of Achyuta's son as Veṅkaṭadeva, and states that he reigned a short time and died deeply regretted, being succeeded by a *relative* named Sadāśiva, who was son of Raṅgarāya and his wife Timmāmbā. But the inscription at Hassan, of which Mr. Rice gives a translation in his *Mysore Inscriptions* (p. 228, No. 129) states (as far as I gather) that Sadāśiva was son of Achyuta.

No doubt the further study of inscriptions will make these matters all more clear. At present it is useless to theorize.

One thing, however, must be noticed. Whether it arises from oral tradition, or from the number of inscriptions and grants made to temples in his reign, it is a fact that the name of Kṛishṇadeva Rāya is held by all natives of the peninsula to this day as that of one of the greatest monarchs that ever ruled the country ; whereas Muḥammadan writers absolutely ignore him and his successors, and declare that the ministers usurped the entire sovereignty, keeping the Rāyas in absolute subjection. This apparent discrepancy needs solution. One fact only I am able to assert positively ;—if the ministers were so powerful, as stated by the Musalmān historians, at least in all inscriptions that I have met with their sovereigns were recognized as paramount and the names of Rāma Rāja, Raṅgarāja and the others never appear as those of supreme rulers.

---

[1] Called Bukka by the first of the two inscriptions under notice. Ferishta states that Īśvara was Raja of Kurnool (*Asiatic Researches* XX, 10).

[2] This prince actually came to the throne and was succeeded by Kṛishṇadeva Rāya, according to an inscription published by Mr. Rice (*Mysore Inscriptions*, p. 242, No. 135).

Krishnadeva was crowned in A.D. 1509.[1] He extended the conquests of the Vijayanagar family considerably. He is said to have first settled the *Drâviḍa* country about Conjeeveram, and then to have crushed a refractory râja in the Maisûr country, the Gaṅga Râja of Ummatûr. In the war against the latter Krishṇa Râya captured the strong fort of Śivasamudram and the city of Śrîraṅgapaṭṭaṇa (Seringapatam), after which all Maisûr submitted to him.[2] In A.D. 1513 he conquered the fortress and dependencies of Udayagiri in Nellore, and brought thence an image of *Krishṇasvâmi*, which he set up at Vijayanagar and endowed.[3] In A.D. 1515 he conquered the hill fort of Koṇḍavîḍu south of the Krishṇâ from a Gajapati ruler who then held possession,[4] Timma Arasu being the general commanding the victorious army. By this conquest, which followed the capture of fortresses further south,[5] the whole country along the east coast of the peninsula was reduced to subjection. In the following year (A.D. 1516) he defeated a hostile army north of the Krishṇâ.[6] In 1529 Krishṇadeva endowed the great statue of *Narasiṁha*, which forms so prominent a feature of the rock-cut remains at Vijayanagar, and which was carved by a Brahman, or at his expense.[7]

The reign of Achyuta seems to have been as remarkable for the number of gifts to Brahmans and endowments of temples as was that of his predecessor Krishṇa. He finally reduced the Tinnevelly country in A.D. 1532-3.[8]

From the inscriptions examined by me, or of which information has been sent to me, I gather the following names as those of certain of the great ministers and chiefs during the reigns of Krishṇa, Achyuta, and Sadaśiva :—

Names.	Dates.	References.	
Sâḷuva Timmarasu	A.D. 1518 ...	See above, Vol. I, p. 48. Inscription at Bezvâḍa.	Kistna District.
Do.	Do. ...	Do. do. p. 82. Bâpaṭla.	
Sâḷuva Timmayya	Do. ...	Do. do. p. 75. Kâkâni.	
Do	Do. ...	Do. do. p. 82. Bâpaṭla.	
Sâḷuva Timmarasa Ayyaṅgâr ...	Do. ...	Do. do. p. 70. Koṇḍakâvûru.	
Timma Râja, son of Chikka Timmayyadeva Mahâ Arasu.	A.D. 1520 ...	Do. do. p. 107. Vijayanagar.	
Salaka Râja Chinna Tirumalayyadeva.	Do. ...	Do. do. p. 118. Mallinâyanipalle, Anantapur.	
Râma Bhaṭlu, first Governor of Udayagiri, and Veṅkaṭâdri, his subordinate	A.D. 1536 ...	Do. do. p. 139, 140. Mâlyakoṇḍa, Nellore.	
The son of Salaka Râjendra and Tippâmbikâ.	In reign of Achyuta.	Do. Vol. II, p. 4. C.P. No. 25.	
Chinna Timmayyadeva, son of Râma Râja.	A.D. 1545 & 1548.	Do. Vol. I, p. 125. Niḍujuvvi, Cuddapah, and Do. do. p. 120. Pennakoṇḍa.	
Aliya Râma Râjayyadeva	A.D. 1547 ...	Do. do. p. 138. Podile, Nellore.	
Râma Râja Veṅkaṭâdrideva	Do. ...	Do. do. p. 95. Guṇṭanâla, Kurnool.	

[1] Inscription at Vijayanagar (*supra*, Vol. I, p. 107; J.B.B.R.A.S. XII, 343; *Ind. Ant.* V, 73).

[2] Mr. Foulkes in the *Salem District Manual*, p. 45. The account is taken from the summary of a manuscript given in the *Madras Journal*, XIV (I), 39.

[3] (*Above I*, 107), Inscription at Vijayanagar, A.D. 1513.

[4] Inscription at Maṅgalagiri (*supra*, Vol. I, p. 75).

[5] See above, p. 187, under the "REDDI CHIEFS of KONDAVÎDU."

[6] Inscription at Mêdûru, Kistna District, (*supra*, p. 51).

[7] Inscription at Vijayanagar (*supra*, Vol. I, p. 107).

[8] Inscriptions at Conjeeveram (Vol. I, p. 181, No. 86, and p. 182, No. 115).

Names.	Dates.	References.
Rāma Rāja Viṭṭhaladeva	A.D. 1547 to 1556.	See above, Vol. I, p. 292. Madura.
Timma Rāja, son of Timmayyadeva ...	A.D. 1551 ...	Do. do. p. 129, Yerraguḍipāḍu, Cuddapah.
Rāma Rāja	A.D. 1552 ...	Do. do. p. 62, Taṅgeḍa, Kistna.
Rāmadeva		
Tirumaladeva		
Tirumalayyadeva, son of Raṅga Rāja, son of Āra Vijaya Rāma Rāja.	A.D. 1555 ...	Do. do. p. 130, Vaṇṭimiṭṭa, Cuddapah.
Tirumala, son of Raṅga Rāja	A.D. 1556 ...	Do. do. p. 107, Vijayanagar.
Rāma Rāja, son of Tirumaladeva ...	A.D. 1565 ...	Do. do. p. 120, Pennakoṇḍa.
Pāpa Timmayya, son of Rāma Rāja Timma Rāja.	*Grant given in reign of Sadāśiva.*	Do. do. p. 124, Bollavaraṁ, Cuddapah.

It has already been mentioned [1] how, after repeated struggles, the whole strength of the Muhammadan kingdoms of the Dakhan combined against Vijayanagar, and, in the battle of Talikōṭa, crushed for ever its widely-extended power, reducing the members of the ruling house to the position of mere zemindars. In spite of the entire loss of power, however, the feeling of the Hindu population of the south seems to have been always loyal to their old rulers, for, even as late as the year 1793, I have seen copper-plate documents which acknowledge the representatives of the family as paramount sovereigns.

Inscriptions at Ahobilam [2] show that there at least the authority of Sadāśiva was recognized up to the year 1568, three years later than the fatal battle which ruined his family. But at the same time (*i.e.*, in 1567) we find Tirumaladeva, the second of the three usurping brothers who had kept Sadāśiva captive —the elder brother, Rāmadeva, having been captured and killed at Talikōṭa—giving a grant in his own name.[3] Other grants of this Tirumala's in 1567, 1568, 1572, 1573, 1577,[4] are to be found amongst the inscriptions noted in Volume I. He retired to Pennakoṇḍa in A.D. 1567.[5] The inscription at Pennakoṇḍa in 1577 notes the name of his minister as Chinnappa Nāyuḍu

With Sadaśiva expired, or sank into obscurity, the old line of Narasiṁha, and the family of the usurping ministers were recognized both by Hindus and Muhammadans as rightful sovereigns. Several inscriptions appear to recognize Rāma Rāya as the founder of this dynasty, as they affix his name (*more Indicorum*) to that of the reigning sovereign or scion of the house specially requiring notice. We may therefore call the three Vijayanagar dynasties by the names of (1) the Dynasty of Harihara, (2) the Dynasty of Narasiṁha, (3) the Dynasty of Rāma Rāja. We are now concerned with the latter.

It has been stated above that the Muhammadan historians believe Rāma Rāja and his brothers to have been sons of "Heem" Rāja; Dr. Burnell [6] calls them sons of "Vīrappa Nāyak"; an inscription at Devanhaḷḷi in Maisūr [7] styles him "Śrī Raṅga." Rāma Rāya married the younger of Krishṇadeva Rāya's daughters, and was therefore called "Aḷiya" Rāma Rāja, *aliya* meaning son-in-law. Dr. Oppert [8] points out that in the "Local Records," Vol. XLVII, p. 65, his wife's name is mentioned as "Tirumalāmbā." He was killed at Talikōṭa.

---

[1] See above, p. 247.
[2] Above, Vol. I, p. 101.
[3] Above, Vol. I, p. 132, Kandukūru, Cuddapah District.
[4] At Pennakoṇḍa, Khairuvvala, and Chintakuṇṭa in the Kurnool District, and at Conjeeveram. (See Vol. I, pp. 119-93, 181, 102, 119).
[5] According to Purchas II, p. 1705. (Burnell's *South-Indian Palæography*, p. 55, n.)
[6] *South Indian Palæography*, p. 55, n.
[7] Rice's *Mysore Inscriptions*, p. 252, No. 140.
[8] *Madras Journal* for 1881, p. 269, n.

From Mackenzie's "*View of the Principal Political Events that occurred in the Carnatic, from the dissolution of the Ancient Hindu Government in* 1564 *till the Mogul Government was established in* 1687"[1] we gather some valuable information; but it must be confessed that all is, at present, singularly confused, the different lists varying in most important particulars. From the inscriptions which I have examined, or of which I have received information (if the dates given are reliable) it would seem that Rāma's brother Tirumala, and the latter's son, Śrī Raṅga, ruled from 1567 till A.D. 1585, or for twenty years after the battle of Talikōṭa. The inscriptions tabulated above (p. 137) give Tirumala in 1567, Raṅga 1572, Tirumala 1573, Raṅga 1574, Tirumala 1577, and then Raṅga 1578—1585. The "Traditional List" published by Ravenshaw (*Asiatic Researches* XX, 1) and repeated in Mr. Kelsall's *Bellary Manual*, gives us Tirumala (1564—1572), Raṅga (1572—1586), and the list tabulated by Ravenshaw from inscriptions gives Tirumala (1560—1571) and Raṅga (1574—1584). In this uncertainty we can only be sure that Tirumala became head of the family after Talikōṭa, that he removed the seat of government to Pennakoṇḍa after the sack of the capital, and that he was succeeded at Pennakoṇḍa by his eldest son Śrī Raṅga I.

Some writers have definitely fixed the accession of Śrī Raṅga at the year A.D. 1574. We learn a little more, however, from other sources. After the battle which decided the fate of the Hindu monarchy, the allies marched as far as Vijayanagar and Ānēgundi. They plundered the capital, committing all sorts of excess, and only retired on receiving the cession of all the lands north of the Tuṅgabhadrā which had been captured by the Hindus. The acknowledged head of the family was then Veṅkaṭa, Rāma Rāja's youngest brother, Timma being for the time ousted. This state of things did not, however, last for very long.[2] Almost immediately after the Dakhāṇī allies had broken up their joint camp at Raichūr, where they fixed their rendezvous after their victorious campaign, Ḥusain Niẓām Shāh of Aḥmadnagar died, and was succeeded by a minor. This event encouraged 'Alī Ādil Shāh of Bijapur to attempt largely to add to his dominions. Timma Rāja applied to him for aid in order that he might regain his position as chief of the family—a position which Veṅkaṭa had usurped—and 'Alī Ādil moved with an army to Ānēgundi ostensibly to his aid, but in reality with the view of adding, first Ānēgundi, and afterwards Vijayanagar itself, to his own dominions. This design was frustrated by Veṅkaṭa calling on the other Dakhāṇī sovereignties to aid him to maintain his position, and 'Alī Ādil was forced by fear of his rivals to retreat back from Ānēgundi.

In 1577 the Muḥammadans advanced against Pennakoṇḍa, which was so bravely defended by Jagadēva Rāya, son-in-law of Śrī Raṅga, that the invaders were defeated and driven back. Jagadēva was rewarded by large grants of land added to the territories of the province (parts of Maisūr and Salem) that he governed. His governorship was then widely extended.

Śrī Raṅga was succeeded in A.D. 1585 by his brother, Veṅkaṭapati, who removed the seat of government to Chandragiri. Veṅkaṭapati ruled with some degree of magnificence at Chandragiri and Vellore, having his territories governed by viceroys. Mackenzie gives the names of some of the principal viceroys and their provinces about the year A.D. 1597. They seem to have been—

Krishṇappa Nāyakka	at Jiñji (Gingee).
? Nāyakka	at Tanjore.
Kumāra Krishṇappa Nāyakka	at Madura.
Jagadēva Rāya	at Çhennapaṭṭaṇa.
Tirumala Rāya	at Śrīraṅgapaṭṭaṇa.
?	at Pennakoṇḍa.

About the year 1593 or 1595 he seems to have roused himself to make an effort for the recovery of at least part of his patrimony from the Musalmāns. "Taking advantage of the attention of the Golkoṇḍa Government being taken up by the invasion of Aḥmadnagar by the Mogul forces under Prince Murād, son of Akbar, he approached the limits of Guṇṭūr with a view of recovering that province; but speedily retreated on finding the Golkoṇḍa officers were disposed to receive him in force, and apologized, alleging that his movement was from motives of religion" to visit and perform ablutions "at the great tank at Cummam." In 1599 Veṅkaṭapati was at war with the Nāyakka of Madura, his vassal.[3] The European missionaries were well received by the sovereign at Chandragiri, and he encouraged the trade of the East India Company. The Dutch were then established at Pulicat, where they had recently built a fort. He died in A.D. 1614. Floris, the traveller, heard of his death while at Masulipatam, on October

---

[1] J.A.S.B. XII (1844), p. 421.

[2] J.A.S.B. XII (1844), p. 421.

[3] Pimenta's account. He was a "visitor" of the Jesuits. "Purchas (Vol. II, pp. 1744—1750) gives an abridgment of it, as also does Jarric ("Thesaurus," I, pp. 625—690)." Burnell's *South-Indian Palæography*, p. 55, n.

25th of that year. He states that the king's three wives burned themselves on his funeral pyre. One of them was "Obiama, Queen of Paleakate," or Pulicat.

His death was followed by great confusion and disturbance. The various viceroys throughout the south of India began to assume an independent attitude and emancipate themselves from their position of vassaldom. The government of the Vijayanagar territories above the ghāṭs was virtually destroyed by the capture of Śrīrangapaṭṭaṇa (Seringapatam) in 1609 A.D. by Rāja Uḍaiyār of Maisūr from Tirumala Rāja, the aged viceroy, who retired and died at Tālkāḍ. And all over the country the Poḷegars began to acquire more and more power.

The following genealogical table exhibits the relationship of the kings of the Rāma Rāja dynasty down to Veṅkaṭapati :—

?
Married Ballāḷikā.[1]

Rāma Rāja,[1]
married Lakkāmbikā.
Called elsewhere[2] Bukka Rāja, *his queen's name being given as* Mallāmbikā.

Śrī Raṅga *or*
Śrī Raṅga Rāma Nṛipatiḥ,[3]
Married Tirumalādevī or Tirumalāmbikā.
He was minister to the sovereign.

- Rāma Rāja. *Governed the kingdom in reign of Sadāśiva. Married Krishnadeva Rāya's younger daughter Tirumalāmbā. Was killed at Talikōṭa A.D.* 1564.
  - Kṛishṇa Rāja.[4] *Acquired Ānēgundi for himself, but died without issue.*
  - Tirumala Rāja.[4]
- Timma *or* Tirumala, (1564—1574 ?). *Married* (1) *Veṅgalāmbā,* (2) *Rāghavāmbā,* (3) *Pēdāvamāmbā,* (4) *Krishṇavāmbā. He removed the seat of government to Pennakoṇḍa in A.D.* 1567.
  - Raṅga I *or* Śrī Raṅga, *alias* Viśākhi[4] (A.D. 1574 ?—1585), *Married* (1) *Tirumalādevī and* (2) *Katāmbā.*
    - A daughter, *married* Jagadeva Rāya.
  - Tirumaladeva *or* Śrīdeva. "*Reigned for a short time.*"[4]
  - Veṅkaṭapati, (1585—1614). *Removed the seat of government from Pennakoṇḍa to Chandragiri. Married three wives, one of whom was "Obiama, Queen of Pulicat," according to Floris. Died without issue.*
- Veṅkaṭa *or* Veṅkaṭādri.

My information regarding inscriptions gives me the following list, the dates being those of the inscription of sovereigns (so-called) who succeeded Veṅkaṭapati.

	A.D.
Śrī Raṅga II	1619
Rāma	1620—1622
Śrī Raṅga II (?)	1623
Veṅkaṭappa	1623
Rāma	1629
Veṅkaṭapati	1636
Śrī Raṅga III	1643—1665

[1] Inscription at Devanhaḷḷi ; Rice's *Mysore Inscriptions*, p. 252, No. 140. The genealogy is partially confirmed by my copper-plate inscription No. 12 (*see above, pp.* 2, 3).
[2] See above, pp. 2, 3, copper-plate inscription No. 12.
[3] I go by inscriptions. Muḥammadan historians call Rāma's father "Heemraaje," as given in Scott's Ferishta. Burnell styles him Vīrappa Nāyak.
[4] According to information supplied to me by the present Rāja of Ānegundi.

This seems to accord well with the "Traditional List" as published by Ravenshaw (*Asiatic Researches* XX, 1) so far as the order of names is concerned, except that my inscriptional list interpolates a Śrī Raṅga and Rāma at the beginning; but all my stone inscriptions require examination. Śrī Raṅga, however, certainly began to reign before the year 1639, for it was he that gave the site of the city of Madras to the English in that year.

Mr. Ravenshaw's list runs—

Śrī Raṅga II.
Veṅkaṭa.
Rāmadeva.
Veṅkaṭapati.
Śrī Raṅga III.

We then have—

	A.D.
Śrī Raṅga IV	1665—1678
Veṅkaṭapati	1678—1680
Śrī Raṅga	1692
Veṅkaṭa	1706
Śrī Raṅga	1716
Mahādeva	1724
Śrī Raṅga	1729
Veṅkaṭa	1732
Rāma	1739 (?)
Veṅkaṭapati	1744
(?)	(?)
Veṅkaṭapati	1791—1793

In a letter to Government, dated 12th July 1801, Munro gave an account of the Ānēgundi Rāj so far as he had been able to gather it. He states that the then Rāja was a descendant of the Vijayanagar family by the female line, his ancestors having obtained the territories of Ānēgundi, part of Harpanahaḷḷi, and part of Chitaldurgam in jāghīr from the Muḥammadan Governments. Early in the eighteenth century they paid a tribute of Rs. 20,000 to the Mogul Emperor. In A.D. 1749 the jāghīr fell under the Mahrattas and paid tribute to them till 1775, when it was reduced by Ḥaidar 'Alī, who fixed the tribute at Rs. 10,000 and the obligation of furnishing a force of 1,000 foot and 100 horse. In 1786 Tīpū completely subverted the jāghīr. The Rāja fled to the Niẓam's dominions, where he remained a fugitive till 1791, when he tried to regain his jāghīr during the war. In 1799 he seized Ānēgundi on Tīpū's fall, and refused to submit to the English. This he was compelled to do, and the estate was handed over to the Niẓām, when the Rāja was made a pensioner. His name was Tirumala Rāja. He died in 1824.

From him the present Rāja of Ānēgundi is descended, as shown by the following pedigree:—

Tirumala Rāja.
Pensioned by the Niẓām's Government in A.D. 1801.
Died 1824.

- A son; (*died before his father*).
  - (A daughter).
    - Tirumaladeva. *Married Lakshmīdevamma.* *Died* 1866.
      - Veṅkaṭa Rāma Rāya, *married Śrī Raṅgamma.* *Died* 1871.
        - *A daughter.*
        - *A daughter.*
      - Krishnadeva Rāya, *married* (1) *Kuppamma*, (2) *Ijjamma*. *Died in* 1872.
      - (*daughter*) Veṅkamma.
      - Narasiṁha Rāja. *Born* 1870; *the present chief.*
    - Lakshmīdevamma, *married* Narasiṁha Rāja.
- Vīra Veṅkaṭapati Rāja, (*died unmarried*, 1831).

VIJAYAPURA, OR BIJAPUR, 'ĀDIL SHĀHI DYNASTY OF—.

(*See* Dakhaṇ, Muḥammadan Kings of the—.)

WARAṄGAL, SOVEREIGNS OF—.

(*See* Gaṇapatis of Oraṅgal.)

WESTERN CHĀLUKYAS.

(*See* Chalukyas.)

YĀDAVAS OF DEVAGIRI.

(See Mr. Fleet's *Dynasties of the Kanarese Districts*, pp. 71—78, for an account of this family. From it the following summary is compiled.)

On the downfall of the Kaḷachuris, the southern parts of their dominions fell into the hands of the Hoyśala Ballāḷas, or Yādavas of Dvārasamudra, while the northern were appropriated by another family of Yādavas, who eventually settled at Devagiri (*hod.* Daulatābād.) The device of their house was a golden *garuḍa*. The following is the genealogy of the dynasty:—

Siṅghana I.
|
Mallugi.
|
Bhillama (A.D. 1187 to 1191).
|
Jaitugi I, Jaitrasiṁha, *or* Jaitrapāla, (A.D. 1191—1209.)
|
Siṅghana II, Siṁha, Siṁhala, Siṁhana, *or* Tribhuvanamalla, (A.D. 1209—1247.)
|
Jaitugi II.

- Krishṇa, Kanhara, Kanhāra, Kandhara, *or* Kandhāra, (A.D. 1247—1260).
  - Rāmachandra, *or* Rāmadeva, (A.D. 1271—1309).
    - Śaṁkara, (A.D. 1309—1312).
    - Bhīma.
    - *A daughter, married to* Haripāla.
- Mahādeva *alias* Uragasārvabhauma, (A.D. 1260—1271).
  - Amana.

Siṅghana I is stated in an inscription to have subdued the "King of the Karṇāṭaka," whom Mr. Fleet identifies with the Hoyśala king Vishṇuvardhana.

In Bhillama's lifetime, his son Jaitugi seems to have been defeated by the Hoyśala king Ballāḷa II in a battle fought, according to tradition, at Lakkundi in the Dhārvāḍ District.

Jaitugi I resided at Vijayapura or Bijapur. He is stated in a later inscription to have slain the "King of Trikaliṅga" and seized his kingdom. Whether this is true or not remains to be proved. The king of "Triṅkaliṅga" would, apparently, be the Choḷa sovereign, or his viceroy in his northern possessions. Kulottuṅga II appears to have reigned over the Choḷa country till after the year A.D. 1158; and I have received copies of inscriptions about the Krishṇā and Godāvarī rivers which would give us a Choḷa prince named Rājendra reigning till at least 1194; after which we hear nothing of any sovereign till the Gaṇapatis of Oraṅgal appear on the scene, the country being apparently in the hands of a number of petty chiefs. It is therefore not at all improbable that the Choḷa sovereign or viceroy of Teliṅgāna (*Trikaliṅga*) was conquered by a Yādava sovereign between the years 1191 and 1209, the date of Jaitugi's reign.

It is in the reign of Siṅghana II, viz., in the year A.D. 1210-11, that Devagiri is first mentioned as the capital. He claims to have conquered the "King of Telunga" (Teliṅgāna), the Kaḷachuri king, and the Āndhra king. Thirty-eight inscriptions of his reign are extant, which prove that the kingdom had extended in size.

Siṅghana II was succeeded by his grandson Krishṇa, whose viceroy (*Mahāpradhāna*) in the southern provinces was the son of a general who is declared to have conquered the Raṭṭas, the Kādambas of the Koṅkaṇa, the Pāṇḍya who shone at Gutti," (?) and the Hoysala king, and to have set up pillars of victory near the Kāverī.

Mahādeva was possibly a usurper. His son Amana seems to have been forcibly ousted by Rāmachandra, who succeeded in A.D. 1271.

Either Rāmachandra or one of his vassals prosecuted a war against the Hoysalas which seems to have been successful. Rāmachandra's sway "extended over all the dominions, in the central and southern parts of the Bombay Presidency, of the dynasties that preceded his." In A.D. 1294 [1] he was attacked by a predatory band of Muḥammadan horsemen under 'Alā-ud-dīn Khilji, nephew of Jalāl-ud-dīn,—their first inroad into the Dakhaṇ,—was defeated and driven into his fort, the town being pillaged by the marauders. Rāmachandra bought off the invaders and concluded a peace, but meanwhile his son Śaṅkara advanced with a large army to the capital. In the battle which ensued the Muḥammadans were ultimately victorious, and the Hindu sovereign had to make further concessions before the invaders would retire.

In 1306 A.D. Rāmachandra having refused tribute, 'Alā-ud-dīn, who, by the murder of his uncle, was now on the throne of Delhi, sent one of his eunuchs, Malik Kāfur, with 100,000 horse, to subdue the Dakhaṇ. Devagiri was defenceless against this host, and Rāmachandra submitted and was sent to Delhi, where he was received honorably and liberally. He was restored, and continued to pay tribute till his death. In 1309 he hospitably entertained Malik Kāfur on his march against Oraṅgal.

In 1310 A.D. Malik Kāfur again marched south, this time against the Hoysalas, and returned to Delhi. Śaṅkara, then sovereign of Devagiri, refused tribute, and in 1312 Malik Kāfur again marched into the Dakhaṇ, seized Śaṅkara and put him to death. He ravaged the Dakhaṇ, and took up his residence at Devagiri. Being summoned soon after to Delhi, Rāmachandra's son-in-law, Haripāla, stirred up the Dakhaṇ to arms, expelled a number of the Muḥammadan garrisons, and asserted his power over the former territories of Devagiri.

In 1318 Mubārak, then on the throne of Delhi, marched in person against Haripāla, who was captured, flayed alive, and decapitated, and his head set up over the gate of his own city.

Thus ended the Yādava dynasty.

YĀDAVAS OF DVĀRASAMUDRA.

(*See* the Hoysala Ballāḷas.)

YĀDAVAS OF MĀNYAKHĒTA.

(*See* the Rāshṭrakūṭas.)

---

[1] Mr. Fleet's summary of what follows is taken from Ferishta.

SUPPLEMENTARY NOTES.

BĀṆA KINGS, THE—.

The publication of Mr. Le Fanu's *Manual of the Salem District* with Mr. Foulkes's Historical Paper in Vol. I, and his exhaustive notes on inscriptions in the Appendix to Vol. II, enables me to make some additions to the above sketch of the dynasties of Southern India.

I had omitted to notice the Bāṇa Kings of Maisūr. This was a very ancient dynasty and apparently ruled over the eastern portion of Maisūr. (*Op. cit.* II, 395, etc.)

At an early date, in the reign of the Gaṅga King Koṅgaṇi I (*see p.* 190), the Bāṇa kings were conquered, but they subsequently recovered their power and prestige. They were conquered again by a chief in the reign of Pṛithivī Koṅgaṇi, prior to the year A.D. 777.[1]

Mr. Foulkes's inscription (*id., p.* 369) gives us a certain chief named Hasti Malla, king of the Bāṇas, who was subject to the Gaṅga Kings of Maisūr, who in turn were feudatories of the Cholas. The Gaṅga Prince Kesarī "Pṛithivīpati" consecrated Hasti Malla, of Padivipurī, king of the Bāṇas by permission of the Choḷa "Parakeśari." A short time previous to this the Bāṇas were conquered "suddenly" (*id., p.* 372, *Ins., verse* 9) by the Choḷa Vīra Nārāyaṇa, and since the inscription in question bears an endorsement in the fifteenth year of the said Vīra Nārāyaṇa, it would appear that this conquest, followed by the giving back of the kingdom and consecration of the Bāṇa king, took place within the first fifteen years of his reign, and therefore that "Parakeśari" or "Koppara Kesari" was a title of this Vīra Nārāyaṇa Choḷa. In the endorsement the latter is mentioned by the title of "he who took Madura."

In another grant the same Bāṇa chief, Hasti Malla, is represented as having captured a Pallava fort, and being in consequence highly honored by the Choḷa sovereign and the Gaṅga King Pṛithivīpati. Mr. Foulkes argues (*id., p.* 388), and I think rightly, that this must have taken place before the conquest of the Pallavas by the Choḷas, and probably only shortly before.

Another grant published in the same work (*id.*, 391) gives us the following table of eight kings. Bāṇa was the first sovereign. A long time after him came Bāṇādhirāja. Again a long time after him came Jayanandivarmā, who ruled as far as the "Andhra country," *i.e.*, the Telugu country.

Jayanandivarmā.
|
Vijayāditya.
|
Śrī Malladeva, *alias* "Jagadekamalla."
|
Bāṇa Vidyādhara.
|
Prabhumerudeva.
|
Vikramāditya.
|
Vijayāditya, *alias* "Pukaṛavippava Gauda."
|
Vikramāditya, *alias* "Vijaya Bāhu."

The last is called the "friend of Krishṇa Rāja." Another Bāṇa king is mentioned in inscriptions at Gūlgānpōde in the Kōlār District of Maisūr, 15 miles north of Kōlār (*Mysore Inscriptions*, pp. lvi, 304, 305), viz., the "Śrī Mahāvali Bāṇarasa," Vikramāditya, surnamed "Bāṇa Vidyādhara."

Reference to the sketch of the rulers of the Malayāḷam country given above (p. 196) will show that one of the early Perumāḷs was Bāṇa Perumāḷ "from Bāṇapuram in *Paradeśa*."

---

[1] Inscription at Nāgamaṅgalam (Rice's *Mysore Inscriptions*, p. 287).

CHALUKYAS.

Mr. Fleet (*Ind. Ant.* XII, 218, 220) mentions an Eastern Chalukyan inscription from the Krishṇā, which states that King Vijayāditya Narendra Mṛigarāja fought 108 battles in twelve years with the Rāshṭrakūṭa feudatories, the Gaṅga *Mahāmaṇḍaleśvaras* and the Raṭṭas; that Guṇagāṅka-Vijayāditya was successful in the war with the same opponents; but that, after his reign, Veṅgī was overrun and crushed by the "Raṭṭa claimants,"—for the time, of course.

CHOḶAS.

Mr. Foulkes (*Manual of the Salem District* II, 369) publishes a grant which gives a genealogy of three Choḷa sovereigns, which seems to correspond with a set of three mentioned in the *Koṅgudeśa Rājākkaḷ*.

Mr. Foulkes's Grant.	*Koṅgudeśa Rājākkaḷ.*
Vijayālaya.	Vijayada.
|	|
Āditya.	Āditya.
|	|
Vīra Nārāyaṇa.	Vīra Choḷa Nārāyaṇa.

We learn that previous to these there had reigned a "Karikāla Choḷa," since the grant states (v. 4) that "in his line, which the fame of Kokkiḷḷi Choḷa Karikāla rendered illustrious, and which was the original stock from which Kochchaṅkaṇa and other founders of royal dynasties sprung, the victorious and wealthy Vijayālaya was born............" Vīra Nārāyaṇa is said to have married the daughter of the King of Keraḷa, and to have conquered (1) the Bāṇa kings, (2) King Tumba and other kings, (3) Rāja Siṁha Pāṇḍiyan, (4) the King of Ceylon. He assumed the title of "Saṅgrāma Rāghava."

Mr. Foulkes (*id.*, *p.* 367) thinks that the Choḷa Ādityavarmā, who conquered the *Koṅgudeśa* about the year A.D. 894 according to his computation, and who had a son Vīra, is the same as the Choḷa Parakeśari, who seems to have had a son Vīra; but the whole history of the Choḷas is, at present, so confused that it is, as Mr. Foulkes remarks, dangerous to theorize.

The Koṅgu chronicle mentions a Choḷa "Arivarideva," or "Harivarideva," *alias* Rājarāja, as great-grandson of Vīra Nārāyaṇa. On page 380 of the same publication Mr. Foulkes gives us a list of seven Choḷas and the dates he assigns to them. But as a great deal of his reasoning seems to be based on the Koṅgu chronicle, neither the dates nor names can be trusted.

	A.D.
Vijayālaya	855—880
Aditya	880—905
Vīra Nārāyaṇa	905—930
Desotya	930—950
Parāntaka	950—970
Divi	970—990
Harivari *alias* Rājarāja	990

One thing is quite clear, that if the Vīra Nārāyaṇa of this list be the same as Rājendra Kulottuṅga Choḷa, the date must be wrong.

Another list has kindly been given to me by Dr. Burgess, who got it from Dr. Burnell. This also is from a chronicle, the *Bṛihadīśvara Māhātmya*, or legend of the great temple at Tanjore. Dr. Burnell had no confidence in it, though he thought that some of the names were doubtless real ones. It will be observed that the list does not at all correspond with the lists drawn from inscriptions.

Kulottuṅga.	Kīrtivardhana.
Deva Choḷa.	Jaya Choḷa.
Śaśiśekhara.	Kanaka Choḷa.
Śivaliṅga Choḷa.	Sundara Choḷa.
Karikāla Choḷa.	Kālakāla Choḷa.
Bhīma Choḷa.	Kalyāṇa Choḷa.
Rāja Rājendra.	Bhadra Choḷa.
Vīra Mārtāṇḍa.	

GAṄGAS OF MAISŪR.

In a grant published by Mr. Foulkes in Mr. Le Fanu's *Manual of the Salem District* (Vol. II, p. 372) is a short Gaṅga genealogy. In the royal line was born Śiva Māra, who had a son named Prithu-yashā *alias* Prithivīpati. He saved a certain Diṇḍikojeriga from Amoghavarsha. [The first of these latter names sounds like a Pallava name. Amoghavarsha was probably one of the three Rāshtrakūta kings of that name (*see above, pp.* 233-4).] He also saved Nāgadaṇḍa (another Pallava?) from death. Prithu-yashā seems to have lost his life in battle with the Pāṇḍiyan King Varaguṇa.[1] His son was Narasiṁha, and the latter's son was named Keśari, *alias* "Prithivīpati." The latter was subject to the Choḷa king Parakeśari (or Kopparakeśari?) and consecrated Hasti Malla king of the Bāṇas. The Bāṇas had been shortly before defeated by the Choḷa king, the same Parakeśari, also called Vīra Nārāyaṇa.

KALIṄGĀ.

The kingdom of Kaliṅgā was one of the oldest in India. Though not actually mentioned by name in the Rig Veda, the sage Kakshīvat is frequently alluded to, and he was the son of a female slave of the queen of Kaliṅgā. The country is mentioned in all the most ancient chronicles. According to Buddhist legends, when Buddha's relics were divided at his death, Brahmadatta, the King of Kaliṅgā, obtained his left canine tooth. Kaliṅgā is also mentioned in the *Jātakas*, such as the *Wessantara Jātaka* and others. In the time of Aśoka (B.C. 250) the country was of sufficient importance to justify that king's engraving his celebrated rock-edicts there for the enlightenment of the people. Pliny divides the country into three portions, *Kaliṅgā*, *Madhya Kaliṅgā*, and *Mahā Kaliṅga*. With all this, very little is known of the names of the kings who reigned over the country, except through native chronicles, which, as before stated, are very untrustworthy.

Dr. Rajendra Lāla Mitra, in his *Antiquities of Orissa* (Vol. II, pp. 12, etc.) gives us some Pāli inscriptions in the Lāt character on the caves in Orissa, which mention King Vīra (or *Vera*, according to the Pāli letters as they appear in print), Prince Vidhuka and King Aira, who seems to have defeated a king of Kaliṅgā named Nanda, and seized his kingdom. The author thinks that this Nanda is either "Sunanda, son and successor of Kāsi, and grandson of Brahmadatta" above alluded to, or one of the nine Nandas of Magadha. Aira's date is the fourth century B.C.

Mr. W. Taylor, now residing at Parlakimedi in Ganjam, has sent me a newly discovered copper-plate inscription of Indravarmā, King of Kaliṅgā, found at Kimedi. It is on three small plates, and dates apparently from about the eighth or ninth century. Two other inscriptions of this king are known (*see above, page* 183), dated respectively in the 128th and 146th year of the "victorious reign" of the dynasty. This is similarly dated in the 91st year, proving either that Indravarmā enjoyed a very long reign, or that there was more than one king of that name.

MAISŪR.

Mr. Foulkes (*Manual of the Salem District*, II, 403—430) has published a grant of Doḍḍa Krishṇa Rāja (A.D. 1714—1731), and has printed (pp. 426—430) several genealogies of this royal house from different sources. My table (*above, p.* 194) is defective, but it is at least as reliable as any other, seeing that seven different tables compiled by Mr. Foulkes from different sources vary in important details.

RĀSHṬRAKŪṬA KINGS.

Mr. Fleet has just published a number of new grants in *Ind. Ant.* XII, 215, from which we gain the following principal particulars:—

(11.) Amoghavarsha I was surnamed "Atiśayadhavala" and "Nripatuṅga I." He defeated the Chalukyas, and built (restored?) the city of Mānyakhēṭa. He came to the throne in A.D. 814-15 or 815-16, and enjoyed a long reign.

---

[1] Mr. Foulkes points out that Kamban, the great Tamil poet, is said to have lived in the reign of Varaguṇa Pāṇḍiyan, while "local tradition" makes Kamban also a contemporary of Rājendra Kulottuṅga Choḷa. This would help in the identification of Vīra Nārāyaṇa with Rājendra Kulottuṅga Choḷa were it not that so much confusion exists in regard to all these dates and names. Patient working will probably throw light on all this before very long.

An Eastern Chālukyan inscription from the Krishṇā states that a long war took place in the time of Vijayāditya Narendra Mrigarāja of that dynasty with the Gaṅgas and Raṭṭas. These Gaṅgas were feudatories of the Rāshṭrakūṭas. 108 battles were fought in twelve years.

(12.) Krishṇa II was also called "Kannara," "Kandhara-Vallabha," and "Krishṇa-Vallabha." His wife was of the family of the Kaḷachuris of Tewar or Tripura.

The Eastern Chālukyan inscription mentioned above states that the wars between that dynasty and the Rāshṭrakūṭas continued into the reign of Krishṇa II. Guṇagāṅka-Vijayāditya was successful in his wars, but after him "the province of Veṅgī was overrun by the army of the Raṭṭa claimants, as if by dense darkness on the setting of the sun."

(13.) Jagattuṅga II. Mr. Fleet has ascertained (*p.* 222, *note* 47) that the name "Jagadrudra" might be expunged both from this king's names and those of his great grandfather Govinda III. The title "Jagadrudra" is due only to a mistake in reading an inscription. Jagattuṅga II gave a grant in A.D. 929-30 under the title of "Prabhūtavarsha." His son,

(14.) Indra IV, gave a grant in A.D. 916-17.

Mr. Fleet (*Ind. Ant.* XII, 248) mentions two royal *insignia*, which it seems were formerly adopted by the Guptas, acquired from them by the Chalukyas, and wrested from the Chalukyas by the Rāshtrakūṭas. These are the figures of the rivers Gaṅgā and Yamunā.

Govinda V is called "Gojjigadeva," "Nṛipatuṅga," "Vīra Nārāyaṇa," and "Raṭṭa-Kandarpa" in an inscription at Kaḷas in Dhārvāḍ. (*i.d.*, p. 249). An army of his was defeated by Rāja Bhīma of the Eastern Chālukyas.

VIJAYANAGAR.

On page 436 of the Chingleput District Manual, Mr. Crole has printed a translation of an inscription in the *Varadarājāsvāmi* temple at Conjeeveram, which gives some interesting details of Krishṇadeva Rāya's conquests (*see above*, p. 249) and of his visit to Conjeeveram after his return. He is described as capturing, first, the hill forts of Udayagiri, Bellamkoṇḍa, Vinukoṇḍa, Koṇḍaviḍu and others, from Nellore up to the Krishṇā river, subduing some chiefs whose names are given;[1] then Bezvāḍa, Koṇḍapalle, and many places north of the river; and finally Rajahmundry, north of the Godāvarī, where "the youngest of his wives, Tirumalādevī, was caused to make many gifts. In A.D. 1516 he went and worshipped at Conjeeveram and gave gifts."

[1] It is interesting to notice that this inscription confirms the Koṇḍaviḍu chronicle (*see above*, *p.* 188) that the Gajapatis of Orissa had possession of that fortress in those days, and that the last of them, Vīrabhadra, son of Pratāpa Rudra Gajapati, was conquered by Krishṇadeva Rāya in A.D. 1515.

INDEX.

A.

B.

C.

E.

F.

G.

H.

I.

L.

M.

N.

O.

P.

Q.

R.

S.

T.

U.

V.

W.

Y.

Z.